HANOCH LEVIN: SELECTED PLAYS ONE

T0348011

Hanoch Levin

SELECTED PLAYS ONE

Krum
Schitz
The Torments of Job
A Winter Funeral
The Child Dreams

OBERON BOOKS
LONDON

WWW.OBERONBOOKS.COM

First published in 2020 by Oberon Books Ltd
521 Caledonian Road, London N7 9RH
Tel: +44 (0) 20 7607 3637 / Fax: +44 (0) 20 7607 3629
e-mail: info@oberonbooks.com
www.oberonbooks.com

PB ISBN: 9781786829139
E ISBN: 9781786829153

Cover design by James Illman
Cover photo by Gadi Dagon

Contents

Preface   vii

Hanoch Levin: A Short Biographical Note   xvii

Krum   1

Schitz   67

The Torments of Job   141

A Winter Funeral   203

The Child Dreams   291

To David Lan, for believing

Thanks

Howard Gooding, Amir Nizar Zuabi, Noam Semel,
Mulli Melzer, George Spender, Dani Tracz, Gal Canetti,
Shimrit Ron and The Hanoch Levin Institute of Israeli Drama

Preface

It was sometime in 1997 that the decision was made to publish a comprehensive edition of all of Hanoch Levin's works. He had just been diagnosed with cancer, and our time with him had started to run out. And so we began – Levin's closest friend (and my publishing partner) Dani Tracz, as managing producer, and me, as editor – to work frantically on the project, in the hope of finishing everything while Levin was still with us. Many others helped, too many to mention. Needless to say Levin himself was more than eager to see all his works in print. He had a huge amount of work to do on the project, all the while continuing, with amazing tenacity, his own work on directing his plays.

One of the challenges we met was that, on top of Levin's already rich oeuvre as we knew it, we were led to 'discover' that he still had, in various states of completion, some 30 (thirty!) additional plays – more than the number of plays he had already published up to that point... Where had he found the time to write all these plays? That question has yet to be answered. He certainly gave all of them a final edit during the years 1997–1999, whilst preparing them for print. We finally completed our task: Levin was able see and touch all 16 volumes before leaving this world. A very small consolation, indeed.

I came to know Hanoch Levin sometime before 1985, and started working with him as editor that same year. The work on the Complete Works edition was perhaps the most demanding, exciting, emotionally-loaded experience I have ever had – not only in our fifteen years of cooperation until then, but in my entire career as an editor. Over a period of roughly eighteen months, every two or three weeks I would receive a 'new' play to read and comment on; we would then meet to discuss my notes, and – often in one or two sessions of intense work – lock down the final version of the play. Time and time again I found myself astounded at the level of perfection he had achieved with these 'drafts'; I was aware that some of the work had been written just days earlier. All that was left for me to comment on was the rhythm of a verse here, the syntactic structure of a sentence there, sometimes the choice of a particular word – and that's it. Rarely did I have to question a whole scene or the structure of a play. Levin, for his part, was always attentive, always willing to hear a different voice.

There's one session I remember more than the others. We weren't yet sure that we would manage to go over all the plays together and, while discussing a few options for a particular phrase, I said to him: 'Listen, Hanoch, you're the author, it's up to you to decide here.' He gave me this direct, uncompromising look in the eyes and said, carefully weighing his words: 'You know, Mulli, as long as I'm here I will do it, but *when the bells of Hell toll*, you'll have to take the decisions yourself.'

I can still feel that shudder down my back. *The bells of Hell* – since when did Hell have bells that toll?! What a way of uttering the unutterable.

***

A lot has already been written (mostly, but not solely, in Hebrew) about Levin's world, and much more is sure to be said in the years to come. Even putting aside all his non-theatrical works, there's no end to what can be discovered in his rich output of some sixty or more plays, of which but a quarter are presented in these three volumes. I would like to elaborate on one particular feature that seems, to me at least, crucial in trying to embrace Levin's world, and maybe understand the impact it has on us, his readers and spectators.

The same effect happens to anyone who watches a play by Levin: this feeling that what we hear and see is radically alien to what we are used to – in life as well as on stage. There's something unexpected, unpredictable, in everything that happens there, and we can't immediately put our finger on what it is. Why, this is not the theatre we're used to, this is not the world we're acquainted with, people don't talk or behave that way, at least *we* don't, we're not the kind of people who act like this, or utter such horrible, insulting words!

And yet, some wicked demon, down in our bellies – the very place from which all those nasty laughs originate, whenever one Levin character humiliates another – this demon keeps whispering to us that maybe we're not so different from these 'Levinians' after all. Could it really be that deep down we, too, feel things that way, and that we'd love to be able to say these unbearable, cruel phrases out loud, only we're too kind to pronounce them, too civilized, too polite?... Too conscious, maybe, of what we're saying?... What would our therapist say if we came up with such an idea?...

Well, let's see what Levin has to say about consulting a professional therapist. In a scene from *The Labour of Life* (vol. 2), Yonah's wife, Leviva (whose name, incidentally, means something like 'potato fritter'), is trying to convince her husband not to leave home (and her) after thirty years of marriage. And it goes like this:

> LEVIVA: I hope you're old enough to
>   understand by yourself that the problem
>   isn't me.
>
> YONAH: Not you?
>
> LEVIVA: Not me. I'm the pretext.
>
> YONAH: So who is the problem?
>
> LEVIVA: You. And there's nowhere for you to
>   run, because anywhere you go you'll be
>   carrying yourself around with you.
>
> YONAH: You don't say! That's some deep
>   insight, eh?
>
>   A real revelation!
>
> *(To himself.)*

> Now she's going to suggest I see a
> psychologist.
>
> LEVIVA: And I also think you should see a
> psychologist.
>
> YONAH: What good will a psychologist do me?
>
> He also wants to run away from his wife.

You could say: what the heck, a little joke at psychotherapists' expense – after all it's a comedy, isn't it? But the deeper you delve into Levin's work, the more you understand how firmly this attitude is embedded in his dramatic world. His work is strewn with passages and situations that mock – sometimes quite bitingly – the very idea of psychology as something that can help. And it's not just that Levin doesn't have too much sympathy for psychotherapy; he simply does not accept the whole idea of psychological baggage as a basis for treating our innate human nature. In Levin's world, psychology is almost illegitimate.

Some 120 years after the appearance of Freud's *Interpretation of Dreams* (1900), we sometimes tend to forget how deeply the development of psychoanalytical and psychological concepts has changed our view of ourselves, our relations with each other, our way of seeing things and talking about them. Can we possibly imagine ourselves today without a solid, busy 'unconscious'? Don't we laugh daily at the 'Freudian slips' of others (and ourselves)? This 'psychologese' is so pervasive that it is nowadays an inseparate – and inseparable – part of our language, of our thought, of our whole umwelt (the way we see the world).

And so here comes a playwright who mercilessly, in one stroke, strips us of this conceptual blanket we wrap around ourselves, leaving us bare, uncovered, unarmed, facing a cold, ruthless world. Levin's plays do not offer us, for example, the luxury of the modern assortment of 'inhibitions', 'anxieties', 'phobias' etc. No, in his world there's only this one big, old-fashioned, but oh how truly human, Fear: we are afraid to die.

Or, as he has put it, with ironically positive formulation, in the title of one of his plays: *Everyone Wants to Live* (vol. 3). It's surprising how much you can achieve by limiting yourself to this 'reduced' stock of pre-Freudian feelings – love, hate, desire, pride, jealousy, contempt, and the like; you can, that is, if you're Hanoch Levin. In his world, people don't keep anything in their unconscious (they don't appear to have one): they just hurl everything right in each other's face.

There's another side to it. When we say psychology, we generally associate it with digging into one's memories, one's childhood, one's past. But Levin's characters, well...they just *don't have* a past, or they usually don't have one, or very little of it – just what is directly connected to their actions in the present, and certainly not enough for a decent therapeutic session. What do we know, for example, about the characters' pasts in *A Winter Funeral* (vol. 1) or in *Suitcase Packers* (vol. 2)? And the almost-abstract characters of *Walkers in the Dark* (vol. 2), what past do they have? Nothing, or close to nothing. And the same holds of most of Levin's plays, comedies and tragic/dramatic plays alike. Levin's characters are all stuck in their miserable – funny or scary – present, without any past (and with no perspective for a better future, either). And where people have no past, what kind of 'psychology' can we extract from them?...

Much has been said about Levin's attraction to Greek tragedy, with his growing tendency to combine poetry and drama as a means of achieving that powerful impact theatrical art can have; his achievements in this field are comparable, in my opinion, to those of the greatest playwrights. Similarly, in ways very close to those of Greek tragedy, Levin is interested first and foremost in the *actions* of his characters, not in their emotional background. To us – constantly flooded as we are with TV series and films, novels and plays, that always ask 'Why did he/she do it?', or in other words, 'What is the psychological motivation of his/her actions?' – such action-only, psychology-free drama comes as a bit of a shock. Levin's characters certainly have their motives, but it's always those 'simple' ancient passions – the struggle to have power over others, the naked sexual desire, the effort to preserve your life at all cost – the very basic needs of the flesh; it never goes 'inside' or 'backwards', to childhood experiences, traumas, complexes, and the rest.

I never discussed any of this with Levin – he wasn't much of a talker (was I?...), least of all when it came to his work; but I'm pretty sure he was very much aware of this, his sweeping aside of the whole psychological pile. As a matter of fact, in one of his plays he goes as far as to explicitly ridicule any psychological/psychoanalytical *interpretation* of his plays, a practice that is, sadly, quite common. To be sure, this kind of interpretation tends to be the norm for most of today's literary productions which, in turn, are indeed based on psychological patterns, and so easily lend themselves to such procedures. Levin, however, is made of different stuff.

In *Walkers in the Dark* there is a group of characters called 'Thoughts', including Vague Thought, Murky Thought, Pickled Herring Thought and others. One of them, a female one (most of the Thoughts are males), is called *Lajan Thought* – a name clearly referring to Jacques Lacan, the famous French psychiatrist and psychoanalytical theoretician, who had (and still has) some enthusiastic followers in Israel, especially in literary academic circles. Here is how the Narrator presents Lajan Thought in the play:

> NARRATOR: In our city, another thought
> has recently been wandering the streets:
> abstract, complex, the last word in post-
> modernist theory à la the elderly professor
> Lajan. She is beautiful, bold, heavenly,
> refined, contemplated by young students
> with long straight hair on autumn nights in
> Paris…

Approached by the wooing Ass Thought and Pickled Herring Thought, at their first meeting all she has for them is condescending contempt:

> LAJAN THOUGHT: Who are you? I'm from the Sorbonne!
>
> ASS THOUGHT: I'm from the undies.
>
> PICKLED HERRING THOUGHT: I'm from the barrel.

But on their second meeting, though Lajan Thought starts by treating Ass Thought as 'ugly', and 'rude', and 'shallow and primitive and naïve, and practically an imbecile…' – she suddenly changes her tone to announce that 'you intrigue me' and you 'amuse me' with 'that spark in your eyes' 'and your lips'… *Bref,* Lajan Thought (how French of her) has fallen in love with Ass Thought. But a happy ending is nowhere in sight. Act 5 opens, and:

> *(Enter ASS THOUGHT and LAJAN THOUGHT arm in arm. ASS THOUGHT is trying to extricate himself.)*
>
> LAJAN THOUGHT: My love…
>
> ASS THOUGHT: No, it won't work.
>
> LAJAN THOUGHT: I love you.
>
> ASS THOUGHT: With sorrow I tell you, Lajan's theory doesn't turn me on. I am a simple thought. Since childhood I have been carrying only myself, bearing the load, the torments, but also the pleasure. And that is how I shall remain, with myself, the burning nights of delirium, alone, in bed, with

pounding heart, feverish, with palpitations
and hoarse moans. I wish you the best.

LAJAN THOUGHT: Goodbye. I'm flying off to
try my luck elsewhere, before I grow old.

ASS THOUGHT: Try Eastern Europe – Warsaw
or Prague – they've just purged themselves
of Communism.

LAJAN THOUGHT: Farewell to you, close study
of the ass!

ASS THOUGHT: Farewell to you, alluring
cultural musing!

LAJAN THOUGHT: Au revoir, Orient!

ASS THOUGHT: Adieu, Paris!

(Exit LAJAN THOUGHT.)

You don't have to plainly identify Levin with this Ass Thought
of his (you can always blame *me* for having done just that), but
what do you otherwise do with these words, 'Lajan's theory
doesn't turn me on. I am a simple thought'? And if anything
is not absolutely clear, Ass Thought is still here to sum up the
situation for you – and don't miss the generalizing plural form,
very loyal to the original Hebrew, of the opening verb: it's a
Credo we have here, a Declaration of Faith (italics are mine):

ASS THOUGHT: What more can we say about
the ass that has not been said. The heavenly
softness, without bones, without nuances,
without psychology, without nonsense, softer
than the skull, firmer than the breast, a
midpoint between steel and water, and
between the two sides a riverbed runs deep

– oh, the painful, promising, dark crevice,
the great rift valley, a place for all seasons,
oh ass, sweet-and-sour suffering, a whole
world unto itself, which, like our world,
is also meaningless, but *who cares about
meaning*, meaning be damned as long as it is
firm and valid, standing strong!

***

In a 1964 article called 'Against Interpretation', Susan Sontag
discusses the role of art criticism in our modern world. Perhaps
today her words are worth listening to even more than they
were at the time (italics are hers):

Interpretation takes the sensory experience
of the work of art for granted, and proceeds
from there. This cannot be taken for granted,
now … Ours is a culture based on excess, on
overproduction; the result is a steady loss of
sharpness in our sensory experience.

…

What is important now is to recover our
senses. We must learn to *see more*, to *hear
more*, to *feel more*.

Our task is not to find the maximum
amount of content in a work of art, much
less to squeeze more content out of the work
than is already there. Our task is to cut back
content so that we can see at all.

The aim of all commentary of art now
should be to make works of art – and, by
analogy, our own experience – more, rather

than less, real to us. The function of criticism
should be to show *how it is what it is,* even
that it is what it is, rather than to show *what
it means.*

***

Go and see Levin's plays. Go and you will *see more, hear more,
feel more.* And you're sure to realise for yourself *what it is* and
that no interpretation is needed, because really, *who cares about
meaning* (dixit Ass Thought).

Mulli Melzer, February 2020

Mulli Melzer is the editor-in-chief of
Levin's *Complete Works* in Hebrew.

Hanoch Levin:
A Short Biographical Note

By almost unanimous consent, Hanoch Levin is Israel's greatest playwright ever, and he remains, to this day, one of Hebrew culture's most important and diverse artists. His oeuvre encompasses some twenty published volumes, and includes a strikingly wide-ranging variety of genres: comedies and tragedies, satirical cabarets, short stories and other prose, songs, poetry, humorous sketches, radio plays and screenplays. Throughout this comprehensive body of work, Levin created a world full of unmistakable characteristics and formulated a language that is unparalleled in Modern Hebrew.

Levin was born in Tel Aviv, in 1943, the second son to parents who fled Poland in the 1930s. The impoverished family lived in a small apartment in the south of the city. His father, a religious Jew, owned a grocery store and struggled to provide for the family. When he died suddenly, Hanoch, who was only thirteen, went to work to help support the family, and continued his studies at evening school. He abandoned the religious lifestyle completely at a young age, and after his compulsory military service he went to Tel Aviv University. In 1965, he began publishing poetry in literary journals, and wrote satirical features for the student newspaper. This was the beginning of a prolific writing career that would continue right up to his death.

The Six-Day War, in June of 1967, which marked a turning point in the evolution of the State of Israel, was to be a landmark event in Levin's own life. Shortly after the war, at the age of 24, he wrote the political cabaret *You, Me and the Next War*, which sharply scorned Israel's euphoric reaction to its victory in the war, and shattered the ethos of heroism and patriotic sacrifice. Levin was one of the first Israeli voices to criticize Israel's occupation of the Palestinian territories and its dire consequences for both sides. As a result of the cabaret, as well as two others that followed, Levin began to gain a reputation as a talented but controversial artist.

Alongside the cabarets Levin began writing plays, mostly comedies at first, such as *Ya'acoby and Leidental, A Winter Funeral,* and *Suitcase Packers* – comedies, but invariably tinged with biting criticism of Israeli society. In the early 1970s, Levin also began directing his plays, mostly meeting enthusiastic audience and acquiring critical acclaim. It was during these years that he developed his distinct theatrical language, as both playwright and director, and the name Levin began to be associated with unique, high-quality theatre.

Toward the end of the 1970s and early 1980s, Levin staged his plays *Execution, The Torments of Job* and *The Great Whore of Babylon,* which portrayed ruthless, cruel, and often bloody scenes, although even these were not devoid of a macabre humour. While audience members were frequently shocked, Levin's unique blend of horror and humour, colloquial language and poetic eloquence positioned him as a one-of-a-kind dramatist. These were the first of Levin's great plays – tragedies, human dramas, mythologies – that engaged with universal themes far beyond the scope of Israeli or Jewish reality. He went on to write and direct incessantly, working on both dramas and comedies – and a constant mingling of dramatic genres. His status as a leading playwright in Israel (and director of his own plays) became firmly established, in particular after his productions of *The Child Dreams, Walkers in the Dark,* and *Requiem.* In the last few years of his life, there was no longer any question that this was an extraordinary phenomenon in the Israeli cultural landscape.

In 1997, when Levin was diagnosed with cancer, an initiative to publish his complete works was launched, and almost thirty previously unknown plays were discovered in his files. All the same, the 16-volume edition was completed and published in 1999, shortly before his death. Levin continued writing right up to his final days, and even began directing his play *The Lamenters* from his hospital bed, but he died before he could complete his work.

Since his death in 1999, more and more of his plays continue to appear on Israeli stages, alongside new productions of his classics, and his work has also reached audiences worldwide. Plays by Levin have been translated into over 20 languages, there have been hundreds of productions, and every year brings new translations of his works into various languages. International audiences are becoming familiar with Hanoch Levin's world, and he is on his way to joining the ranks of the finest international playwrights.

Hanoch Levin was married three times, and is survived by four children.

Mulli Melzer
Translated by Jessica Cohen

KRUM

A Play with Two Weddings and
Two Funerals

Translated from the Hebrew by Jessica Cohen
and Evan Fallenberg

This 'play of two funerals and two weddings', in Levin's words,
is a comedy about the dreams, wishes, and complete failures of
a couple of people that live their feeling of worthlessness as a
fate. Even though it is set up, like many of Levin's comedies, in
a Tel Aviv neighborhood, the action could take place anywhere.

KRUM

Cast of Characters

KRUM

THE MOTHER *(Krum's mother)*

SILENTI

GLOOMER

DOLCE

FELICIA *(his wife)*

TAKHTIKH

TRUDY

DOOPA

TWEETY

BERTOLDO

DR. SHEBOYGAN

ORDERLY, BARBER, NURSE, GROOM, BRIDE,
PHOTOGRAPHER, UNDERTAKER

Premiere	Haifa Municipal Theatre, 1975
Director	Hanoch Levin
Costume and Stage Design	Ruth Dar
Lighting Design	Yekhiel Orgal

Cast:

KRUM	Ilan Toren
THE MOTHER	Fanni Liubitch
SILENTI	Shmuel Wolf
GLOOMER	Alex Monte
DOLCE	Mordechai Ben-Ze'ev
FELICIA	Ruth Segal
TAKHTIKH	Ilan Dar
TRUDY	Hanna Roth
DOOPA	Rachel Dobson
TWEETY	Maya Rothschild
BERTOLDO	Shmuel Calderon
DR. SHEBOYGAN	Giora Shamai
BARBER, PHOTOGRAPHER, UNDERTAKER	Shlomo Bar-Abba
ORDERLY 1, GROOM	Makram Khoury
BRIDE, NURSE	Dalia Cohen
ORDERLY 2	Yossi Kalman

ACT ONE

SCENE 1

Airport. Early evening. THE MOTHER, SILENTI.

THE MOTHER: They've announced the plane has landed. In a moment I'll see my son. Here he comes.

(KRUM enters with a suitcase and hugs THE MOTHER.)

KRUM: I had no success overseas, Mother. I didn't make money and I didn't become happy. I didn't have fun, I didn't get ahead, didn't get married, didn't get engaged, didn't meet anyone. I didn't buy anything, didn't bring anything. In my suitcase there is dirty underwear and toiletries. That's all, I've told you everything, and I want you to leave me in peace.

THE MOTHER: *(Eyeing the suitcase.)* There must be a surprise in there for me.

KRUM: No.

THE MOTHER: There must be a surprise for Mother.

KRUM: No! No!

MOTHER: What are you shouting for?! Who wants anything from you?! Did you come back home to argue?! *(She cries.)*

KRUM: Getting on my nerves already. You're very lucky I don't want to make a scene at the airport. Hello, Silenti. *(Pointing to the crying MOTHER.)* It's from joy. Why didn't Gloomer come?

SILENTI: He doesn't feel well. He's waiting for you at his place.

KRUM: Let's go.

(They exit.)

SCENE 2

GLOOMER's balcony, next to the balcony of DOLCE and FELICIA. Early evening. GLOOMER is sitting.

GLOOMER: Mr. Dolce! Mr. Dolce! *(DOLCE steps out onto the balcony.)* Excuse me for bothering you. In today's paper it says that crying opens up the diaphragm, and that a healthy person should cry from time to time.

DOLCE: You want us to cry together? But my wife and I are about to leave for a wedding.

GLOOMER: I thought I might ask you to put on a sad record. Sad music brings me straight to tears.

DOLCE: You'll have to cry quickly because we're on our way out.

GLOOMER: Could you possibly lend me your record player? I'll take care of it.

(FELICIA enters.)

FELICIA: You know we don't take the record player out of the house, except in cases when we're moving.

DOLCE: But you can hear it from our apartment; after all, the windows are open.

FELICIA: Put something on for him already and let's go.

GLOOMER: A singer, if possible. If the singer cries, it's easier for me to cry.

FELICIA: Put the Italian on for him.

(DOLCE exits.)

GLOOMER: Thank you. I feel that if I could only open up my diaphragm…

6

FELICIA: I heard. *(She exits. Sad music by an Italian vocalist can be heard. GLOOMER tries to cry. The music stops. DOLCE and FELICIA appear in fine clothes, out on the street. They look in GLOOMER's direction.)*

GLOOMER: I couldn't get it out. Not enough time.

DOLCE: We're sorry, we don't want to miss the appetizers.

FELICIA: Using our records to be happy, our records to be sad – do I dance to someone else's music?! Always taking advantage! People who don't have a record player should learn to cry from silence! *(DOLCE and FELICIA exit. GLOOMER tries to sing the song from the record, unsuccessfully. He stops.)*

SCENE 3

GLOOMER's house. Evening. GLOOMER. KRUM enters.

KRUM: Hello, Gloomer. I came back this evening.

GLOOMER: You saw a few things, did you?

KRUM: I didn't see anything. Most of the time I slept. They say life abroad, you know… Well, I didn't find it. I guess I like thinking about travelling more than travelling. You know me: I want lots of wants, but without any doing. Waiting as usual for the great novel of the century to be written by me. Waiting as usual to meet one day on the street, completely by chance of course, a rich, beautiful woman who suddenly desires me, and only me…

GLOOMER: Of course not *me*, I'm no competition for you, I'm ill.

KRUM: …and above all, waiting to miraculously find myself one day outside this neighborhood, outside this city, in a white house surrounded by a garden, far from the buses and the fumes, with a beautiful, seductive wife and two children.

GLOOMER: Name one of them after me.

KRUM: One thing you have to admit I've managed to this very day, despite all my loafing: not getting married. Because to get married and have children here, in this neighborhood, on a clerk's salary, that's the end of your dreams. Look around at everyone here. It's a disgrace. No. Not me. I want a year or two for myself. To sit and write a novel about this neighborhood, to make money off it and take my leave. Farewell, people, I made myself a little living off your lives and your suffering, and now I'm going to live. Good riddance. *(Pause.)* I'm only sorry about my mother. She's getting old. Wanted to live to see a grandchild.

GLOOMER: Krum…

KRUM: What's happened around here meanwhile?

GLOOMER: Nothing. You probably heard that Trudy's going with someone else. His name is Takhtikh. Graduated from technical college, or will soon.

KRUM: Trudy is mine the minute I call her. At the moment I'm just not interested. *(He stands up.)*

GLOOMER: Krum, I wanted to ask you something.

KRUM: I refuse to hear that question anymore.

GLOOMER: Just one more time, Krum.

KRUM: Absolutely not.

GLOOMER: Be a mensch, Krum. Look, I'm sick. One little question with one little answer. Just tell me, 'Yes' or 'No.'

KRUM: God, why did I come back!

GLOOMER: When is it better to exercise, in the morning or in the evening?

KRUM: In the morning.

GLOOMER: First let me list the pros and the cons for you.

KRUM: I know all your pros and cons by heart already.

GLOOMER: Let me give you the arguments one last time, and then you give me a last and final answer. It's no secret that the problem with my health is that to this day I can't decide if I should exercise in the morning or the evening. If I do it in the morning, before work, there's a risk that the exercising will wear me out and I'll be tired at work; and if I do it in the evening, before bed, there's a chance it'll be refreshing, and then I'll have trouble falling asleep. And midday is out of the question, because I'm not a man of compromise: with me it's either the start of the day or the end. There are other problems involved, like showering for example. If I decide to exercise in the morning, I take a shower afterwards, and then, what happens after work? Do I shower again? That's not realistic, especially in winter. And if I exercise at night, before bed, of course there's no point in showering in the morning, but then the question arises again: perhaps the water is refreshing, so the morning would be better. Fifteen years I've been grappling with the problem, and every time I make up my mind, I read an article in the newspaper that proves the opposite. Why don't they, once and for all, hold an international medical conference on this issue and make a final decision? Honorable doctors: you are killing us. Now tell me your final answer, on condition that you've considered all the arguments.

KRUM: Morning.

GLOOMER: But what if the exercise tires me out?

KRUM: Goodbye.

GLOOMER: Answer me, you see how much I'm suffering. It's not like I enjoy these questions, but they're eating me up. Come on, tell me already, if done in the morning, does exercise tire you out?

KRUM: Gloomer, you are a man with a morbid passion for health, and I have no more patience for you. That is my final answer.

GLOOMER: Meaning, you answered 'morning' just to get rid of the question. See? How can I take your answers seriously? What is the basis for your answer, when you say 'morning'? Huh? Are you a doctor?

KRUM: Good night. *(He exits.)*

GLOOMER: *(To himself.)* As a result of all these gnawing doubts, I have taken ill. Taken ill. Exercising is out of the question now. Even crying, I can't do.

SCENE 4

Café. Evening. TRUDY and TAKHTIKH sit at a table. SILENTI sits at a different table. KRUM enters.

KRUM: Hello, Trudy. I came back today.

TRUDY: I see.

KRUM: I wanted to write...

TRUDY: Do you know each other? Takhtikh, Krum.

KRUM: May I join you?

TRUDY: We were just thinking of leaving.

KRUM: It's not ten yet.

TRUDY: I'm tired. *(TRUDY and TAKHTIKH stand up.)* Good night. *(Turns to leave with TAKHTIKH.)*

KRUM: I'll come to your place later.

(TRUDY and TAKHTIKH stop. Pause.)

TAKHTIKH: He can walk you home.

TRUDY: Why?

TAKHTIKH: Because. He can walk you home.

KRUM: Why not? Shall I? *(To TAKHTIKH.)* It was nice to meet you.

TAKHTIKH: I'm sure it was. *(Sits down at SILENTI's table. KRUM approaches TRUDY, who has moved away a little.)*

TRUDY: You don't love me and I'm trying to forget you. Why do you keep showing up again?! *(Pause.)* You *do* love me a little.

KRUM: No.

TRUDY: Why do you torment me?

KRUM: What do you want? I suffer from this, too. *(He buries his head in her breast.)*

TRUDY: What am I doing, what am I doing? Once again sticking my head into something that can only end in sadness. *(KRUM pulls her outside. They exit.)*

TAKHTIKH: *(To SILENTI.)* Me and her… Nothing. Just friends. What do I care. They used to be together, didn't they? *(Pause.)* No? *(Pause.)* It's no good to be alive. Especially for someone who doesn't believe he deserves it. Have you ever felt your life, not from the inside, but outside, on your back, like a hump? *(Pause.)* Have you? *(Pause.)* You probably think you're really smart with those deep

11

silences of yours. A Chinese philosopher. Do you want to become known for being silent? It won't do you any good, you're not the first. In this neighborhood, chatty people have died and silent people have died. *(Pause.)* I myself keep silent for an hour sometimes, and I don't make a big deal out of it. *(He stands.)* Shall we take a walk?

SILENTI: I'm staying put.

TAKHTIKH: Me too. *(Sits down.)*

SCENE 5

TRUDY's house. Night. KRUM and TRUDY are getting dressed.

TRUDY: Takhtikh is in love with me and is driving me crazy about marrying him. And that's what I'll do in the end. *(KRUM tries to knead her breast.)* No, I've had enough. Don't play with my breasts, and don't ruin my life. I want a decision from you.

KRUM: I can't get married. Not now. It clogs up all my plans. I'm starting to write regularly, which is why I need a period of quiet to be free. Financially, too. After that...

TRUDY: There won't be any after that. I'll marry Takhtikh, we'll move to a new neighborhood, we'll have a kid, and when I run into you back here, arm in arm with your mother, with those same pants, those same plans, I'll laugh in your face.

KRUM: You'll laugh in my face and I'll put that in my novel.

TRUDY: Novel! I love that crap, and I myself don't know why. *(KRUM embraces her.)*

KRUM: Trudy.

TRUDY: *(Allowing him to embrace her.)* You don't believe a word that comes out of your mouth. You don't even try to convince me anymore. You know I'm yours, you just come and take.

KRUM: Trudy.

TRUDY: You're cold, so cold. When water gets dumped on your head, you come to me to dry off.

KRUM: I'm a big louse, I know it. But you can see I'm trying, really. Look, who do I come to when things are bad, if not to you? Whose bed do I climb into when I don't have another, if not yours? And who do I keep trying, unsuccessfully, to love, if not you? I really am a big louse. Slap me! *(TRUDY slaps his cheek, hard.)* Whore, you'll never see me again. I was just about to propose to you, now it's all over. *(Exits.)*

SCENE 6

Street in front of TRUDY's house. Night. TAKHTIKH. KRUM enters, sees TAKHTIKH, stops.

TAKHTIKH: Yes, it's Takhtikh. Standing here waiting half the night while you enjoy yourself upstairs with Trudy. I saw, I saw. At first the light was on, then you turned it off for an hour, then it was on again.

KRUM: What do you want?

TAKHTIKH: To get to know the man who has Trudy.

KRUM: My conscience is a little tired this evening, and I'm not sure you'll manage to wake it up.

TAKHTIKH: Let it sleep. And don't worry, I won't try to take Trudy back. I'm patient. So don't be in a hurry. And enjoy yourselves.

KRUM: Tell me, why do you do that to yourself? You graduated from technical college.

TAKHTIKH: I didn't graduate from anything. I'm a technician. I make a decent living, but I'm just a technician.

KRUM: You make me feel big. Get out of here already.

TAKHTIKH: Of course I'll leave if you tell me to, you're the boss. You have a free hand with Trudy. I just want you to know that even if you're small, I'm even smaller.

(They exit.)

SCENE 7

Street outside GLOOMER's balcony. Night. GLOOMER is on the balcony. DOLCE and FELICIA enter the street, heavy with food and drink.

GLOOMER: Hello, Mrs. Felicia and Mr. Dolce. How was the wedding?

FELICIA: It was.

GLOOMER: You ate a little, huh? What did you eat?

FELICIA: Excuse me, but we're digesting now. Let's go in, Dolce.

GLOOMER: Krum is back.

FELICIA: *(Stopping.)* Did he bring you something? Probably nothing. Well, I'll be making a visit tomorrow morning to Krum's mother.

GLOOMER: Was there chicken?

FELICIA: *(Laughing contemptuously.)* Chicken? Chicken is a fly compared to what they had there.

GLOOMER: You don't say!

FELICIA: Finally, a contractor's wedding. But who has the strength to talk now, Dolce? We'll go inside to digest.

DOLCE: I want to breathe a little more air.

FELICIA: He doesn't want to see me undress. *(She exits.)*

DOLCE: *(Laboring to breathe.)* Oy, I'm full.

GLOOMER: What else did they have there?

DOLCE: Don't ask.

GLOOMER: I won't dare even begin to be jealous.

DOLCE: Oy, I'm full. I'm dying.

GLOOMER: Probably had a band and dancing, too.

DOLCE: Who could think about dancing? Who could even move? From the table to the toilet, from the toilet to the table – oy, I'm full. How full I am. One more bite and I'm dead. I'm going to go kill myself with a piece of cake. *(Exits.)*

GLOOMER: *(To himself.)* I can't believe they didn't have dancing. Men and women dancing together, body to body, and with the music in the background, quietly making plans to get married.

SCENE 8

TRUDY's house. Early evening. TRUDY and DOOPA face the mirror.

DOOPA: I'm so unattractive. When one's eye flutters over me and keeps going, it finds a certain charm in me, but when stared at, my full ugliness is revealed. How, Doopa, can I make the eyes merely flutter, the eyes merely flutter and not stare?

TRUDY: A big butt. That's my problem.

DOOPA: You can afford to say that because you know you're more attractive than I am. You've got Krum, and before that you had Takhtikh, and even before that you had Krum again.

TRUDY: Great catches, the both of them. Krum comes and goes, comes and goes.

DOOPA: With me, they don't even come. I'm frisky and cheerful and I chirp like a bird, and I have no one. I'm all closed up inside, I'm exploding. So many things I could give a man, devotion and love, infectious laughter, and I have no one. And I'm still cheerful.

TRUDY: You've shriveled.

DOOPA: From nerves. And I'm still cheerful.

TRUDY: Krum has a friend, his name is Gloomer – would you be interested?

DOOPA: Gloomer? What a name. Gloomer. Gloom and doom? *(She laughs.)* Is he serious?

TRUDY: Who?

DOOPA: Gloomer! I mean, is he thinking about marriage or about fooling around?

TRUDY: Only marriage. He's not a guy for having a good time.

DOOPA: Oy, how I've been wanting one of those! Someone who will sit around the house with me in pajamas, who will be completely mine, and I'll serve him and I'll tickle him. I pray he'll be handsome. And cheerful. I don't much care if he's smart, but let him be cheerful, and let him have good skin. And be financially sound. Nothing excessive, but sound. I really don't care about his brains. And I pray that he's—

TRUDY: But why do you need to pray so much? Just ask me, I know him.

DOOPA: What's he like, Trudy? I'm begging you, have mercy.

TRUDY: Of all your prayers, I'm afraid there's only the
pajamas. Haven't I lost weight off my hips? He's ugly.
Very. So much so that it stops being an issue. If you find
any charm in him, you'll be the first. If you find any
cheerfulness in him, you'll be the first. Some of the time,
he's sick. The rest of the time, he thinks he's sick. Pajamas,
you wanted pajamas, you got it. What else? Money. If
you find any money there, you'll be the first. And the last
thing, in my opinion he's also stupid, but that you said
doesn't matter to you. A big butt, that's my problem.

DOOPA: But why?

TRUDY: Why, why! Look at this butt, I'm also asking why!

DOOPA: *(Bursting into tears.)* Why? Why?

TRUDY: But what kind of question is that, my dear Doopa?
These are the men destined for us, and these are the ones
we must take. Where is Doopa's famous cheerfulness?

DOOPA: *(Laughing.)* I'll find something nice in him, if it's the
last thing I do. You'll see.

TRUDY: If you can only get his pajamas off. Should I tell him
to wait for you at the café this evening at eight?

(DOOPA nods.)

SCENE 9

*Café. Evening. GLOOMER is sitting at a table. DOOPA enters and sits
down at a different table.*

GLOOMER: *(Eventually rising with hesitation.)* I think it's me.

(DOOPA draws near.)

Are you already disappointed? *(Pause.)* My name is
Gloomer.

DOOPA: Doopa.

GLOOMER: Sit.

(DOOPA sits down.)

What are you drinking?

DOOPA: A beer.

GLOOMER: I never drink beer. I would like to be a man
who drinks juice and milk. In reality, I drink tea. *(Pause.)*
They're in no hurry to serve you here. It's not such a nice
place. We could buy a bottle at the corner store and drink
it at my place on the balcony.

DOOPA: Not a good idea. I'm in a bit of a hurry anyway, I
have something to take care of this evening. *(Glancing at
her watch.)* Oy, it's already eight-fifteen. *(She gets up.)*

GLOOMER: I could walk you.

DOOPA: No need. Good night.

GLOOMER: Could we... Could we meet again tomorrow?

DOOPA: I'm busy tomorrow.

GLOOMER: And...

DOOPA: And after tomorrow too. Good night.

(GLOOMER touches her hair fleetingly. DOOPA leaves.)

SCENE 10

*KRUM's house. Morning. KRUM is sitting and eating. His MOTHER
sits across from him.*

KRUM: I can't stand it when people watch me while I'm eating and pin their hopes on me.

THE MOTHER: Who's got hopes?! Who wants anything from you?!

KRUM: You sit and watch me and pin your hopes on me day and night!

THE MOTHER: What does he want from my life?! I was sitting here watching a fly! I'm not allowed to watch a fly in my own house?!

KRUM: The fly is going to eat in a restaurant.

THE MOTHER: Go, go to a restaurant! A meal you begin as a son, you'll finish as an orphan!

(KRUM exits. FELICIA enters.)

FELICIA: Hello, Mrs. Krum. I saw Krum leaving, he looked angry.

THE MOTHER: Emotional. He's emotional because he came back yesterday from abroad.

FELICIA: If you say so. *(Looking around.)* He didn't bring you anything?

THE MOTHER: I have everything.

FELICIA: A little television?

THE MOTHER: I have a television.

FELICIA: A domestic brand.

THE MOTHER: The picture's fine.

FELICIA: A leather jacket? A purse? A handkerchief? *(Sniffing around.)* Oh well.

THE MOTHER: Madam Felicia, my son returned from abroad in good health, and that is what is important. He is healthy, he works and makes a living, what more could I ask for? Look, he even managed to save a little from his wages for a trip to Europe.

FELICIA: Mrs. Krum, Europe is not the issue here. Yes, he travelled. Although everyone travels these days. What is travel? A plane takes you and a plane brings you back. But never mind, he travelled. The real question is, is a person travelling toward something? Is he progressing to something, is he building something? And in particular, are there wedding bells in his future?

THE MOTHER: Look, Mrs. Felicia, under no circumstances could I say that I'm disappointed in my son. He has talent, people have always said that.

FELICIA: Of course, there's no need to skip right to disappointment. One can always keep waiting and hoping. Still, the question is, how long? A man does not stay forty forever.

THE MOTHER: My son is thirty-eight.

FELICIA: If you say so.

THE MOTHER: And for hoping, thank God, I still have the strength.

FELICIA: Of course you have the strength, Mrs. Krum, the question is whether there is any point.

THE MOTHER: As long as he is healthy and feels well…

FELICIA: 'Healthy and feels well!' What is that, Mrs. Krum? Everyone is healthy, the question is what one does with one's health. Does a person know how to use the time when he is healthy? Does he have anything to show for being healthy? Furthermore, who among us can say, 'I am healthy?' Illness, after all, gets the last laugh. *Pardonnez-moi.* I have no complaints, each to his own life. One person becomes a doctor, another a decorator. As long as you're pleased.

THE MOTHER: Mrs. Felicia, I am absolutely pleased with my son.

FELICIA: You are a stubborn woman, Mrs. Krum. Oh well. If you say so. You're pleased with your son, your son is pleased with you, and all I can do is envy you. *(Pause.)* Nothing? A little French cheese? Swiss chocolate? Oh well then. Now I've made myself hungry. I'm going to make lunch. Goodbye.

THE MOTHER: Goodbye.

(FELICIA exits. To herself.) Another attack we've fended off. All one's life, fending off attacks. Widowhood attacks you from the front? Deprivation is already attacking from the rear. You fended off a rent attack? The municipality comes at you from the side. You fended off the municipality? Felicia is lying in wait. You fended off everyone? Climb into bed to fend off a long, empty night.

SCENE 11

KRUM's house. THE MOTHER is sitting. KRUM enters.

KRUM: Mother, why aren't you asleep? *(Pause.)* Don't you feel well? Mother? Why don't you answer?

THE MOTHER: Pressure.

KRUM: Pressure where? Your heart? Do you have pain? Why aren't you talking?

THE MOTHER: Pressure.

KRUM: Should I call a doctor? Sometimes I have pressure in my heart, too. It goes away.

THE MOTHER: Mine doesn't. 'Mother, mother!' you'll say over my grave.

KRUM: Mother, I'm warning you, I'm not a well man.

THE MOTHER: You'll have many years left to be sorry.

KRUM: I'm going to die, Mother, I'm warning you, I'm going to die.

THE MOTHER: Who is the old lady here? Me. I'm going to die. I'm the old lady of the two of us. I'll die first. *(Pause.)*

KRUM: All right. I'll marry Trudy. *(Pause.)* Pleased? Happy?

THE MOTHER: Happy.

KRUM: After all, you wanted me to marry. You wanted grandchildren.

THE MOTHER: For me, you're doing this? Thank you very much, I have a television, that's enough for me.

KRUM: You wanted me to get married! You!

THE MOTHER: What are you yelling for in the middle of the night? Go yell at Trudy's. Go, go to Trudy.

KRUM: You, as usual, are not satisfied.

THE MOTHER: Is Trudy satisfied? Trudy doesn't have pressure? Go to Trudy.

KRUM: What do you have against Trudy?

THE MOTHER: I have something against Trudy? I wish you every happiness.

KRUM: So go to sleep.

THE MOTHER: When I want to go to sleep, I'll go to sleep. He likes it best when I'm asleep: I don't see, I don't ask, my nose just honks a little at the sky.

KRUM: When you're asleep I'm innocent, when you're awake I'm guilty.

THE MOTHER: And when I die you will hear the verdict!

KRUM: Oh, blandness, blandness. I'm trapped between walls of blandness. Bland in my mouth. Bland in my veins. Bland in front of my eyes. Bland, bland.

SCENE 12

GLOOMER at home. Evening. DOOPA enters.

DOOPA: Remember?

GLOOMER: I thought I'd never see you again, and I... I've already moved on, emotionally. Sit.

(DOOPA sits down. Pause.)

DOOPA: You want explanations?

GLOOMER: No. But I must say one thing: my nerves aren't built for uncertainties.

DOOPA: I understand you. But what can I say after such a short acquaintance?

GLOOMER: Perhaps I should rephrase my question: Could you explain what reason you could possibly have for not wanting to marry me? *(Pause.)* You have long pauses. Meanwhile, I fall apart.

DOOPA: *(To herself.)* Dear God, don't let me grow sick of this man so quickly. You, who have not handed me many reasons to be happy, but you have granted me happiness itself: do not make me sick of this man. Make his weakness find the appropriate compassion within me, allow his lack of charm to touch my heart.

(GLOOMER tries to caress her face. She turns her face away.)

GLOOMER: Why?

DOOPA: No looking. Eyes are crueler than fingers.

(GLOOMER caresses her face while it is turned away.)

GLOOMER: Except that if we ever want to… kiss, it'll have to be face-to-face.

(DOOPA reaches her hand behind her and probes GLOOMER's face.)

I haven't shaved. I didn't prepare for a woman this evening. *(Pause.)*

DOOPA: My answer is: Yes.

GLOOMER: *(Turning her face towards him at once.)* I fully believe that I am a sick and weak man, that I eat and breathe with supreme effort, and that I will never be able to take my place in the world in a healthful manner. I fully believe that I should be pitied, understood, not shouted at, not startled, not battered, and made no demands of. I fully believe that if I am left in peace, absolute peace, I may manage to live another three or four months, at best six, after which I will decline. In your arms. Such a pity.

(DOOPA laughs.)

You're already laughing at me.

DOOPA: You are so… Picturesque.

GLOOMER: Really? Do I seem picturesque to you? *(Pause.)* I think you're right. I really am picturesque. *(Exuberant.)* Oh… I am picturesque. You hear that? I'm a picturesque man. Picturesque, picturesque. Me. Stay the night.

DOOPA: Turn the light off.

(GLOOMER turns off the light. Pause.)

GLOOMER: I feel nice, I feel good, I'm going to die. *(Self-indulgently.)* I don't want to live, I don't want to live.

(They both laugh.)
And now I want to ask you one more question. Try to concentrate and answer me seriously.

DOOPA: I'm listening.

GLOOMER: When is it healthier to exercise, morning or evening?

DOOPA: Kiss my ass.

GLOOMER: What?

DOOPA: I've been warned about that question.

GLOOMER: *(To himself.)* Around here, I'm all played out. Maybe in Alaska they haven't heard of me yet. That's where I should go one day, to get a serious answer once and for all.

SCENE 13

Street in front of TRUDY's house. Night. KRUM enters.

KRUM: Trudy! *(Pause.)* Trudy!

(TAKHTIKH enters the street, shoes in hand.)

TAKHTIKH: You show up, you're the master, you're the man, you're number one, and I scurry off like a mouse. *(He turns to leave. TRUDY appears on the balcony.)*

TRUDY: Takhtikh…

TAKHTIKH: Make yourselves comfortable and don't worry about anything. *(He exits.)*

TRUDY: The next time you show your face at my place, I'm calling the police.

KRUM: We're getting married.

TRUDY: When?

KRUM: Right away. I mean, right after Gloomer.

TRUDY: Come upstairs.

KRUM: The bed is still warm from Takhtikh.

TRUDY: Nothing's warm from Takhtikh. Come on.

KRUM: So you admit that he was in your bed! Whore!

TRUDY: You were gone for two weeks, what did you want me to do?!

KRUM: *(Getting closer to her.)* Okay, I'm sick of it, I'll marry you, but I'll tell you honestly so all my cards are on the table: above all, what I need is quiet. You know who I am and what I have, and I know who you are and what you have. I don't want any unnecessary tenderness between us, I don't want you caressing me outside of bed. Don't call me pet-names, don't hang on my neck in the street. In general, your expressions of love send chills down my back – like fingernails on a chalkboard. If you just put up with me, that'll be enough. That's all.

TRUDY: If you wanted me to accept a marriage proposal like being spat at – I accept.

KRUM: *(To himself.)* I'm still trying to find something lovely in her and I can't. But there must be something about her, if someone else wants her. But what? What?

(They exit.)

SCENE 14

DOOPA and GLOOMER in DOOPA's house. Evening.

DOOPA: Trudy and Krum are getting married the week after us, and this evening the four of us are going to the movies to celebrate our engagements. I think that's them.

(TWEETY and BERTOLDO enter.)

TWEETY: Hello, Doopa.

DOOPA: Tweety! My God, it's Tweety!

TWEETY: I got the invitation to your wedding. I'm so happy that you're finally getting married. Meet Bertoldo. He's Italian. He speaks only Italian.

BERTOLDO: Molto lieto *(Pleased to meet you.)*.

TWEETY: Speaks only Italian. *(Pointing to GLOOMER.)* The father?

GLOOMER: I'm the groom.

TWEETY: Sorry. It's because you look so…

GLOOMER: Sick. Not old, sick.

TWEETY: Feel better.

GLOOMER: I won't.

DOOPA: Tweety is my good friend from childhood. She used to live here, then she moved to a villa outside the city. Since then we've become exotic to her. She visits once every two years.

TWEETY: You know how busy I am.

DOOPA: But you must come to the wedding.

TWEETY: That's just it, I'm going to Capri two days before
with Bertoldo. So I was passing by and I stopped in to
wish you congratulations.

(KRUM and TRUDY enter.)

TRUDY: Hello.

KRUM: Hello.

DOOPA: Trudy, meet Tweety, my good friend from
childhood. She used to live here. Now she's in a villa.

TRUDY: Nice to meet you. Trudy.

KRUM: Krum.

TWEETY: Nice to meet you. This is Bertoldo, he's Italian.

BERTOLDO: Molto lieto.

KRUM: *(To TWEETY.)* I seem to remember you, vaguely. You
were very little when you moved away.

TWEETY: I was seven.

DOOPA: Seven, and she already moved to a villa outside the
city. Imagine. And now she's going–where? To Capri.

TWEETY: Just for two weeks. I'm very pressed for time.

DOOPA: And she can't even make my wedding. By the way,
Tweety, Krum and Trudy are also getting married.

TWEETY: Bravo! Get married! Have some babies around
here.

DOOPA: We'll have some babies. We'll have some with
pleasure. We're on our way to the movies now, will you
join us, Tweety?

TWEETY: I'm very pressed for time. I promised Bertoldo a
night swim at the Hilton.

BERTOLDO: Ho caldo, voglio audare, ti voglio strappare una tetta sotto l'acqua. *(I'm hot, I want to go already, I want to tear into your tits under the water.).*

TWEETY: Due minuti, Bertoldino, comportati come si deve. *(Two minutes, Bertoldino, behave yourself.)*

BERTOLDO: Mi hanno rotto le balle questi schifosi, ti voglio scopare al Hilton. *(I'm sick of these disgusting people. I want to fuck you at the Hilton already.)*

(He pounces on TWEETY, hugs her and tries to unbutton her blouse.)

TWEETY: Basta, Bertoldo! No! *(Enough, Bertoldo! No!)*

(She pushes him away.)

Forgive him, he's Italian. Are you going to live here?

DOOPA: Until we find something better.

TWEETY: What's wrong with this place? And your man...

GLOOMER: Gloomer.

TWEETY: Groomer? All right, Groomer it is. At least he looks quiet.

GLOOMER: Weak. Not quiet, weak.

BERTOLDO: Madonna mia santa, ti sbatto qui per terra e ti chiavo davanti a questi sorci. *(My holy Madonna, I will knock you down on the ground here and fuck you in front of all these rats.)*

(Pounces on TWEETY again, trying to rip her blouse off, manages to pull off a button.)

TWEETY: Basta, Bertoldo! *(Enough, Bertoldo!)*

Down, you horny thing! Down!

BERTOLDO: Si, si, down, down.

29

TWEETY: *(To DOOPA.)* They're impossible, I'm telling you, they're impossible. *(Trying to button up.)* He knocked a button off.

(KRUM and GLOOMER bend over slightly to look for the button on the floor. They slowly get down on their knees and start crawling on all four and searching in every corner of the room.)

In any case, Groomer, take care of Doopa, she deserves it after so many years of loneliness.

DOOPA: I never complained.

TWEETY: Then why is your face so gray? And why is there no light in your eyes? No, no, you complained, and rightfully so. You cried at night, you couldn't fall asleep because of the suffocating feeling in your throat that you deserved something too. Something. *(Pointing at the crawling GLOOMER.)* And there is the something.

GLOOMER: What color is the button?

KRUM: Maybe it rolled into the hallway.

GLOOMER: But what color was it?

(They both continue to crawl around, searching.)

BERTOLDO: Via, via, andiamo, o ti spruzzo sul soffitto tutto quel che ho qui nei pantaloni. *(We're leaving now, or I'll spray everything I have here in my pants on the ceiling!)*

(He pounces on TWEETY. She tries again to get away from him, but he does not let go. He gives her a deep kiss on her mouth while everyone watches. He comes.)

TWEETY: *(Breathless.)* Oh, these Italians – savages!

(BERTOLDO tries to grab her again.)

Enough, Bertoldo, enough! Down, you horny thing! Down! Cercami il bottone, arza! *(Down, boy! Look for my button!)*

(BERTOLDO grabs her and tosses her in the air. TWEETY laughs.)

All right, I have to go, Doopa. He's like a cat, he doesn't care if it's a public place, especially since he's not in his own country. So congratulations, everyone. You deserve it, all of you. You really do. *(To BERTOLDO.)* Avanti. *(Let's go.)*

BERTOLDO: Che vadano a fan culo con la loro casa, Amen! *(They can go fuck themselves in the ass with their house, amen!)*

DOOPA: Bye, Tweety. Thanks for coming.

(TWEETY and BERTOLDO exit.)

And come visit!

KRUM: The button. *(He picks it up. He and GLOOMER look at the button.)*

TRUDY: A button. Big deal, a button. What, you've never seen a button before?

(KRUM puts the button in his pocket.)

KRUM: She left a faint scent in the air here. The scent of a faraway place.

GLOOMER: My nose is stuffed up.

TRUDY: If I used imported soap like her, I'd also have a faint scent of a faraway place.

DOOPA: All right, let's go to the movies already. We're late.

(They exit.)

SCENE 15

Cinema. Night. TAKHTIKH and SILENTI sit in one row. In the dark, KRUM, TRUDY, DOOPA and GLOOMER enter.

GLOOMER: Is this darkness or have I finally gone blind?

TRUDY: Shhhh, the film's started.

(They sit down in the row in front of TAKHTIKH and SILENTI.)

KRUM: O projectionist,

Darken the cinema,
So we will not see each other,
And will not have to
Look each other in the eye.

And now,
Show us a film,
Let it be riveting, and light and colorful,
With lovely, happy people,
Dressed well,
And beautiful, naked girls,
And houses with gardens, and fast, shiny cars.

And we shall sit in the dark,
Gazing at the light,
And drown the sorrow and indignity of our lives
In it for two whole hours.
And we shall imagine in our hearts that we are the
lovely people,
And with us are the beautiful, naked girls,
And ours are the houses with gardens
And the fast, shiny cars.

O motion picture,
Flickering strip of light,
On you all our hopes are pinned,
And on you, O projectionist,
Seated above our heads, who gives us, for the price of a ticket,
Two hours of true life
Within the lie that is our lives.

(The film ends. The lights go up. Everyone is grinning foolishly.)

Rise, wretched people. The film is over, be ashamed to live.

(They all stand up.)

TAKHTIKH: Hello, Trudy. Hello, Krum.

TRUDY: Hello.

TAKHTIKH: Here we all are.

TRUDY: That's how it is.

(KRUM, TRUDY, DOOPA and GLOOMER exit. TAKHTIKH looks at SILENTI for a moment.)

TAKHTIKH: And I'm stuck with you again, hey? The one I came in with, he's the one I leave with. Tell me, don't you have any girlfriends who are throwing a party right now, or who we can ask out? A cousin? An aunt? *(Pause.)* No miracles are going to happen to me, not to Takhtikh.

SCENE 16

TRUDY and KRUM on the street outside TRUDY's house. Night.

KRUM: Good night.

TRUDY: You're not coming up?

KRUM: I'm going to sleep.

TRUDY: What's wrong with you?

KRUM: Nothing, why?

TRUDY: You liked her.

KRUM: Who?

TRUDY: The one you haven't stopped thinking about for the past three hours. The one with a faint scent of a faraway place and two grown men on their knees looking for her button. *(Pause.)* Hug me.

(KRUM hugs her.)

Kiss me.

(KRUM kisses her.)

More.

(KRUM kisses her.)

Thanks to her, I get your most tender kisses. You know you'll never have her, no matter how hard you try. You have me, only me. I am your beauty, I am your glory. With me you live, for me you work, and from me you expect your children; at my side you fall ill, in my presence you collapse, and before my eyes you die, and beneath me you are buried, and to me you leave your clothes and your money and your name and your pictures! In my memory you still flicker from time to time, and in my oblivion you will be lost forever. I, and me, and beside me, and in me. *(She exits.)*

KRUM: *(To himself.)* Impressive biography, Krum. A woman excreted you – a woman swallowed you. O, holes – the garbage is ready. *(He leaves.)*

SCENE 17

A street outside a wedding hall. Evening. GLOOMER and DOOPA enter wearing wedding clothes. They seem to be in a rush. FELICIA, DOLCE, KRUM, TRUDY, THE MOTHER, TAKHTIKH and SILENTI follow them. GLOOMER turns around every so often and waves his hands victoriously.

GLOOMER: I got married! I got married!

KRUM: Bravo, Gloomer! Bravo!

(FELICIA stands before GLOOMER and opens her mouth wide.)

GLOOMER: Would you like to sing something?

DOLCE: My wife wants to know if, other than a piece of cake and a glass of wine, there's no hope.

DOOPA: You can see this is a hasty wedding. My husband is sick.

FELICIA: But we're healthy.

GLOOMER: *(Waving a hot water bottle in the air.)* I'm sick. Mrs. Krum, thank you for the gift, I'll use it tonight.

THE MOTHER: May you live a long life.

GLOOMER: And here's to your son's marriage!

THE MOTHER: If he doesn't have a little funeral first.

GLOOMER: *(Waving his arms victoriously again.)* Good night everyone, and thank you. I got married!

(He dashes off, followed by DOOPA, KRUM, TRUDY, THE MOTHER, TAKHTIKH, SILENTI. Pause.)

FELICIA: No music, no food. And it's only ten o'clock. Ten.

DOLCE: It's a good thing I pocketed a bottle of cognac right at the beginning. *(He removes a bottle from his breast pocket.)*

FELICIA: This whole wedding has the whiff of a funeral to it.

(DOLCE drinks. She takes the bottle from his hand and drinks. DOLCE grabs it back and drinks.)

What do you think – is the groom going to bury the bride, or the bride the groom?

(DOLCE drinks.)

The bride the groom, I say.

(She grabs the bottle from him and drinks.)

DOLCE: Where is the moon?

FELICIA: And now in a week's time we have Krum and Trudy's wedding. As far as I'm concerned, I'm already dressed.

DOLCE: Where is the moon?

FELICIA: What do you need a moon for?

DOLCE: It reminds me of a banana. I can't find the moon.

FELICIA: *(Pointing at her behind.)* It's here, come in and look for it.

DOLCE: *(Sadly, to himself.)* What a vulgar, stinking woman I got. What a vulgar, stinking woman I got.

FELICIA: What do you think – am I going to bury you, or you me?

DOLCE: *(Grabbing the bottle back.)* Let's go home.

FELICIA: I want to dance.

DOLCE: There's no music here.

FELICIA: We'll wait.

DOLCE: It's the middle of the street. At night.

FELICIA: I want to dance.

(Pause. From far away comes the truncated sound of a wail. GLOOMER appears on his balcony, sobbing and waving his arms victoriously.)

GLOOMER: I'm crying! I've opened up my diaphragm! I'm crying!

(His voice breaks. He buries his face in his hands and keeps crying. His crying slowly turns into a rhythmic sobbing. FELICIA takes DOLCE in her arms, and the two begin to dance to the rhythm of GLOOMER's sobbing.)

END ACT ONE

ACT TWO

SCENE 18

A street outside the wedding hall. Evening. TRUDY and TAKHTIKH enter in wedding clothes. They seem to be in a hurry. Followed by DOOPA, DOLCE, FELICIA, SILENTI.

TRUDY: *(To DOOPA.)* Why didn't Gloomer come?

DOOPA: He suddenly felt a weakness in his legs.

TRUDY: Send him my best.

(FELICIA stands before TRUDY and opens her mouth wide.)

DOLCE: My wife would like to know...

TRUDY: The wedding's over. Thanks to all of you and good night.

FELICIA: But we are people who eat!

(TRUDY holds TAKHTIKH's arm and hurries out with him. DOOPA follows. Pause.)

FELICIA: This one was even shorter than the last one. Obviously, when the groom is switched at the last minute, they try and finish as quickly as possible, out of embarrassment.

DOLCE: I'm going crazy. With me, I'm either starving or stuffed. In the end I'll die.

FELICIA: *(To SILENTI.)* When's your turn?

(SILENTI exits.)

DOLCE: *(Pointing to his empty breast pocket.)* No luck.

(FELICIA scowls. DOLCE takes out a bottle from his other breast pocket. FELICIA's face lights up. They exit.)

SCENE 19

TRUDY and TAKHTIKH's balcony. TRUDY is in her nightgown.)

TAKHTIKH: *(Offstage.)* Trudy. *(He enters.)*

Trudy. Are you getting some fresh air, or do you regret settling for me?

TRUDY: What a pain in the neck!

TAKHTIKH: I'm feeling such wonderful tranquility now that I'm constantly afraid I'll lose it. *(Pause.)* Shall I make us tea and cookies?

TRUDY: That's the most brilliant idea you've had in the last two weeks.

TAKHTIKH: *(Excited.)* Tea with cookies. Oh, tea with cookies. *(He exits, humming to himself.)* Trudy, Trudy, my Trudy...

TRUDY: *(To herself.)* Trudy. That's my name. I won't pretend it doesn't move me to hear someone singing it. Trudy. I never knew my name could be whispered so sadly, so tenderly, that it would suddenly take on such meaning. And when I hear him sing my name, that sensitive, devoted man who is now putting the kettle on, I can't help but feel something for him.

(TAKHTIKH enters.)

TAKHTIKH: The tea...

TRUDY: Oh Takhtikh, Takhtikh, if only you weren't such an idiot, with those puppy-dog eyes you look at me with...

TAKHTIKH: *(Looking at her, holding his breath in wonder.)* Trudy, you are a princess.

TRUDY: Stop talking nonsense.

TAKHTIKH: I'm telling you, you are a princess. Trudy. *(She kisses him with affection.)*

TRUDY: I understand what you mean, but I'm not a princess. Maybe a manager, that I could see, but not a princess.

TAKHTIKH: *(Brimming with emotion, embraces her.)* Oh manager, manager. I have a manager. And what a manager! Chairman of the board of managers! *(He leads her out.)*

SCENE 20

FELICIA, DOLCE and SILENTI stand on the street outside GLOOMER's house. KRUM enters.

KRUM: What happened?

FELICIA: Gloomer lost his balance and fell.

KRUM: He fell?! Just like that?

FELICIA: Gone are the days when it took a man months to fall. In the twentieth century you get up and next thing you know you fall down.

(KRUM turns to enter GLOOMER's house.)

Dr. Sheboygan is with him.

(KRUM stops. Pause. Everyone waits.)

DOLCE: The doctor is coming out, the doctor is coming out!

(DR. SHEBOYGAN enters, stands in the doorway of the house, regards the onlookers.)

SHEBOYGAN: I have given instructions to move the patient, Gloomer, to the hospital. I suspect a disorder in the nervous system. He must undergo thorough examinations.

FELICIA: Thorough!

SHEBOYGAN: I will not go into the details at this point. The reason for the disorder might be profound or it might be superficial, it might be physical or it might be mental, it might be temporary or it might be eternal.

FELICIA: Eternal!

KRUM: Pity him, Doctor, he has only just found joy in his life.

FELICIA: Pity all of us, Doctor. *(She turns her behind to him.)* And give us one big shot for a life of joy.

DOLCE: *(Turning his behind to the doctor, too.)* A shot for a healthy life, a life of good earnings, Doctor.

(SILENTI hesitates for a moment, then turns his behind to the DOCTOR.)

FELICIA: A shot for a different life, a different life, Doctor.

DOLCE: A life of healthy appetite, Doctor.

FELICIA: And a warm, full belly.

SHEBOYGAN: *(Silencing them with a wave of his hand.)* The medical profession firmly rejects your petition for mercy. The medical profession will feel no sorrow for your illnesses and your deaths. The medical profession will not pity your poverty, your crowded houses, the polluted air that you breathe and the noise that rattles your sleep at night. Furthermore, the medical profession will not collude with your dreams of a different life, a better life, life as it should have been. All that the medical profession is capable of doing is to heal you if it can, and in most cases it cannot. *(He walks past the rear-ends and exits.)*

41

SCENE 21

GLOOMER and DOOPA at home. Evening. GLOOMER is in bed.

GLOOMER: I must take my leave of this room. I will never see it again. Now someone else will live here, someone healthy, who will enjoy my bed and my hotplate. With you: you are healthy.

(The ORDERLY enters with a stretcher.)

And here's another healthy person.

(The ORDERLY approaches GLOOMER's bed.)

The thing I have been awaiting has truly arrived. It has truly arrived. I can't believe it. I don't understand. Where exactly am I?

(The ORDERLY is about to help GLOOMER onto the stretcher.)

No, wait a minute, it can't be. I'm always sick, I'm Gloomer, ask anyone, it's nothing serious with me. I was joking. I was joking all these years. Is this what I deserve? I swear, I wasn't being serious.

ORDERLY: Come on.

GLOOMER: Me? Are you talking to me? Honestly, he means me. That I should go. That I should go with him to the hospital. God, he really means that I should go with him to the hospital. To the hospital. Me. But why? After all, I am me. Do you hear, Sir? I am me. *(Shouting.)* If this is a dream, I demand to wake up now!

(The ORDERLY grabs his shoulder.)

You're not a dream, are you?

ORDERLY: Why should I be a dream? I have a wife and kids, I want to live, too. *(He tries to drag GLOOMER onto the stretcher.)*

GLOOMER: Thank you, I can do it myself. I'm healthy. See
for yourself. *(He is barely able to stand. He wobbles.)* No,
on my own. *(He cannot stand.)* In any event, it's best to
reduce the distance between the head and the floor. *(He
gets down on all four.)* Here we go. This way. This should be
proposed to the Minister of Health. *(Falls flat on his belly.)*
Even better. Safer yet. Slowly but surely. *(Crawling.)* See?
Healthy. *(He stops. His head falls to the floor.)* Healthy.

(The ORDERLY and DOOPA lift him and place him on the stretcher.)

ORDERLY: Let's go.

DOOPA: *(Running her hand over GLOOMER's face.)* I'll come
tomorrow morning.

(The ORDERLY begins to push the stretcher.)

GLOOMER: *(To The ORDERLY.)* She won't come.

(They exit.)

SCENE 22

*Hospital. Evening. GLOOMER lies in bed. KRUM and SILENTI are
next to him.*

GLOOMER: You see? You see I'm sick? And you made fun
of me all this time, and I was tempted to believe you. You
led me astray. What kind of people are you? One should
never, ever believe one is healthy. One is always sick –
always! When you're sick you're sick, and when you're
healthy you're sick. Where is Doopa?

KRUM: I don't know.

GLOOMER: Why isn't she here? I wanted to die in the
presence of a woman crying in the room – is that such a
grandiose ambition? What kind of people are you?

43

(To SILENTI.) Why don't you say something? What do the doctors say, Krum? Am I going to live?

KRUM: Yes.

GLOOMER: Oh sure. If a doctor tells me I'm going to live – that's the end. I don't see them curing me. They aren't even doctors, they're just models in white coats.

(The BARBER enters, pushing a small cart with his instruments. He walks to the head of GLOOMER's bed.)

Doctor, how many white blood cells? How many?

BARBER: Sorry, I'm the barber.

GLOOMER: You see? White coats! They're all barbers! They've brought me to a barbershop!

BARBER: Please sit up. I'll shave your head.

GLOOMER: Why?

BARBER: For the operation. *(He begins shaving GLOOMER's head.)*

GLOOMER: Operation. They'll cut me open. And where? In the hardest place to open – the head. They're not going to cut me. No. Not Gloomer. With Gloomer they'll carve me up. Not much to do on this head, huh?

BARBER: Just a little in the back.

GLOOMER: Mother Nature herself prepared me for the operation.

BARBER: I used to have a barbershop on the outside. Mostly for kids. I don't like kids, they go wild, they won't sit still. I like it better in here. The customers are quiet, they let me do my job. *(He finishes and holds a mirror up to GLOOMER.)* Take a look. *(He puts his instruments on the cart. To KRUM.)* Be well. *(He leaves.)*

KRUM: We'll go now, too. Good night, Gloomer. We'll see you in three days, after the operation.

GLOOMER: And make sure Doopa comes. I want a crying woman. Tell her: It's included in the marriage.

SILENTI: Good night.

(KRUM and SILENTI leave.)

GLOOMER: You'll miss me yet! *(To himself.)* God, forgive me. I was a man of surfaces, I lived a life on the surface. But if I never got around to having a sublime thought, it's only because I didn't have time to solve my exercise problem. And when I ask you today to forgive me and make things easier for me, it's only because I believe that my suffering from the exercise issue was great, so great, and could have stacked up to any sublime suffering. The amount of my suffering, God, is the only thing to my credit, because without it I have nothing. Nothing.

(NURSE enters, holding a syringe.)

What now? Manicure? Pedicure?

NURSE: A shot to help you sleep well. *(She injects him.)* Now sleep.

GLOOMER: *(Slightly drowsy.)* Don't go. Why are you going? Have you forgotten me? Have you forgotten everything between us? The fire, the passion, the power? Come with me. I've made you a nice little house, where we will spend the rest of our days, and in the house there is a bathtub large enough for the two of us, I will soap you and the two of us will know nothing but joy.

NURSE: Good night.

(She leaves.)

GLOOMER: I have made many women happy, and I will make you happy too.

SCENE 23

DOOPA at home. Evening. BERTOLDO enters.

BERTOLDO: Ciao, buon-giorno. *(Hello. Good day.)*

DOOPA: Ah, the Italian. Time to start singing. What are you doing here? Where's Tweety?

BERTOLDO: *(Gesticulating.)* Partita ieri, tornera fra due giurni, Bertoldo solo, solo. *(She went abroad yesterday. She'll be back in two days. Bertoldo is alone, alone.)*

DOOPA: *(Laughing.)* Tweety's gone for three days, and you're looking for company? Is that what you're trying to tell me?

BERTOLDO: Si, Si. *(Yes, yes.)*

DOOPA: Sit down.

> *(BERTOLDO sits next to her, places his hand on her shoulder. DOOPA removes it.)*

> My husband is sick. *(She tries to explain with hand gestures.)* My husband. Sick. Hospital. *Hospitale.*

BERTOLDO: Si, si, hospitale. *(He returns his hand to her shoulder, DOOPA removes it again.)*

DOOPA: Actually, maybe you know – what do you Italians say, when is it better to exercise? Morning or evening? *(She tries to explain using hand gestures.)* Exercise. Sport.

BERTOLDO: Si, si sport!

DOOPA: *(Starts demonstrating exercises, raising her arms up and to the sides. BERTOLDO looks at her breasts, and suddenly comes from behind and puts his arms around her so that his hands are on her breasts. DOOPA does not protest. She freezes for a minute, then, to herself.)* Here you are, Doopa. Italy.

> *(BERTOLDO hugs and kisses her, and she responds. KRUM enters.)*

46

KRUM: Excuse me.

(DOOPA stands up.)

I just came to tell you about the operation. It was a success. The tumor they removed was malignant. *(Pause.)* It would be nice if you visited him, at least once. There's not much time left.

BERTOLDO: *(Rising.)* Ma cosa vuole quel cazzo. *(What does he want, the prick?)*

KRUM: I have the doctors' permission to take him to the seashore tomorrow, to watch the sunset for the last time. So if you would like...

BERTOLDO: *(Approaching KRUM.)* Ma cosa vuoi, perche disturb! Perche non ci lasci in pace, non vedi che siamo ocupati! *(What do you want? Why are you disturbing us? Why don't you leave us alone? You can see we're busy!)*

(KRUM exits. BERTOLDO returns to DOOPA and puts his hand on her shoulder. She removes it.)

BERTOLDO: O, tutto da capo! *(Oh, back to square one!)*

(He puts his hand on her again, she removes it. He tickles her neck, she shakes her head. He tickles her breast, she refuses.)

DOOPA: To the Hilton.

BERTOLDO: Hilton?

DOOPA: Hilton!

BERTOLDO: Ma va' fan' culo col tuo Hilton! *(Go fuck yourself in the ass with your Hilton!)*

(They exit.)

SCENE 24

Park facing the sea. Twilight. KRUM enters quickly, followed by SILENTI pushing a wheelchair in which GLOOMER sits, wearing a large hat.

KRUM: Because of all those traffic jams, we're late, and now there are only a few minutes before the sun sets. Over here, Silenti, quick. Here's the park, from here we can watch the sea and the sunset. Turn him with his face to the sun.

GLOOMER: Fresh air, air that smells of sport.

KRUM: Gloomer, look at the horizon. The sun is almost setting.

GLOOMER: Why are you rushing me out here to see the sun? What's the big deal…

KRUM: Look, look at the color of the sky. And have a look at the flowers around us, too.

GLOOMER: Had I only breathed in this kind of air my whole life…

KRUM: To your left is the Hilton Hotel. Silenti, turn him toward the Hilton. Look, Gloomer. Tweety went to swim in the Hilton pool. Remember Tweety?

GLOOMER: Tweety. But what's with you guys, bringing me out here to see –

KRUM: Oh, the sun, the sun! We're going to lose the sun! Seize the sun, Gloomer! Seize it!

GLOOMER: *(Straightening up in his wheelchair, startled.)* Krum! Am I seeing the sun for the last time?! The last time?!

KRUM: The sun! The sun!

GLOOMER: *(Taken aback.)* No! The sun hurts me!

48

KRUM: Hilton!

GLOOMER: Hilton hurts me!

KRUM: Look at the sea, Gloomer, seize the blue. Gloomer!

GLOOMER: The blue hurts me! The sea hurts me! The whole world hurts me!

KRUM: Look, look Gloomer, look! A ship! That way, a ship!

GLOOMER: The last one? The last one, Krum? Won't there be any more ships? Not even one?! A boat? A drawing of a boat?!

KRUM: It's sailing away! Seize it!

GLOOMER: No!

(A PHOTOGRAPHER, BRIDE and GROOM rush in.)

PHOTOGRAPHER: We're missing the sunset. Stand over there on the boulder facing the sea.

(The BRIDE and GROOM position themselves in front of GLOOMER.)

KRUM: And here are a bride and groom.

GLOOMER: No! They're hurting me! They shouldn't get married!

PHOTOGRAPHER: Look at one another and smile.

(The BRIDE and GROOM smile at each other. The PHOTOGRAPHER snaps pictures.)

KRUM: Look: a bride smiling with a sunset in the background.

GLOOMER: I want my picture taken with them.

PHOTOGRAPHER: *(To GROOM.)* Embrace her.

(The GROOM embraces the BRIDE.)

49

GLOOMER: I want to be in the picture too.

(KRUM approaches the BRIDE and GROOM.)

PHOTOGRAPHER: Sir, you're in the way. We have to catch the sun.

KRUM: *(Quietly, to the GROOM.)* My friend is sick. He's come to take his leave of this world. He wants to have his picture taken with you.

GROOM: Sick? We're happy people, getting our wedding pictures taken.

KRUM: One shot. For him. So he'll remain in a picture with a happy couple.

GROOM: *(To BRIDE.)* What do you say?

BRIDE: I'm sorry, but that'll bring us bad luck.

PHOTOGRAPHER: Kiss.

(The BRIDE and GROOM kiss.)

GLOOMER: With them! With them!

BRIDE: Take him away from here.

GLOOMER: I got married too! Where's Doopa?! *(He holds his hand out to the BRIDE and GROOM. The PHOTOGRAPHER shoots pictures.)*

PHOTOGRAPHER: That's it. Sun's gone. To the wedding hall. *(He leaves. The GROOM approaches KRUM.)*

GROOM: With all due respect to a man taking his leave of this world, we don't get the chance to get married every day. *(He turns to leave with the BRIDE.)*

GLOOMER: *(Calling after the BRIDE.)* Show me your ass!

(The BRIDE and GROOM, alarmed, huddle together and run off.)

KRUM: It's getting dark. Let's get back to the hospital. *(To GLOOMER.)* One last glance at the sea?

(GLOOMER's head sinks between his shoulders and he does not react. They exit.)

SCENE 25

TRUDY's house. Early evening. TRUDY, pregnant, is sprawled in an armchair. DOOPA enters with a suitcase.

DOOPA: Hello, Trudy. I came to say goodbye.

TRUDY: Gloomer is on his deathbed.

DOOPA: I'm going away.

TRUDY: Where to?

DOOPA: I've been offered a job in a supermarket up north. Check-out girl. Lots of men go through the check-out, maybe one will stop. *(Pause.)* What's there between him and me, Trudy? I don't know him at all, I only know his illnesses. The wedding didn't take. The few times I managed to sleep beside him in bed and listen to him moaning, that didn't take either. There was nothing between us. We didn't have the time. *(Pause.)* You're looking at me like a whore. What? It's very convenient to have a Doopa in the world. Doopa will marry the dying ones. Doopa will lay them in their graves. Doopa will take it on herself, all the filth. *(Pause.)* Doopa is on her way, people! To the great expanse of the supermarket! My laughter will chime with the coins in the register. A cheerful man will pass by and buy American cigarettes and aftershave and he'll tear me from the cashier's stool straight to the airport.

(Meanwhile, TRUDY has fallen asleep without DOOPA noticing.)

I feel a little sorry for him and I kind of make myself sick. So what? Trudy? *(Pause.)* You've fallen asleep. You get tired quickly these days. Absorbed by your pregnancy. You've made yourself a nice home, too. *(She gets up and takes her suitcase.)* And you'll be holding a baby soon. *(She sneaks out. TAKHTIKH enters. He wakes TRUDY.)*

TAKHTIKH: Chairman of the board of managers.

(They leave.)

SCENE 26

Hospital. Early evening. GLOOMER lies in bed. KRUM and SILENTI are next to him.

KRUM: Doopa's gone. She won't be back.

GLOOMER: Doopa? She's ugly. Let her go. Krum, go to a sporting goods store tomorrow and buy me a pair of tennis shoes and a racket. In the end I've decided: afternoon, tennis. If I play tennis with beautiful girls in the afternoon, I'm getting exercise *and* I'm spending time with women. Tennis in the afternoon is best.

KRUM: Tomorrow I'll buy you sneakers.

GLOOMER: Krum, I want to be healthy, I want to be healthy! What I've lived until now, that wasn't living. I was just preparing for life, I was just making plans, that's not called living, that's not called living! *(Quietly.)* The worse it gets for me, the more I cling to life. Like a fly to filth. What a disgrace. *(He cries silently.)* They don't give you a minute's rest, then they lay you to rest. *(Pause. Stops crying.)* And what's outside? Spring? What else? I'm in the hospital and outside what else would there be but spring?

KRUM: Outside it's cold and gray. The weather is unpleasant.

GLOOMER: But I can see the sun from here.

KRUM: The clouds have covered it up.

GLOOMER: I miss out on so many things if I die.

KRUM: You're not missing anything.

GLOOMER: Yes I am. I'm missing so much.

KRUM: You're not missing anything, Gloomer, I'm telling you you're not. Look at us, look at our lives, look at the lives we still have to drag out – what are you missing out on?! Look at our houses. Look at our women. Think of the daily effort to make a living, to get a little more! Think of the lack of grace in our lives, the lack of beauty, the lack of love, because no one taught us how to grab it when it's handed to us! Think of the senseless running around from place to place, the endless roaming at night, and the never-ending games we have to play – what are you missing out on? What are you missing out on, Gloomer?!

GLOOMER: *(His voice weakening.)* I'm missing, I'm missing…

KRUM: *(As if shrinking; SILENTI does the same.)* Look at us, Gloomer, is this what you're missing out on? This? This face? This back? These knees? These last few convulsions on Earth before they put us in?!

(He and SILENTI shrink inward. And suddenly GLOOMER starts to shrink inward too, as if taking part in their game. KRUM and SILENTI, in response, shrink even further, and then, all at once GLOOMER stops and lies motionless. KRUM and SILENTI freeze for a moment, then try another movement or two to awaken GLOOMER, but GLOOMER does not react.)

Gloomer? *(Pause.)* Gloomer, do you understand? *(Pause.)* Gloomer?

(DR. SHEBOYGAN and a NURSE enter quickly. SHEBOYGAN leans over GLOOMER, then straightens up, covers GLOOMER's face with a blanket, and turns to KRUM.)

(Defensively.) Don't tell us that... *(Trying to dodge.)* Don't tell us that...

SHEBOYGAN: He's dead.

(KRUM stands still.)

He's dead. He has moved from the domain of medicine to a no-man's-land. This man is forsaken. The years of his upbringing and molding, the food he ate, the books he read, the medicine he took, the dreams his brain produced, the huge amount of work and the money of the people who prepared his life for him, all of it, all the investment has now come to nothing, and its remnants— forsaken.

KRUM: Nevertheless, he made us laugh a little.

SHEBOYGAN: He made you laugh? Who are you?! You will be forsaken, too.

(The ORDERLY enters, wheels out GLOOMER's bed, leaves with the NURSE. SHEBOYGAN turns to leave.)

KRUM: Doctor.

(SHEBOYGAN stops.)

You will forgive me, but you're speaking like an undertaker. You are a doctor. You must leave some hope, if not for the dead then for the living.

SHEBOYGAN: Yes. There is still one hope.

KRUM: You see?

SHEBOYGAN: You must hope for exhaustion.

KRUM: For exhaustion?

SHEBOYGAN: Yes. There is still one hope. You must hope for exhaustion. What will ultimately heal you is exhaustion. You will grow old, you will weaken, and with weakness comes rest. And just as you will have no more strength to be happy, so will you also be too weak to shout, to protest, to suffer. Serenity will then come to you, and you will sink into it. You will be very, very peaceful, you will be the peaceful remnant of a low, sunken, orderly life. A thick layer of ash will cover all the loves that have ended, that were cut off, that you dreamed of and never were, and that left you, in the end, alone. And then, very quietly, without defiance or bitterness, you will begin one day to die. You will take no interest in life, in God, in hope, in the meaning of your life. A tiny sliver of strength will remain in you, just enough to face hope with a blank stare, a stare that will also gradually blur. Until you die. So hope for exhaustion.

SCENE 27

Street outside DOLCE and FELICIA's house. Late morning. FELICIA is dressed up.

FELICIA: Dolce! We're late! The bris is at noon, and as I remember their wedding, they have a tendency to finish quickly.

(DOLCE enters, dressed nicely.)

Do you think they'll have table service or just a buffet?

(The UNDERTAKER enters across the stage, pulling a gurney with GLOOMER's body on it, shrouded in black. Behind the gurney are KRUM, THE MOTHER, SILENTI carrying a suitcase. FELICIA and DOLCE see the funeral procession and try to quickly get away to the other side. KRUM notices them.)

KRUM: Mr. Dolce! Mrs. Felicia! The funeral procession is here!

DOLCE: I'm sorry, but we've got Trudy and Takhtikh's bris.

FELICIA: We can't do everything. We're not birds.

(DOLCE and FELICIA leave in haste.)

SCENE 28

Cemetery. Midday. The UNDERTAKER pulls the gurney with GLOOMER on it. He is followed by KRUM, SILENTI and THE MOTHER.

UNDERTAKER: No relatives?

KRUM: None.

UNDERTAKER: We'll keep things short, then. *(He lowers the body into the grave.)*

KRUM: Be gentle. He was sick.

(The UNDERTAKER buries GLOOMER. He holds his hand out to KRUM. KRUM takes a bill out of his pocket and gives it to him. The UNDERTAKER puts the cash in his pocket and holds out his hand again.)

UNDERTAKER: For being gentle.

(KRUM gives him another bill. The UNDERTAKER leaves. THE MOTHER leaves after him.)

KRUM: *(To the grave.)* And now from your death, Gloomer, from your death and from your suffering, I'll gather momentum and finally start writing seriously. Because I may never have this opportunity again.

(He exits with SILENTI.)

SCENE 29

Street outside GLOOMER's house. Afternoon. DOLCE and FELICIA come back from the bris. They stop.

FELICIA: Well, just like I said, the groom died first.

DOLCE: I'll miss him a little. The music, the medications.

FELICIA: May God forgive him for the wedding he had. Some people are born for weddings, and some people are born for bar-mitzvahs. You have to accept that.

(DOLCE gives her a long stare.)

Isn't that so? What are you looking at? I'm still alive. With a healthy man at my side, doing everything that needs to be done. With a good appetite. And the result: I'm not lonely. I'm not lonely.

(DOLCE does not take his eyes off her.)

You won't die so fast either. With me, you'll stick around. Felicia will look after you. You are my natural backdrop, my 'taken for granted,' my 'there is no doubt,' my 'of course,' my sweet 'of course.' *(She pinches his behind.)* Oy, such a *tuches*, such a *tuches* that God split into two – half for me, half for you.

DOLCE: What a vulgar, stinking woman I got. I don't want to share my *tuches* with you! I don't want to share my bed with you! I don't want to share my toilet with you! I don't want to share anything with you! I thought you would die over time! I was wrong! You'll never die! You and your refrigerator, you're both immortal! I'll die! Me! Like Gloomer, I'll die! I will die!

(FELICIA slaps him hard across the face.)

57

FELICIA: You'll live! We came together in the fresh air. We laughed together in the stench. We will rest together in the suffocating dirt.

(They exit.)

SCENE 30

Street. Night. SILENTI walks with a suitcase. KRUM enters.

KRUM: Silenti, where to?

SILENTI: *(Shrugging his shoulders.)* Going away.

KRUM: Where to? Did something happen?

SILENTI: No.

KRUM: Then why?

SILENTI: *(Shrugging.)* I'm bored. In particular…

KRUM: Go on.

SILENTI: In particular, I'm bored.

KRUM: What are you going to do in a different place?

(SILENTI shrugs.)

After all, it'll be the same wherever you go. At least here, people know you.

SILENTI: I'm bored.

KRUM: Looking for action, are you? You want to try your luck in another place? Tell the truth.

SILENTI: No. Just because.

KRUM: I know, I know, you want to succeed, you want to be rich, you want a wonderful woman you'll bring back here in an American car to show her the neighborhood you grew up in. Tell the truth! I don't believe you! You kept quiet the whole time, you hid your ambitions. I know these silent types. Secretly dreaming of success, of women!

SILENTI: I give you my word: I will remain poor, lonely and bored.

KRUM: In that case, stay with us in the muck!

SILENTI: I just wanted to get away. I'm bored. Goodbye.

KRUM: Who do you think you are, going away and leaving the rest of us here?! Who do you think you are?! Not even a human being! You are one of the comical elements of the landscape of my youth! Your face, like the crumbling plaster on the walls of the houses on this street, exists only as the backdrop to my life, a page in my novel, it has no other existence – none at all!

(SILENTI exits.)

None at all!

SCENE 31

KRUM's house. Night. THE MOTHER is seated. KRUM enters.

KRUM: Why aren't you sleeping?

THE MOTHER: I can't.

KRUM: Take a sleeping pill.

THE MOTHER: I want a grandchild. A grandchild I could rock in a cradle would put me to sleep.

KRUM: What can I do?

THE MOTHER: A grandchild. I was preparing for a wedding.

KRUM: So was I.

THE MOTHER: You had Trudy.

KRUM: I wanted to have something more than Trudy.

THE MOTHER: You don't.

KRUM: I have desires.

THE MOTHER: You have Trudies. Trudies. In your world, in your arm's reach, in the portion fate has granted you – there is nothing more than Trudies. Trudies, and working in an office, and feeding a child, and another, and a mortgage for the rest of your life. There's nothing more for you, my dear son, there are no more toys for you in the world. *(Pause.)*

KRUM: But I do have desires.

THE MOTHER: Give them up.

KRUM: I'm going to start writing now.

THE MOTHER: Writing?! Don't bring up that nonsense with me again.

KRUM: Try to fall asleep, Mother.

THE MOTHER: There are no more toys in the world for you.

KRUM: Sleep, sleep.

THE MOTHER: There are no more toys in the world for you!

KRUM: Sleep, Mother, sleep.

THE MOTHER: There are no more toys in the world for you!!

KRUM: *(Almost strangling her.)* Sleep, Mother. Close your eyes, already. Close them.

THE MOTHER: You won't rest until I close them forever. I am the final witness to your failure – murderer!

(KRUM exits.)

SCENE 32

Hilton ballroom. TWEETY and BERTOLDO are dancing. KRUM enters.

KRUM: Remember me?

TWEETY: Remind me?

KRUM: Krum. We met at Doopa's, before her wedding.

TWEETY: Oh, yes. The button.

KRUM: I have the button.

TWEETY: Keep it.

KRUM: Thank you.

TWEETY: How is Doopa? How's her marriage?

KRUM: Her husband died.

TWEETY: Oh, poor Doopa. She is so unsuited to happiness. Weren't you supposed to get married right after her?

KRUM: Yes, but I didn't.

TWEETY: Oh, you people, really. Did something happen?

KRUM: No. In fact, if I can speak candidly, I called off my marriage on… the same evening I met you. *(Pause.)* How was Capri?

TWEETY: I've already forgotten. I'm leaving again tomorrow morning.

KRUM: Where to?

TWEETY: Los Angeles.

KRUM: I've always dreamed of that city.

TWEETY: I can only envy you that a place like Los Angeles still evokes such excitement in you.

KRUM: And I envy you that you've reached the level where Los Angeles no longer evokes anything in you.

TWEETY: And with that mutual envy, let us part.

KRUM: Forgive my impertinence. I look at your bottom and I say to myself: that is a bottom that has sat in California. One young lady's bottom has seen more of the world than my mother and I have seen put together. Where is the justice in that?

TWEETY: *(Laughing.)* Which does occasionally make me think: such a bottom, that has seen so much, shouldn't God have exempted such a bottom from having to go to the toilet?

KRUM: Take me with you to Los Angeles.

TWEETY: Why would I?

KRUM: No?

TWEETY: No.

KRUM: I thought maybe. I mean, I love you. *(Pause.)* Sorry.

TWEETY: Why? You're nice.

KRUM: Yes? So shall we?

TWEETY: Someone's waiting for me there.

KRUM: A man?

TWEETY: A man.

KRUM: Will you get married?

TWEETY: Of course. He's finishing his doctorate, and then – to Brazil.

KRUM: And Bertoldo?

TWEETY: Bertoldo is temporary.

KRUM: Does he know that?

TWEETY: He will tomorrow morning.

KRUM: *(Going over to BERTOLDO.)* Did you hear that? You're temporary! You're out of here tomorrow! Psssss…

BERTOLDO: *(Jerking his head.)* Ma cosa vuole quel cazzo? *(What does this prick want?)*

TWEETY: *(To KRUM.)* That's it. I think I'll go home.

KRUM: I apologize for speaking out of place. I'm trying to write a novel and I'm collecting material.

TWEETY: An artist…

KRUM: Something like that.

TWEETY: Explain to me how it is that you all start off as writers and you end up as waiters.

KRUM: That's why it's so important for me to get out of here. I feel it's a matter of life or death. If only I could get out into open spaces…

TWEETY: Who's stopping you?

KRUM: How? Where to? Who would pay? What would I live on? And my mother?

TWEETY: I don't believe that if you want something badly enough it's impossible.

KRUM: You don't believe. You float in here on a pink cloud of 'everything's possible,' perfuming the air with a thin scent of 'everything's possible,' and you don't believe. And yet there are people for whom 'impossible' is not a word to be toyed with.

TWEETY: Perhaps one really should feel sorry for people of your type once in a while. The trouble is, I'm pressed for time and I forget.

KRUM: I don't forget. People like you are born to hurt people like me.

TWEETY: You really are nice. I'll allow you to give me a kiss before you leave.

KRUM: With a taste of Los Angeles on your lips – goodbye.

(He leaves.)

SCENE 33

Night. TAKHTIKH sits alone on his balcony. KRUM is on the street.

TAKHTIKH: Hey, Krum.

KRUM: Alone again?

TAKHTIKH: So what? Just because I married Trudy and I have a child, does that make me an insensitive person? I have sensitivities, I have insomnia, you bet I do. And I'll tell you something else: Sometimes I look at Trudy's face and suddenly I want to cry from the affront to all the aspirations and dreams I used to have. Me, with my talents... Instead – Trudy. Every night I knead her buttocks like a baker. She has black hairs on her thighs and under her nose, I'm sure that's not news to you. But her flesh – you may not be up to date on this – her flesh has begun to ooze. And I love that yellow, hairy spillage more than I love my own life. 'More than my own life' – well, I may have gone a little too far. But I can't live without her. I have a terrible attraction to her. Sometimes when I don't see her for half an hour I feel like I'm going to go crazy. Do you see the contradictions? And it's all bouncing around inside me. So who says I've stopped being sensitive and complicated? Why don't you come in?

KRUM: I'm in a hurry. Have you finished?

TAKHTIKH: No, I haven't. You're quiet, you're probably laughing to yourself, saying: 'Thank God, this guy's suffering too.' Nonsense. Don't be so quick to rejoice. These are just little bumps in my happiness and Trudy's. You wouldn't understand that, of course. You're a cucumber. Nothing happens to you in life. You don't know what it is to have a burden, to have a home, to have love, to have your own child, yours.

KRUM: Good night. *(He turns to go.)*

TAKHTIKH: Your mother died. Two hours ago.

(KRUM stops.)

SCENE 34

Street outside KRUM's house. Morning. UNDERTAKER pulls a gurney with THE MOTHER's body on it, shrouded in black. KRUM follows.

UNDERTAKER: No relatives?

KRUM: I'm the son.

(They keep walking.)

Here's the house. Wait.

(They stop. To the corpse.) Rise from the dead, you dear, rotten soul, and reawaken in me my childhood faith that your powers are invincible. Rise, you who birthed me and raised me, whom I trusted that one day would redeem me, that one day you would tear off a mask and behind the façade of suffering and desolation a face of joy would be revealed, and we would laugh, laugh at the bad dream

65

we'd had. Rise, Mother, and come inside to make lunch for me, for I will not accept any other possibility. I will not. I will not.

(He lets out a howl, as if he is about to burst into tears, but he manages to hold it in.)

No, no, not yet. I am not yet ripe for this kind of crying.

(The sobbing mounts in him again, but he holds it in again.)

No, there will be time for such terrible grief, and I am not yet ready. Later. One has to prepare, to gather strength, to eat well, sleep well, exercise every morning. One has to ripen, to shore oneself up in preparation for that day, and that day will arrive, and I will burst out in a huge tempest of emotion, and a massive wave of tears will wash over me, and every crevice of my soul will open, and I will cry and cry, about everything, about my mother and my life and my loves, and about all the wasted time that will never return, and I will break through the suffocation once and for all, and then I will be pure and fresh – on that day, which I believe is yet to come – pure and fresh and finally ready for life.

(The tears well in him again, and again he manages, with difficulty, to hold them in.)

Not yet. I will exercise every morning. Later.

(The UNDERTAKER pulls the gurney. KRUM follows. They exit.)

END

SCHITZ

A musical play

Translated from the Hebrew by Naaman Tammuz

A four-person 'musical play', later adapted into a full-scale opera.
The bourgeois existence of an elderly couple, seeking only to
marry off their daughter (and get rid of her, while they're at it),
is disrupted by the eruption into their life of not one, but two
wars. A unique blend of musical comedy and biting satirical
themes typical of Levin.

Cast of Characters

FEFECHTZ SCHITZ

TSESCHA, *his wife*

SCHPRACHTZI, *his daughter*

TCHARCHES PELTZ

First Act

SCENE 1

A room in the Schitz household. Evening. TSESCHA, FEFECHTZ, SCHPRACHTZI. Eating.

TSESCHA: Hard times,
 Schprachtzi my girl,
 lock your backside up at home,
 preferably in a safe
 hungry men with axes are roaming the streets,
 they'll finish off
 your rump fillet
 and you'll have nothing
 left to offer
 when your man finally arrives.

(To the meat.)

Fifty lira a kilo. Shocking. Human flesh is getting cheaper than pig meat.

(To SCHPRACHTZI.)

Come on, hurry up and get married.
Hurry up and get married, come on.
Why aren't you getting married?!
You're already dry,
any second now you'll crumble into little grains of dirt;
What do you think I got married for? For myself?
You think I need this?
I got married in order to marry off a daughter!

Get married already! Come on! Get married already! Get married already, come on!

SCHPRACHTZI: Oh, why don't you just die already!

TSESCHA: Get married and then I'll die.

SCHPRACHTZI: Die and then I'll get married. Dying first. I'll be free, my face will soften, the spark will return to my eyes, and then a man will see me leaning on a double gravestone and reach his arm out to me.

TSESCHA: But can't you see that your mother and father are already dying?!

(The Song of Anticipation for a Man.)

SCHPRACHTZI: Oh, for some man to show up, God, please,
let me see a man's shadow fall across my dress,
because my heart's already tired and my blood's getting cold,
my flesh which was firm is now limp and weak,
and from one year to the next, my smile gets more bleak,
soon the time will come around
soon I'll be well overdue
for getting a small poodle to carry me through.

FEFECHTZ: I don't understand what's missing in my daughter Schprachtzi that no one wants to take her? I mean, it's a real bargain. It's all meat, clean meat, no bones at all. And whichever side you approach from – you've got plenty. You've got plenty. You like leg – you've got leg. Like the breast – take breast. Tongue – here's tongue. You wanted kidneys – here are the kidneys. And everything's tender and fresh and melts in your hands. You rest your head – and your head sinks in. You tickle – it laughs. You stroke – it moans. You talk politics – it listens and simultaneously makes you a salad, and you look quietly at the backside

70

and get aroused. I don't get it, I mean in terms of meat I'm giving away two women's worth in one!

SCHPRACHTZI: Oh, for some man to show up, God, please,
let me see a man's shadow fall across my dress,
he can be not much to look at, he can carry a purse,
he can be a little tired and a bit past his prime
he can be mediocre in bed and not show me a good time,
but he'll rest his head on my chest
and I'll have something of my own and feel blessed.

It's Saturday evening. And instead of being an orphan I'm single. I'll go to the party at my good friend Tsfarvadila's, I'll eat and dance, and maybe I'll leave my nipple-marks on some man's chest.

(Exits.)

FEFECHTZ: Television!

(TSESCHA and FEFECHTZ exit.)

SCENE 2

The living room in TSFARVADILA's house. Night. A party. Music and dancing. SCHPRACHTZI is sitting alone.

SCHPRACHTZI: I ate twenty sausage sandwiches out of hunger, ten out of anticipation and anxiety, and five more out of disappointment, and now I'm full of energy. Everyone's dancing and I'm waiting.

(Starts crying.)

No, I mustn't. I must be appealing, appealing!

(Tries hard to look appealing.)

This time I must! I must! Mm! Mm!

No! The effort's making me ugly! I mustn't!

I must be calm, calm.

But the minutes are passing

and I'm not getting younger by the minute!

Oh, another minute has passed!!

No, no, composure.

A little composure.

Time, please stop. Give me a moment to recover, to sort my hair out, to wipe my face. Don't wash over me. Please don't! It's not stopping. From the moment you step into it, you're travelling, travelling, till the day you die. Help! Take me out of time! Now I've grown even uglier. How do I look?! Thirty-five sandwiches are crying out from my flesh. Enough, this time I must! I must!

(Tries hard to look appealing.)

Mm! Mm!

(TCHARCHES enters, looks at her.)

TCHARCHES: I also sometimes suffer from constipation.

(SCHPRACHTZI leaps into his arms, drags him off to dance. Suddenly she stops, raises one hand with her little finger pointing in the air.)

I love the brutal contrast between your body and your little finger.

(SCHPRACHTZI brings a finger from one hand close to a finger from the other hand without them touching each other.)

I love the torn differential void on either side of which reside your fingers' dynamic self-restraint in not touching one another.

(SCHPRACHTZI points at her backside with her thumb.)

I love the shattering of your finger's direction against the absolute firmness of the wall of your backside.

(SCHPRACHTZI places her foot on a chair, passes one hand from behind, under her thigh, waves it out in front and touches her breasts which are hanging from above.)

I love the sneaky twisting deception of your hand's trajectory, to the point of gripping contact with the frontal lines of your breasts' dynamic, breaching force.

(SCHPRACHTZI stands motionless.)

That's the pinnacle, that's the greatest thing in the realm of operational achievability, and by that I'm referring to the stunning stillness of your body as its mighty mass crushes any possibility of movement.

SCHPRACHTZI: I'm Schprachtzi.

TCHARCHES: I'm Tcharches.

SCHPRACHTZI: Tcharches!

TCHARCHES: Schprachtzi!

SCHPRACHTZI: Schprachtzi.

TCHARCHES: Tcharches.

SCHPRACHTZI: Do you like me?

TCHARCHES: Yes.

SCHPRACHTZI: Of course you would say 'Yes'. And how do I know you're telling me the truth? And even if it is the truth, how do I know it's not just a transient truth?! How do I even know it's serious?! How do I know it's eternal?! Maybe in half an hour you'll think otherwise?! And if not half an hour, maybe in a week, a month, ten years?! Tell me, will you think otherwise in ten years?! Yes?! Because

I can't stand things which aren't eternal, I'm sick and tired of it being first this way then that way, I want things once and for all, forever: Are you mine, or aren't you mine?! Huh?!

TCHARCHES: Yours. Signed: Tcharches.

SCHPRACHTZI: Obviously, signed! But how do I know that your signature – which so far I've only heard about and not actually seen on paper – how do I know it's eternal?! How, how, how do I know it's eternal?!

(The Army Officer's Song.)

TCHARCHES: I was an officer in the army,
　　I led a unit on the battleground,
　　into the fire we ran,
　　I ordered them all to lie down.
　　Some are still lying there, unable to leave.
　　and I'm not what I used to be,
　　looking for someone with their heart on their sleeve
　　and a woman who knows how to weave.

SCHPRACHTZI: That's me, that's me, that's me!

TCHARCHES: When will you introduce me to your father, who owns two trucks and a fifty percent stake in a front end loader , and tell him about our engagement?

SCHPRACHTZI: Tomorrow, tomorrow I'll present you to my father, who owns two trucks and a fifty percent stake in a front end loader and we'll tell him about our engagement.

(They kiss.)

What's Schprachtzi eaten?

TCHARCHES: Lakerda[1].

SCHPRACHTZI: When?

TCHARCHES: Yesterday.

SCHPRACHTZI: That is indeed the lakerda I ate yesterday at
the vegetarian restaurant with my good friend Shoshkes.
Was I full from the lakerda?

(They kiss.)

TCHARCHES: You had halva for dessert.

SCHPRACHTZI: The halva's from today.

TCHARCHES: There's also some from yesterday.

SCHPRACHTZI: I eat halva every day, every day, every day!
Tell me about today's lunch!

(They kiss.)

TCHARCHES: Steak fat on your gums.

SCHPRACHTZI: From what time?

TCHARCHES: Fourteen oh five.

SCHPRACHTZI: He's precise and likes sticking his tongue into
filth.

TCHARCHES: I hate it when there isn't enough oil on the salad.

SCHPRACHTZI: I love the fact that we both hate the same
things. And now I'll tell you about one of my weaknesses:
Chips. When I see chips I get weak at the knees.
Oh, chips, chips!
Soft, fried, a little burnt,
like a brave tanned man in the desert sun,
a legendary figure from an Asian dream.

1 A pickled bonito dish eaten as a mezze in the Balkans and Middle East.

(The Love Song to Chips.)

I'd like to get married to chips,
Firm, tanned, hot as can be,
I'd wrap them up in a bag,
And go for a stroll by the sea.

I'd sit there on a little rock
And chew them nice and slow.
And then, facing towards the setting sun,
I'd let a little burp go.

TCHARCHES: The sun's already coming out of the night's arse.

SCHPRACHTZI: See you tomorrow.

(Exits.)

TCHARCHES: What can I do, I'm not very picky. My
desires are small and my aspirations are small as well.
Schprachtzi, two trucks and half a front end loader , so
what? If your desires are small, your disappointments are
small as well. And the nausea's equally small. Here, now
I'm a bit nauseous, so what? Do I throw up? Of course
not. If I throw up now, what'll I have left for later?

SCENE 3

A room in the Schitz household. Evening. FEFECHTZ, TCHARCHES.

TCHARCHES: Mr Schitz, your daughter and I are a match.
You'd be surprised at just how much. I like lakerda and
she likes…what?

FEFECHTZ: Skip it. What my daughter likes is deeply
engraved in my wrinkles.

TCHARCHES: Also lakerda. And sausage, and steak, and
pickled cucumber, and for the steak to be tender, tender

not tough, and for the blanket to be warm, and we laughed so much – it was the laughter of a spiritual fusion – when we discovered that neither of us – yes, neither of us – like it when the toilet seat's cold when you sit on it in the winter, and that's why we decided we'd upholster it. That's it for now regarding our world-view.

FEFECHTZ: In short, a wedding.

TCHARCHES: The ceremony, the hall, the food, the band, the clothes and the flowers – from the bride's side.

FEFECHTZ: And from the groom's side?

TCHARCHES: From the groom's side – the groom.

FEFECHTZ: That's not much.

TCHARCHES: Perhaps, but we can't do without it.

FEFECHTZ: You'll forgive me for interfering, but I'm the father, and the father's asking how the young couple's expecting to feed themselves.

TCHARCHES: That depends on how much the father gives.

FEFECHTZ: The father's poor. He doesn't have any money.

TCHARCHES: The father has two trucks and half a front end loader , and that's just on the surface.

FEFECHTZ: The trucks are losing money.

(TCHARCHES laughs.)

They're losing.

TCHARCHES: And the front end loader .

FEFECHTZ: Rumours. The father denies them.

TCHARCHES: In that case, the father will give a three-bed flat in town, or, alternatively, a three-bed flat outside town plus a car, plus two hundred and fifty thousand in cash, whether that's in town or outside town.

FEFECHTZ: The father has no choice but to smile sadly.

TCHARCHES: The father will smile when he's left with his daughter sitting on his knees.

FEFECHTZ: The father will bring the groom into his business and give him a decent wage.

TCHARCHES: If the father wants the daughter to raise a grandson on bread and onions, then that makes the groom think twice about the whole deal.

FEFECHTZ: The father will give a decent wage plus a two-bed flat until the first child.

TCHARCHES: The first is already on the way.

FEFECHTZ: The father will give three bedrooms as long as the ceremony takes place before the belly's showing.

TCHARCHES: The flat will be in town.

FEFECHTZ: Ten minutes from town – that's as good as in town.

TCHARCHES: Ten minutes from town brings us to the car clause.

FEFECHTZ: The father has no choice but to laugh despairingly hellwards.

TCHARCHES: Which is what'll happen sooner than the father thinks.

FEFECHTZ: Let it happen. The father doesn't have any money.

TCHARCHES: If the father wants to see his grandson more than twice every two years, the father will make an effort and give a car.

FEFECHTZ: The father will come to see the grandson by himself.

TCHARCHES: They won't open the door. The grandson will come to the father.

FEFECHTZ: The father will donate a pickup truck.

TCHARCHES: The groom isn't a chicken transporter, the groom is a grandson transporter.

FEFECHTZ: The father will swap it for a car when he sees the grandson.

TCHARCHES: The father won't see the grandson until he gives a car.

FEFECHTZ: The groom said the grandson was on the way.

TCHARCHES: So what if he did.

FEFECHTZ: The father won't let himself be made a fool of.

TCHARCHES: The groom will get a car and give the father respect.

FEFECHTZ: The father will think about it.

TCHARCHES: The father will decide now, because there's a child on the way.

FEFECHTZ: The father wants to know once and for all if there is or isn't a child!

TCHARCHES: The groom will only discuss the matter in the presence of a car.

FEFECHTZ: The father will give one.

TCHARCHES: Four doors.

FEFECHTZ: Why four?

TCHARCHES: The groom's sick of negotiating over everything! The groom feels like he's at a cattle market! The groom also has his honour, the groom is a sensitive creature, it's costing him enough of his health just to fall in love with the father's daughter, what does he need all this for, but he was an officer in the army and he knows what it means to do his duty, and that's why he's making every effort, but there's a limit! Four doors, for the last time!

FEFECHTZ: The father will give one. Is there a child on the way?

TCHARCHES: And two hundred and fifty in cash.

FEFECHTZ: Why? The father's bringing the groom into the business.

TCHARCHES: The groom has ideas of his own.

FEFECHTZ: The father's glad there are ideas, but the father doesn't have any money.

TCHARCHES: Doesn't have, but will give.

FEFECHTZ: The father swears he doesn't have any, he has nothing in cash!

TCHARCHES: The father will give, second time.

FEFECHTZ: The father's running from the IRS, running from debt collectors, only goes out in the street at night, the father's ruined!

TCHARCHES: The father will give, third and final time.

FEFECHTZ: The father will give, the father will give, the father will give! Why does the father even have to give?! The father's an orphan, no one's giving to the father! That's it, the father's had enough, the father wants a father. To receive, to receive for once instead of giving!

TCHARCHES: The groom's pleased to meet you, and now he's in a hurry, a wealthy female tourist from Los Angeles is waiting for him at the Hilton. Good luck to you.

(Gets up. TSESCHA enters.)

TSESCHA: Throw that Romanian some more. He's not leaving here on his own, I swore it, and Schprachtzi's not getting into bed with peanuts any more.

(Exits.)

FEFECHTZ: The miserable father will give a hundred thousand.

TCHARCHES: The miserable groom will take nothing less than two hundred.

FEFECHTZ: A hundred and fifty.

TCHARCHES: To the Hilton. Good luck to you!

(Gets up. TSESCHA enters.)

TSESCHA: Throw in some more. The Romanian thinks he's taking the money, but Schprachtzi's taking the money as well as the Romanian.

(Exits.)

FEFECHTZ: A hundred and seventy-five, and then the father's completely empty.

TCHARCHES: *(Sits down.)* Two hundred, only because the groom is fond of the father.

(FEFECHTZ shakes his head.)

Still two hundred.

(FEFECHTZ shakes his head less assertively.)

Two hundred.

(FEFECHTZ shrugs his shoulders.)

Good luck to you.

(Stands up.)

FEFECHTZ: Fine, two hundred.

(TCHARCHES sits down.)

Without a car.

(TCHARCHES stands up.)

With a car.

TCHARCHES: With a car! With a flat! With furniture! With money! Money! Everything! Everything!!!

FEFECHTZ: Everything! Take everything!
You don't have an ugly daughter to marry off,
and a wife with a little beard to make into a grandmother.
If you got a malignant tumour in your armpit,
you'd also give everything in order to remove it.
Take. Take everything.

(Throws some coins from his pocket.)

You wanted everything, didn't you?
You'll get the trousers soon.

TCHARCHES: Why are you angry? Party A wants a wedding, Party B wants a living. Both sides met and have reached an understanding, that's all. Can Party B call you Dad?

FEFECHTZ: And about the trucks and the front end loader – hands off! Because before you manage to stick your hand in I'll chop it off. In general, I'll squash you. You're a Romanian thief, but I'll make a Persian rug out of you. Call me Dad.

(TSESCHA and SCHPRACHTZI enter. They all hug.)

SCENE 4

A room in the SCHITZ household. Evening. Everyone.

TCHARCHES: Big daddy,
daddy with two pockets,
full, jingling,
two oases in an arid world.
Ay, pockets, pockets,
a man's real balls,
in you resides the power
which fertilises the world;
You, curators of the sperm
of business, of the buying, the selling, the pimping.
The oils tanks which turn
the wheels of industry and commerce,
Horns of plenty of the stock exchanges, of religion and
culture!
You herald construction and destruction, birth and death.
Not in individual units or by the dozen,
But in global wholesale:
You are the intoxicating, arousing drug,
Which spreads so many legs
on so many soft beds at night.

(Gets down on his knees and passionately kisses FEFECHTZ's pockets.)

FEFECHTZ: Yes. The time which has filled my pockets
has in the meantime also emptied my balls.

(The Song of the Pockets and the Balls.)

When I was twenty years old
I had myself two balls
Dreams and power came with ease,
But my pockets, my pockets were small
When I was twenty years old,
And flapped empty in the breeze.

When I was sixty years old
My pockets had filled with gold
Full of jangling and tunes,
But oh the balls, the balls.
When I was sixty years old,
Were two deflated small balloons

SCHPRACHTZI AND TSESCHA: But your money melted on
  our flesh
  And your sperm was lost between our legs,
  And when we lead your coffins past,
  With you cold, empty and small,
  No pockets and no balls
  It's us who will laugh last.

TCHARCHES: When you're twenty years old
  And in your pockets there's no gold,
  You'll stink in your bed all alone,
  And with both of your balls,
  When you're twenty years old,
  You'll have absolutely no one to bone.

So when you're twenty years old
Fill your pockets with gold
And keep your balls on ice,
And when you're sixty years old

With what's left of your balls

You can bang, if you want, the moon twice.

SCHPRACHTZI AND TSESCHA: But your money will melt on
our flesh

And your sperm will be lost between our legs,

And when we lead your coffins past,

You cold, empty and small,

No pockets and no balls

It's us who will laugh last.

TCHARCHES: *(To SCHPRACHTZI.)*

It's ten. We're late.

Tsfarvadila and her fiancé Schmargitskes will be here soon
to take us for an evening swim.

Are you dressed? Have you taken a hundred lira from
your father?

SCHPRACHTZI: Five minutes.

TCHARCHES: I'll be in the loo in the meantime.

(Exits.)

SCHPRACHTZI: I'm going for an evening swim with
Tcharches. I need a hundred lira.

FEFECHTZ: You're better off going to sleep. That's a cheap,
enjoyable and healthy activity.

SCHPRACHTZI: I don't have time now,
You can see:

(Wiggling her hips.)

This flesh has got to run, to take in
lots of juice and air and moonlight
and thousands of loving fondles.

TSESCHA: Schprachtzi,
    You've been appointed by your parents to take a man
    and enslave him to the family enterprise.
    Instead you've rising up with your hips
    against me and your father.

SCHPRACHTZI: I'll take this opportunity to tell you:
    I won't tolerate another word which isn't to my liking.
    We're done. There's no more sitting at home in the
    evenings under your pressuring gazes.
    I'm going to be a sovereign woman,
    I'll fill a different flat with my presence.
    In this flat I'll leave behind my prominent absence.
    Absence of my body, my movements, my laughter,
    in this flat there'll be left
    old smells, old furniture.
    Soon also the smell of medicines,
    the sound of bones cracking, a sigh,
    dense air, heavy breaths, grunts, end.
    This chair? – soon mine.
    These cushions? – soon mine.
    This flesh? – was once part of you,
    today it's separating.
    And when you feel the agonies of death,
    it's not this flesh which will be hurting.

FEFECHTZ: This flesh, it's me!

SCHPRACHTZI: *(Pats her own backside.)*
    You planted a coconut tree, Dad,
    someone else is going to eat the coconut.

TSESCHA: Look at her – Hips! A coconut!
    Just yesterday she was eating peanuts alone in the kitchen!
    I'm warning you Schprachtzi:

I've been full of dirt for thirty years longer than you!

(Pats her backside.)

Dad's still got a coconut of his own!

SCHPRACHTZI: Where? Where's the coconut?
It's only the packaging that's left.
Wrinkles, wrinkles,
crumbling wherever you look.

FEFECHTZ: And that's how, every night,
with yet another scratch on the furniture
the man, bleeding, goes to sleep.

SCHPRACHTZI: I understand that he's bleeding, and you are too.
A hundred lira for me to leave you to bleed by yourselves.

TSESCHA: Think hard Schprachtzi:
Tcharches, who is Tcharches?
Less than a month ago his death would have
mattered to us as much as the death of a Chinaman.
A stranger, just another man,
born to fill the time
between childhood and widowhood.
Decide now: Who does Schprachtzi belong to?

SCHPRACHTZI: Who does Schprachtzi belong to?
Schprachtzi belongs to the sausage, the French cheese,
the soft mattress and the fancy kitchen.
Those are Schprachtzi's small masters
and Schprachtzi's their loyal dog.

(TCHARCHES enters.)

TCHARCHES: Tsfarvadila and Schmargitskes
are waiting for us in the car downstairs.

SCHPRACHTZI: Excuse me Mum and Dad –
A watery delight is calling me.

(SCHPRACHTZI and TCHARCHES leave.)

SCENE 5

A room in the SCHITZ household. Night. FEFECHTZ and TSESCHA in bed.

FEFECHTZ: It won't be an easy fight.
The Romanian wants the money,
and Schprachtzi wants the Romanian.
I could have kicked the Romanian out,
but I'm Schprachtzi's father,
and Schprachtzi needs the Romanian
and the Romanian wants the money.

TSESCHA: Compromise with the Romanian,
do business with him,
give with one hand
and take with the other,
he'll be a good husband to Schprachtzi,
and my fingers are tingling for a grandson.

FEFECHTZ: Tsescha, the Romanian wants it all,
he won't just rip
the smile off our lips,
but also the gold teeth out of our mouths.
Summon all the forces of evil from afar,
and, Tsescha, don't forget whose wife you are.

TSESCHA: At the age of twenty, passion fans the flames of evil
in your soul
At the age of fifty Tsescha's run out of coal.

FEFECHTZ: What do you mean Tsescha's run out of coal?

(Puts his hand on her breast.)

TSESCHA: No. Like Schprachtzi said:
Only the packaging's left.

(The Song of Eternal Hunger.)

FEFECHTZ: Even when I was little, I was a wolf who was
never sated,
I'd eat a cow a day, but my heart would yearn for more,
flowers, sea and sky would leave me feeling deflated,
as soon as night fell – I let a cow into my bed.

And then I kissed her,
my heart tired and cold,
lots of meat in my belly,
and lots of meat to behold.

FEFECHTZ AND TSESCHA: A few years have passed,
we still want to live,
resting on the balcony,
finishing off leftovers.

TSESCHA: Even when I was little, I was voracious in the extreme,
from dawn to dusk I nibbled on apple cakes and honey,
I had so many dreams, I buried them all in whipped cream.
As soon as night fell – I went to bed with a lump of dough.

And then I kissed him,
my heart cold and full of qualms,
cream filling my mouth,
and also cream in my arms.

FEFECHTZ AND TSESCHA: A few years have passed,
we still want to live,
resting on the balcony,

finishing off leftovers.

FEFECHTZ: *(Bends over and addresses the front of his trousers.)*
If you rise up – everything will rise up,
the energy, the persistence, the excitement.
Today I need you, not for pleasure
but for the last drops of strength
with which to stand on my own two feet.
If you fall now –
everything falls.

(Pause. To TSESCHA.)

You've let me down.
Such erosion – I couldn't believe it.
I've read and seen other women –
But I never believed it would be you.
Your whole appearance at the age of twenty
screamed: it won't happen to me.
Well, I married a deception.
If I'd really had a happy life
I wouldn't have devoted fifty years to food.

(TSESCHA gets up.)

FEFECHTZ: Where are you going?

TSESCHA: For a bit of air.

FEFECHTZ: Breathe, breathe, and most importantly:
don't forget whose wife you are, Tsescha!

TSESCHA: *(To herself.)*
Whose are you, Tsescha?
Little Tsescha, weak Tsescha,
that's why little Tsescha likes going
in whichever direction the wind is blowing.

(Exits.)

SCENE 6

A room in the SCHITZ household. FEFECHTZ is in bed.

FEFECHTZ: Stupid life. What good does sleeping do me? If
sleep at least accumulated like an investment fund, I'd
know that I'm investing in something and that afterwards
I'd be left holding something. But in reality you get up in
the morning, and where's the sleep? It's leaked out in the
gaps between your dreams, you've gained nothing, soon
you'll be tired again and then you'll go to sleep again. I
wish I could lock sleep up in a safe. Same with food. You
eat, you invest energy, you've got the amortization on
your jaws and teeth, and then you get up in the morning,
your stomach's whining, where's the food? So far I must
have eaten at least six hundred cows, where are the cows?
I could have had a whole herd by now. And I have to see
all this waste with my heart aching, and then start again
every day. And it reaches the point where I ask: Why am
I alive? Or in other words: What am I going to die with?
Not food, not sleep, not even some little reserves of feeling
up a woman. It's no secret, a man dies empty.

(Gets up, gets dressed.)

(The Song of the Two Trucks.)

I have two pretty trucks,
one is orange, the other pink,
they carry cows by night,
and by day – workmen to the building site.

Once a worker got loaded instead of a cow,
the driver had made a mistake,
he drove him to the slaughterhouse,

where he was cut into a kosher steak.

The judge awarded me damages,
and the worker's family paid out
the price difference which I'd lost
between the worker and the cow.

And in order for it not to happen again,
I set a rule to always be obeyed
that every worker on the truck,
must sing cheerfully all day.

I have two pretty trucks,
one is orange, the other pink,
they carry cows by night,
and in the morning – workmen to the building site.

(Exits.)

SCENE 7

The beach, night. SCHPRACHTZI, TCHARCHES.

TCHARCHES: Forgive me, but every time I see you, I get this little desire in my heart to…

SCHPRACHTZI: I'm listening.

TCHARCHES: No, I'm despicable.

SCHPRACHTZI: You're not despicable. Tell me.

TCHARCHES: I'm despicable, I'm despicable. This little desire for your father not to exist. I'm despicable.

SCHPRACHTZI: No, you're not despicable.

TCHARCHES: I'm despicable, I'm despicable.

SCHPRACHTZI: I said you weren't despicable.

TCHARCHES: Are you sure?

SCHPRACHTZI: Yes.

TCHARCHES: Actually, you're right, why am I despicable?
What have I done? I just wish your father didn't exist,
that's all.

(Fondles her breasts.)

Not for him to die, it's not like I'm despicable, I know that
if he died it might hurt you. No, I'd just like for him to not
exist, meaning that one day he'd be there and the next
day he wouldn't, that's all.

SCHPRACHTZI: It's obvious to me that the despicable one
here is my father.

TCHARCHES: Right? Of course I also wish your mother
didn't exist, but I'm concerned that that's wishing for
too much and that that might already border on being
despicable. Your mother also doesn't haggle over every
penny which a young man starting a family needs in order
to make an honest living.

SCHPRACHTZI: As far as I'm concerned, my mother can also
not exist. Just the two of us.

TCHARCHES: Let her exist a bit longer.

SCHPRACHTZI: Let her exist.

TCHARCHES: But not your father, let your father not exist.

SCHPRACHTZI: Let him not exist.

TCHARCHES: Soon, because our lives are passing.
He's not young man any more, right?
His blood pressure, so I've heard, is a bit high.
So one push here, another push there –

93

And one fine morning the man just doesn't wake up.

(Carries on kneading her breasts.)

SCHPRACHTZI: You should have worked in a bakery.

TCHARCHES: I'm already imagining the moment where
I come into the room and see your father's shirt and
trousers without your father actually being inside them.

(SCHPRACHTZI pulls TCHARCHES into bed. Lying down.)

A sensitive matter like a father's non-existence
Needs to be handled carefully,
slowly and discretely.
First of all to isolate.
Get the mother away from the father.

(SCHPRACHTZI moans.)

Of course, she's loyal to him,
thirty years together
are enough to make even the hunchback loyal to his hump.
Talk to her, stir up some dust,
win her heart over with something,
you can buy an old woman, like you do a Red Indian,
with colourful pieces of glass and some rags.
Open up some new horizons for her,
throw in something about a trip to Los Angeles with us.

(SCHPRACHTZI moans.)

And the other thing I wanted to remind you about:
Take some dishes from them for our new flat.
Not all at once. Again, really slowly.
Take spare kitchenware, a folding table,
an armchair, then move on to entire sets.

I like the look of their fridge, let them buy themselves a
new one.
No, we'll take the new one ourselves.

(SCHPRACHTZI moans.)

I'm giving you pleasure, eh?
And I'm not even sure yet
what I'm getting in exchange.
I don't like seeing people getting enjoyment from me,
makes my heart tense up a bit.
Oh sure, lying there on her back, moaning with pleasure,
letting me sweat onto her flesh,
squeezing, squeezing, pushing, squeezing, squeezing, pushing!

(He looks upwards.)

God, you who looks down from above,
and sees my backside going up and down
like a caterpillar moving under the sky –
Promise me that at least I'm not working for nothing,
not for nothing, God, just not for nothing,
because this spillage comes at a cost,
and I want the pleasure and the money as well!

(Climaxes.)

And also the big carpet from the living room.

SCHPRACHTZI: They told me that people moan – so I moaned.
That doesn't mean I enjoyed it.
In general: you're unfocussed, you're in a rush,
and you're missing a couple of centimetres,
which for some reason got tacked on to your nose.
So lower your nose a bit, officer,
and try harder to grow down there.
I'm in the water.

95

(Exits.)

TCHARCHES: Of course I'd also like for her to not exist, at least part of her. Why do I need all of her? She's full of leftovers. The head, for example. What do I need her head for? It eats all the time, looks at me, tests me, wants things from me. Basically: a burden. No need for it. Let it not exist. And also the hands, taking, poking – a waste. And the feet with the twisted toenails, and the warts, and the armpits, and the back, and the thick neck – two thirds of this woman is waste. Chop it off and throw it away. Leave behind the arse, as a base, and then the breasts directly on top of it. A brarse. A female patty made of three meatballs, soft, useful, decorative, and also rolls up to you by itself. Off to the water, to squirt out more dreams like that one.

SCENE 8

A room in the SCHITZ household. Night. TSESCHA. SCHPRACHTZI enters.

SCHPRACHTZI: We had a great time, we made plans, holidays, we're discussing a trip to Los Angeles. With you, of course. In time there'll also be a grandson. So there's definitely what you'd call a new life for a woman whose horizon is close to disappearing.

(Pause.)

At the University of Los Angeles there's a widowed professor. An athletic, tanned gentleman. He's looking for a life partner, a widow about fifty years old, who knows how to live and loves life.

TSESCHA: My husband's still alive.

SCHPRACHTZI: Ah. He happened to see a photo of you, the professor. It's exactly what he's looking for. Exactly like that.

TSESCHA: My husband's alive.

SCHPRACHTZI: He plays golf. And he's a wonderful dancer. His wife will have black servants. She'll play the piano. And swim in the swimming pool! And eat toast! And buy American magazines! American! American!

TSESCHA: My husband's alive!!!

SCHPRACHTZI: The question is: for how long.

(Exits.)

SCENE 9

A room in the SCHITZ household. Night. TSESCHA.

TSESCHA: I'm a housewife, what you'd call a simple woman,
　　I'm loyal to my husband, nothing complicated,
　　it's true my daughter might need me more now,
　　but that's how I am, with me the husband comes first.

　　And everything would be well and good,
　　apart from one fact, you see,
　　that my daughter's offering me a professor,
　　and I'm so easy to win over with a PhD.

　　Just like the professor has nothing to do with my
　　relationship with my husband –
　　if you can call what we have a relationship –
　　my dreams used to be a little different,
　　and love – who can even remember it?

　　And everything would be well and good,
　　apart from one fact, you see,

that my daughter's offering me a professor,
and I'm so easy to win over with a PhD.

So how long can a person go on sacrificing themselves for
nothing
when they're being given offers like these, horizons like
these, Los Angeles, and more generally...
No, I'm a simple woman, nothing complicated,
Start my journey with a husband, and carry on even
without him.

And everything would be well and good,
apart from one fact, you see,
that my daughter's offering me a professor,
and I'm so easy to win over with a PhD.

SCENE 10

Entrance to the wedding hall. Evening. FEFECHTZ, TSESCHA.

FEFECHTZ: Fifteen minutes to the ceremony.
What do the presents add up to?

TSESCHA: Forty-two thousand,
and four irons.

FEFECHTZ: Who gave me an iron?

TSESCHA: Poor guests.

FEFECHTZ: I didn't invite poor people.
You have to pay for happiness,
the food costs money.
I gave four courses,
there's fruit, cakes,
I put whiskey on the tables,
The band's only semi-automatic,

Seventy thousand lira altogether.
I want a return on the investment.

TSESCHA: *(Receives more presents.)*
Forty-four thousand,
forty-four point two

FEFECHTZ: Fifteen minutes to the ceremony.
Stall for another fifteen minutes,
some guests still need to arrive.

TSESCHA: Forty-six point four,
forty-eight thousand.

FEFECHTZ: Open your wallet, pull out a cheque,
happiness, ladies and gentlemen, isn't about feeling nice,
I have a daughter who needs love
and love has a market price.

TSESCHA: Fifty thousand,
fifty-two thousand.

FEFECHTZ: Dear guests, make a small effort!
If you really want chicken
and not two portions of salt herring!
If you want to hear music
and not the whirring of the air conditioners!
If you want to eat like pigs,
drink like camels and dance like butterflies:
Make another small effort, dear guests!

TSESCHA: Fifty-six point four,
fifty-eight thousand,
sixty thousand.

FEFECHTZ: We're close to the seventy mark!
Ten thousand more, ladies and gentlemen,

Round it up to seventy!

TSESCHA: Sixty-five thousand.

FEFECHTZ: Dear guests,
　　what's five thousand lira
　　when they're standing between you and happiness?

TSESCHA: Sixty-five point two,
　　sixty-six thousand.

FEFECHTZ: Open your wallet, pull out a cheque,
　　and write in a three-digit sum to pay,
　　I've got a son-in-law who's tracking the dollar
　　and a daughter who's tracking the buffet.

TSESCHA: Sixty-six point five,
　　sixty-seven thousand.
　　The maître d' says we can't wait.

FEFECHTZ: Three thousand more lira so we cover our expenses
　　and then we start.
　　Don't let three thousand lira
　　stand between you and happiness.
　　There's chicken, I swear, there's chicken!

TSESCHA: Sixty-seven point two.

FEFECHTZ: You see?
　　You can do it if you want! Ah!
　　Excuse me, I can see a couple over there in the corner
　　who's snuck in without giving anything.

TSESCHA: Those are the bride and groom.

FEFECHTZ: Sorry. Still!
　　And whoever brought an iron, I'm sorry,
　　but we don't have anything to iron.

We take cash. Please.

TSESCHA: Sixty-seven point four.

FEFECHTZ: Same with books.
This isn't a Bar Mitzvah,
we're grown people,
we read newspapers and pay taxes. Please.

(Opens a book.)

Shakespeare?
All of Shakespeare in exchange for Benjamin Franklin[2]!

TSESCHA: Sixty-nine thousand.

FEFECHTZ: Only another thousand.
Now's the time to pull out the final weapon.
I'd like to invite the bride and groom!

(TCHARCHES and SCHPRACHTZI enter.)

Here they are,
soon to be husband and wife.
And afterwards a baby.
They also want to eat, not for pleasure, no,
to survive.
Look at them.

(Squeezes SCHPRACHTZI.)

Bones. A skeleton. They use her to teach anatomy.
And the bride wants to have children after all,
For herself? No, ladies and gentlemen, for you.
To protect our borders, little soldiers, yes yes.
Let my daughter protect the homeland!

TSESCHA: Sixty-nine point three.

2 Benjamin Franklin's portrait graces the US $100 bill.

My husband's an orphan and I'm an orphan,
And my daughter will also become an orphan soon.
Thank you. Sixty-nine point nine.

FEFECHTZ: Just a hundred lira. What's a hundred lira, you
ask yourself, for a man like me, to get down on his knees
for?!

(Kneels down.)

I don't have them, I simply don't, good people, my
humanity, I don't have them. Would I be talking if I did
have them?

TSESCHA: Seventy thousand! We've covered our expenses.

FEFECHTZ: Another hundred so that it doesn't turn out I've
invested in a business and come out of it with just the
original fund. Another hundred and that's it, eh? Another
hundred, another hundred, another hundred…!

(A note is thrown at him. He picks it up.)

Like that, eh? Throwing. I'd empty your pockets and strip
you all naked. I'd take the money from your wallets and
the wallets themselves. I'd look between your teeth, down
your throat, through your guts, I'd open you up, ladies
and gentlemen, I'd open you up like a tin of sardines and
grind you up and check every single gram and take and
take and take…

(To TSESCHA.)

We're a hundred lira up. After the wedding we'll go to a
small restaurant somewhere and get something to eat.

SCENE 11

The wedding hall. Evening. TCHARCHES and SCHPRACHTZI under the chuppah. FEFECHTZ and TSESCHA beside them.

FEFECHTZ: The ring!

TCHARCHES: The cheque!

FEFECHTZ: What cheque?

TCHARCHES: You haven't given me the cheque!

FEFECHTZ: Repeat after me: 'You are…'

TCHARCHES: 'You are…' The cheque!

FEFECHTZ: 'consecrated…'

TCHARCHES: The cheque!

FEFECHTZ: You're holding up the Rabbi.

TCHARCHES: 'consecrated…'

FEFECHTZ: 'according to the laws of Moses…'

TCHARCHES: Not past Moses! I'm not budging from Moses without a cheque!

SCHPRACHTZI: Oh, I'd so much like to already be after the ceremony, after it all, to already be looking back at my entire life.

(Cries.)

Will I ever cry tears of joy?

TSESCHA: Give him the cheque!

(TCHARCHES turns to leave.)

SCHPRACHTZI: A husband! A husband!

FEFECHTZ: Take it, take the cheque!

TCHARCHES: *(Comes back, inspects the cheque.)* We said two-hundred thousand.

FEFECHTZ: The rest on the first of the month.

TCHARCHES: I'll ruin your daughter so you won't be able to put her back on the market!

(Kicks SCHPRACHTZI.)

SCHPRACHTZI: Ow! Tcharches!

TCHARCHES: A small cheque has separated us from each other. Goodbye.

(Exits.)

SCHPRACHTZI: Ah, the cheque.
It was all too perfect,
A dream like that is better left undreamt.

TSESCHA: Give him the cheque!

(TCHARCHES enters.)

TCHARCHES: And also your wife.

(Kicks TSESCHA. He's about to approach FEFECHTZ, FEFECHTZ takes out the other cheque and hands it over.)

FEFECHTZ: 'the laws of Moses and Israel'!

TCHARCHES: *(Puts both cheques in his pocket.)*
Which shows me I could easily have
demanded another hundred thousand.
The arsehole's drowning in money.
My late mother told me:
'You're gentle, too gentle for them'.
Oh, I wish I could just

have everything I want,
and then another small piece.
'and Israel'!

(Pushes the ring forcefully onto SCHPRACHTZI's finger.)

SCHPRACHTZI: Ah!

(Holds her finger up, looks at it.)

At last. Ownership, belonging.
Just like everyone else. Just like everyone else.
My parents are popping out of me like two blisters
of toxic gas,
In a moment they'll just dissolve into the mist.
Now it's time to chew new meat.
Will I swallow? Will I throw up?
We'll see. But for the time being – it's mine.

(Hugs TCHARCHES.)

SCENE 12

The wedding hall. Evening. Everyone.

TSESCHA: Photo time!

(They line up for a photo. FEFECHTZ is about to join. To FEFECHTZ.)

No, you've accompanied us up to the smiles,
From here on – no!

FEFECHTZ: What do you mean 'no'?!
I'm the father.

TSESCHA: He's the father – what a worn-out argument.
Help me, fresh-faced children.

SCHPRACHTZI: Dad, what are you talking about
getting photographed?

Are you someone to be remembered, Dad?

Why would you push yourself into photos?

Why immortalise a piece of nonsense?

FEFECHTZ: I want to leave proof between two pages of a
photo album that I was also part of this world and that I
laughed a little.

TSESCHA: You weren't, and you didn't. We'll deny
everything. I dreamt you for a bit, like a bad dream, and
now I'm waking up and shaking the leftover pieces of filth
from my head and setting out clean and pure to build a
new life with the support of my daughter and son-in-law.
Did you know that we're discussing a very interesting
introduction between me and an American professor
from the University of Los Angeles? American! He'll take
me to Los Angeles, Los Angeles where everything's so
wonderful, if only for the fact that everything's American,
and the man doesn't need to stare enviously at postcards
from America, no, he's in the postcard himself, dipping
in a swimming pool, or flying in a plane to New York, or
eating toast! New York! Toast! Photographer!

FEFECHTZ: *(To TCHARCHES.)*

Don't love me,

give me the money back.

You're not giving it back?

Then love me.

What? You don't love me?

And you're also not giving the money back?

For two-hundred thousand lira

I've bought a son, love and warmth!

Schprachtzi. I gave you a flat and a car.

Where's the heart overflowing with emotion?

So far you've cost me
decades of hard labour,
a whole life.
Even the bank, which is the biggest rip off,
pays some interest –
What does my own flesh and blood pay me?
Tsescha, that dress you're wearing
was paid for with my money!
Will you cry over me when I die?
Will you cry over me?
Will you eat biscuits bought with my money
and cry over me?
Will you wash with the soap I bought you in Paris
And cry over me?
Will you cry over me, my loved ones?
Or just tell me, goddamit, how much does your crying at
funerals cost?

TSESCHA: Yeesh, those eyes are always open and watching me,
constantly demanding and accusing,
those eyes I've been surrounded by
for thirty years like a room covered in mirrors,
with every embarrassment, every failure, magnified in
them a thousand times –
If only those eyes would close already! Enough!

SCENE 13

The wedding hall. Evening. Everyone's ready for the photograph. The air raid siren sounds.

TCHARCHES: War.

SCHPRACHTZI: War?

TSESCHA: What war? They haven't served the compote yet!

TCHARCHES: What's all the fuss about?

> War breaks out sometimes, doesn't it?
> Over here it comes around with the seasons:
> Winter, Spring, Summer, War.

(Takes SCHPRACHTZI aside.)

> The cheques to the bank – in a tracker account,
> sort out the flat at the land registry,
> what else? – the big carpet in the living room,
> take it, don't forget.
> And with your father – carry on, you know…

(Kisses SCHPRACHTZI and starts leaving.)

SCHPRACHTZI: Tcharches!...

TCHARCHES: Schprachtzi!...

(Exits.)

TSESCHA: War. We need to start stockpiling.

> Schprachtzi, before your father and the guests finish everything,
> collect all the rolls, the cakes,
> the potatoes, the meat, the rice.

SCHPRACHTZI: Mum, I'm so worried.

> If Tcharches dies –
> It'll ruin my marriage.

TSESCHA: Later, later!

> First of all, let's save the food from the guests!
> Take the cognac and the whiskey as well,
> because in times of need it's good to have something to sell.

(The Ballad of the Soldier, the Wife and the Food.)

SCHPRACHTZI: The man gets up and goes to battle,
    On the home front he leaves his wife,
    The wife buys two hundred eggs.
    twenty litres of oil, a hundred kilos of flour,
    and doesn't forget two sacks of rice.
    and doesn't forget two sacks of rice.

TSESCHA AND SCHPRACHTZI: One day, then two, the battle
    rages on,
    The wife cries every night,
    In the morning she buys a hundred kilos of sugar.
    Two hundred and twenty boxes of cocoa,
    And doesn't forget thirty crates of Coca Cola.
    And doesn't forget thirty crates of Coca Cola.

    The battle's over, the husband's dead,
    The wife is left on her own.
    Eating a sausage alone in the kitchen,
    Diluting a tear in a bottle of Coca-Cola,
    Smelling corpses in a slice of Swiss cheese.
    Smelling corpses in a slice of Swiss cheese.

    End of First Act.

Second Act

SCENE 14

A field. Morning. TCHARCHES.

TCHARCHES: After the great victory I had a vision in the middle of the night. In my vision peace and calm prevail. Clear skies stretching to the horizon above blossoming fields. No borders, no barbed-wire fences. In my vision people are working in the field and in the factory without hatred, without fear, they're working together, regardless of nation, religion, race or gender, because everyone's working towards a single goal, they're all working for me. I'll build factories for you, I'll give you machines and tools, and you'll work for me. You'll work willingly, you'll work with a song on your lips, because you've got something to work for, you've got a goal, there's a vision, my vision.

SCENE 15

A room in the Peltz household. Morning. SCHPRACHTZI. TCHARCHES enters.

TCHARCHES: Schprachtzi!

(They hug.)

We're buying a front end loader. The army's digging, the market's hot. For that I need more cash. Which brings us back to the topic of your father. Is he alive? Not good. Time's pressing.

SCHPRACHTZI: His blood pressure is our great hope. Tomorrow I'll recruit my mother to the cause.

TCHARCHES: Don't loosen your grip. Until the stroke.

(Exits.)

SCHPRACHTZI: An old generation wilts,
　　something new is woven,
　　and I, the agent, in the middle,
　　sucking from the old, dripping into the new,
　　a bloated warehouse of food, love and air,
　　whose purpose is passing it all to the next generation with care.

SCENE 16

A room in the Schitz household. Morning. SCHPRACHTZI. TSESCHA.

SCHPRACHTZI: I had a breakfast which included what? Egg,
　　tomato, cucumber, onion, cheese, cream, salt herring,
　　a roll, butter, chips of course, honey, cake, coffee and
　　watermelon with bananas and strawberries. And now I'm
　　going to throw up. No, I'm not throwing up because of too
　　much food, but because I'm pregnant. Pregnant.

TSESCHA: The scene's familiar. You yourself were created
　　inside me out of tons of vomit. Nowadays when I throw
　　up it's a bit more worrying.

SCHPRACHTZI: And rightly so Mummy, there's throwing up
　　and there's throwing up.

(The Throwing Up Song.)

TSESCHA: People throw up because they're unwell,
　　in the middle of the night a heart attack or a nightmare,
　　unrequited love or terrible loneliness,
　　sweating with fear, their face soaking wet;
　　but when you throw up, flooded in morning light,
　　you have no reason to worry, for you it's just a delight.

SCHPRACHTZI: Young women get nauseous,
throw up in the morning, peacefully pregnant,
weigh up their filling breasts in their hands,
get back into bed with the sweetest of smiles:
But when you throw up in the evening in the light of the TV,
you've got reason to worry, for you it's a malignant
disease.

TSESCHA: Happy vomiting and goodbye.

SCHPRACHTZI: Goodbye everyone. A child comes out of all
this filth in the end. A little Schprachtskin.

(Exits.)

TSESCHA: My daughter was impregnated with a sperm and
fertilized. It won't be long now – a matter of months – and
I'll be rocking a grandson on my knee, and he'll warm my
legs like a hot water bottle. A small grandson, cute piece
of human rubber, a warm smooth cut of meat which I'll
be able to lift up and put down and shake and put to bed
any time I want, and he'll be so dependent on me, and cry
because of me and laugh because of me, and beg me to
give him some chocolate – and if I feel like it I'll give him
some and if I don't feel like it I won't – and afterwards
I'll force him to thank me and kiss me and praise me and
ask me for forgiveness. That's how I see the first six years
around my grandson. After that he'll start to stink, he'll
have desires of his own, the scoundrel, and maybe I'll die
in the meantime or definitely dry up. Miserable life.

(SCHPRACHTZI enters.)

You'll let me play with it right?

SCHPRACHTZI: With the vomit?

TSESCHA: The grandson.

SCHPRACHTZI: With both, of course.
You'll feed the grandson,
you'll wipe away the vomit,
likewise you'll clean, serve,
cook and sew, and such other
hallmarks of a beloved grandmother.

TSESCHA: You say beloved and then you neglect me.

SCHPRACHTZI: And who introduced you to a professor?

TSESCHA: You didn't introduce me. You just said you would.

SCHPRACHTZI: That's right, next spring.

TSESCHA: You said next spring a year ago.

SCHPRACHTZI: And I will indeed introduce you to him, like I
said, next spring.

TSESCHA: Allow me to also remind you about the trip.

SCHPRACHTZI: There's a baby on the way.

TSESCHA: It's quite urgent for me.
You see, for every moment that I have left to live
you've got two or three.

SCHPRACHTZI: Lots of time stretching out in front of me, eh?
A big bowl full of time.

TSESCHA: Are we going?

SCHPRACHTZI: No.

TSESCHA: You promised. I want to go!
I want to see America!
I'm so scared that they'll ask after I die:
'And did she see America?'

SCHPRACHTZI: And has she already buried her husband?

SCENE 17

A toilet in the Schitz household. Night. FEFECHTZ sits and sings.

(The Song About Going to Argentina.)

FEFECHTZ: Far, far, far away, to South America,
  to Argentina, where I'll find some refuge,
  from the sweat and the heat and the flies,
  to Argentina, where I can hide myself
  and change my face and my name,
  and turn into someone else, someone else.

(TSESCHA and SCHPRACHTZI listen from outside.)

TSESCHA: Dad's singing nostalgic songs in the toilet!

SCHPRACHTZI: The swan song!
  His mouth is opening and closing – but the heart's already
  gone.

FEFECHTZ: Far, far, far away, to South America,
  to Argentina, to the meat industry,
  the profit's good and the currency hard,
  to Argentina, where I'll buy a lot of cows,
  and fatten them up until they choke
  and take them to the slaughterhouse, the slaughterhouse.

(Looks upwards.)

Ah, sky, sky. Deep, eh? Studded with stars, eh? Have
you come to take away my peace of mind with your dark
magic? With the pale sorcery of the moon? Not here. Not
with Fefechtz.

(Turns his backside to the sky.)

Kiss my arse, broad skies, glowing stars. Kiss my arse, moon. Kiss my arse, universe. I don't recognise your existence, don't recognise it, I recognise sausage.

(Takes a sausage out of his pocket.)

I have a lover and her name is Salami. Salami loves Fefechtz. She lies before me silent, submissive, gentle, not demanding a thing, especially not money. I put Salami in my mouth, chew her very slowly, mix her with my saliva and swallow. Salami loves Fefechtz.

SCENE 18

A corridor in the Schitz household. Night. FEFECHTZ comes out of the toilet feeling unwell.

FEFECHTZ: Air! Sausage!
Tsescha! Sausage! Tsescha!
Air! Tsescha! Sausage!

(TSESCHA, SCHPRACHTZI and TCHARCHES enter.)

TSESCHA: A doctor! A doctor!

SCHPRACHTZI AND TCHARCHES: Get him a gravedigger fast!

FEFECHTZ: Air! Air!

TSESCHA: He can't breathe!

SCHPRACHTZI AND TCHARCHES: Get him a nitrogen mask!

FEFECHTZ: Oh, doctor, doctor,
give me another chance,
I'll stop living like a pig,
I'll donate to hospitals every month;
Oh, doctor, doctor, give me one more chance to stay,
I'll miss the borscht in Winter if in the Autumn I pass away.

TSESCHA: A doctor! A doctor!

SCHPRACHTZI AND TCHARCHES: Get him a gravedigger fast!

FEFECHTZ: Air! Air!

TSESCHA: He can't breathe!

SCHPRACHTZI AND TCHARCHES: Get him a nitrogen mask!

FEFECHTZ: Oh, doctor, doctor,
    give me another chance,
    my life has passed without me being prepared for them,
    I've never been to a concert;
    Oh, doctor, doctor, let me breathe for one more day,
    so I don't go to the grave with the steaks from yesterday.

    (Remains paralyzed.)

TCHARCHES: Alive? Alive?

FEFECHTZ: I can't feel my legs.
    I can't feel my hands.
    I can't feel my genitals.
    I can't feel my throat.

TCHARCHES: According to my calculations the head's left.
    Paying in installments, eh?
    A generation which doesn't know what tempo is.

SCENE 19

A room in the Schitz household. Night. FEFECHTZ is in bed. TSESCHA, SCHPRACHTZI and TCHARCHES at the head of the bed.

SCHPRACHTZI: And now Mummy, me and Tcharches
    are going to our new flat to have intercourse in peace,
    without being surrounded by this atmosphere of illness,

and tomorrow morning Tcharches will get up to do
earthworks, and me – to the café.

TSESCHA: So we'll meet tomorrow at the café?

SCHPRACHTZI: You've got a sick husband at home!

TSESCHA: Take me with you to the café!
I want to go to the café so much,
morning, sunshine, coffee, a magazine,
who's gotten sick, who's died, who's gotten married.

SCHPRACHTZI: Women like you don't sit in cafés anymore.
Women like you walk past cafés
on their way to the doctor's clinic,
and look at the people sitting there with a sense of exile.
After a while women like you
stop even walking on the street which has cafés on it.
The waiting room in the clinic
becomes your café.
Listen carefully to the coughs and the groans,
those are also juicy gossip stories in their own way,
order an Ice Valerian[3]
and a portion of Undecyl eczema cream,
enjoy yourself.

TSESCHA: What about Los Angeles? What about the
professor?

SCHPRACHTZI: Professor, professor, professor – there is no
professor!

TSESCHA: There's no professor?

SCHPRACHTZI: No!

---

3 Valerian is a flowering plant sometimes used as a herbal sedative and anti-
anxiety medicine.

TSESCHA: I want the professor!

SCHPRACHTZI: Tcharches – home! I'm worried the baby's hearing too much about matchmaking. We're better off taking him to the British consulate for him to hear a bit of English.

TSESCHA: At least stay with me for the night
In case Dad gets another stroke.

SCHPRACHTZI: What's wrong with you, Mum? Have you gone mad?
Think of the baby!

TSESCHA: Think of your mother!

SCHPRACHTZI: But it's obviously easier for me not to think of my mother,
And whatever's easier for me – that's what I'll do.

TSESCHA: What am I asking?
Nothing substantial.
A symbolic concession.
Stay here for a night. An hour.
Five symbolic minutes!

SCHPRACHTZI: I can't make a concession, even a symbolic one, for your convenience. Because in order to do so you would have had to raise me that way from childhood. But you didn't do that. And don't think that I don't suffer enough because of that. Because in fact I'm keen to compromise on my convenience, to do people favours and to help, but I just can't. My mother spoiled me too much in my childhood, gave me whatever I wanted, shoved bananas into my mouth and wiped my bum, until in the end I turned out a horrible person. What did you do to me, mum?! Why didn't you teach me to compromise?!

Eh?! Now I'll repay you! Old woman, say sorry for me not knowing how to compromise! Get on your knees for me being evil and not staying to help my lonely mother nurse my sick father!

(The Song of the Young and the Elderly.)

SCHPRACHTZI: I am a young person,
     death still has no place in my world,
     hunger strikes me outside the old people's home:
     and if a lonely old man stares out from his window at me
     I show him what he's missing by turning my arse for him
     to see.

TCHARCHES AND SCHPRACHTZI: Because being young,
     isn't picking flowers,
     being young
     isn't being on cloud nine,
     being young
     is looking around
     seeing horror and suffering
     and feeling perfectly fine.

TCHARCHES: I am a young person,
     death is something that only happens on screen,
     at funerals I think about screwing:
     if someone wants my help, I'm always happy to come around,
     to help lower someone else's coffin into the ground.

TCHARCHES AND SCHPRACHTZI: Because being young,
     isn't picking flowers,
     being young
     isn't being on cloud nine,
     being young
     is looking around
     seeing horror and suffering

and feeling perfectly fine.

TSESCHA: I am an elderly person,
   death's hand is touching my shoulder,
   a beautiful sunset to me is but harsh ridicule:
   and when a baby looks at me with innocence and surprise,
   it's my own fate which I see sealed in his eyes.

   Because being old,
   isn't being wise,
   being old
   isn't finding a bench on which to sit,
   being old
   is seeing the spring,
   and flowers in bloom,
   and feeling like absolute shit.

SCHPRACHTZI: Goodbye, Mum, goodbye Dad, we'll come
   and visit you on the holidays, to eat and mess up your
   house.

TCHARCHES: My wife said goodbye, I won't repeat it.

   (TCHARCHES and SCHPRACHTZI exit.)

TSESCHA: No professor's going to come from her any more,
   Or anything else either.
   All the anticipation was for nothing,
   cost me my health.
   Also my honour's at an all-time low
   in my son-in-law's turbid eyes,
   furthermore I've lost the professor himself,
   and who knows how many other losses
   which I don't even know about.
   So what?

Another pair of socks? Another bar of soap?
Living from anticipation of haberdashery to anticipation
of canned food?
The grandson, ah yes, the grandson.
That one'll also piss on me for the first two years
And after that he'll start spitting.

SCENE 20

*A room in the Schitz household. Night. FEFECHTZ in bed, TSESCHA
by his side.*

FEFECHTZ: Sausage.

TSESCHA: The doctors said no.

FEFECHTZ: A small sausage. A cocktail sausage.

TSESCHA: No.

FEFECHTZ: Without cucumber.

TSESCHA: And without sausage.

FEFECHTZ: The doctors won't know.

TSESCHA: Do you even know what I could have had by now?

FEFECHTZ: A professor from the University of Los Angeles.

TSESCHA: Yes. Los Angeles.

FEFECHTZ: Tsescha will give Fefechtz a small cocktail sausage
and the doctors won't know. Tsescha's good, Tsescha won't
rat me out to the doctors.

TSESCHA: Why should Tsescha be good, Tsescha's lost all her
opportunities by being with Fefechtz.

FEFECHTZ: But Tsescha's good, good, Tsescha's not angry, Tsescha understands that you need to compromise a bit in life.

TSESCHA: I don't want to compromise! No one compromises!

FEFECHTZ: But Tsescha's good, good. Tsescha's not like everyone, Tsescha's good.

TSESCHA: Yes, good. What good's that done me? I've lost. I was a girl and I just waited to grow up. So? So I've grown up, so what? You prepare for life like it's a big fancy ball, you wash yourself, perfume yourself, wear the finest dresses and the finest jewelry, then finally you open the door and fall into the sewer. You've got it good, you're sick, you don't have problems of that kind.

FEFECHTZ: Tsescha, sausage. Sausage.

TSESCHA: Who loves Tsescha?

FEFECHTZ: Fefechtz.

TSESCHA: And how much does Fefechtz love Tsescha?

FEFECHTZ: Very. Very, very. Sausage.

TSESCHA: Who does Fefechtz love more, Tsescha or sausage?

FEFECHTZ: Tsescha, Tsescha! Sausage!

TSESCHA: If Fefechtz loves Tsescha more than sausage, then Tsescha's staying and sausage isn't.

(Eats the last piece of sausage.)

Enough, no more sausage.

(Pause.)

I'm a woman, and you're a man,
what do we have to do with each other?

Flesh touched flesh for a little bit,
and then separated forever:
We were born apart –
and we also won't be buried together.
No, I don't want you to make me a widow! I don't have
anything apart from you, you paralyzed piece of meat! I
want you beside me! Always, always beside me! Mine!
Mine!

FEFECHTZ: The only thing keeping me alive is the yearning
to taste a piece of sausage one more time.

TSESCHA: The only thing keeping me at your side is my
ability to withhold the piece of sausage from you.

(Places FEFECHTZ's emaciated hand between her legs.)

(The Oasis Song.)

There was once a little oasis here,
An oasis brimming with life,
And right in the middle, between the foliage,
Burned the flowers of delight.

Come waters, trickle in,
Fill the well up high,
Tomorrow morning I'll wake up
With a rose between my thighs.

The little oasis is long gone,
Cracks and dried up weeds,
And in the stinking hole, in the middle of it all,
Cobwebs hang from wall to wall.

Come waters, trickle in,
Fill the well up high,
Tomorrow morning I'll wake up
With a rose between my thighs.

SCENE 21

A room in the Peltz household. Morning. TCHARCHES.

TCHARCHES: From a pick up truck and half a tractor before the glorious war
to fifteen pieces of heavy machinery, and there's scope for plenty more,
there are plenty of earthworks to do, the army needs trenches all day,
I submit my invoices to them, and the Department of Defense agrees to pay.

I dig dugouts for soldiers, neatly organised in threes,
which in the event of a defeat, automatically become cemeteries,
that way I submit two separate bills for each hole to get funded:
Two thousand lira as a dugout, and as a cemetery – two thousand five hundred.
In total that's four thousand five hundred lira per ditch,
Plus seven hundred on gardening and camouflage for each,
And another five hundred lira 'El Malei Rachamim',
'Yizkor' and Kaddish,
Altogether five thousand seven hundred – ten thousand just to round up,
I simply need to reach out my hand, and the Department of Defense coughs it up.

After digging ten thousand dugout-cemeteries from reinforced cement
It turned out the army was shitting in them, but inside them nobody went,
And so the digging works were stopped, and these bills were handed to the clerk:
Two thousand lira for the hole as a hole – that's the base cost for the work,

Plus two thousand five hundred as a grave, two thousand as a dugout for a platoon,

Plus a thousand lira as a urinal, a latrine and a spittoon,

Plus two thousand lira to fill in the hole on account of its not being used,

Plus a two thousand lira field supplement, to cover the risk of being abused,

Altogether eleven thousand five hundred for not digging anything at all,

Plus one thousand five hundred for expenses, such as yoghurt from the market stall,

Plus ten thousand lira as compensation for breaching what our contract says,

In total twenty-three thousand a unit – and the Department of Defense just pays.

SCENE 22

A room in the Peltz household. TCHARCHES. SCHPRACHTZI enters.

TCHARCHES: Were you at your parents'? Is there a funeral?

SCHPRACHTZI: The paralysis has spread to the face.

TCHARCHES: What's that about? Is every stroke around here going to end up with some kind of partial paralysis?! Another leg, and another finger, and another muscle, and am I going to wait and wait?! And what about the heart itself – when's it going to seize up? Man clings on to his life like a leech, without any written approval, without a single fragment of health to hold onto, a pest of the mammalian family, bloodsucker of the cosmos, breathing and breathing and breathing, and I've got loans to pay off by the end of March! Loans by the end of March, you hear?! You hear, Schprachtzi, you fat woman, you piece of meat for rubbing, who uses my sperm – mine!

– next to her intestines for fertilization?! I've planted a whole orchard in your stomach, good for you, great for you, you're an orchardist, and I, I, can't even become an earthworks contractor?! Loans at the end of March! I'm running out of time, running out, I'm suffocating, I need cash, I have liquidity problems, I'm a financial eunuch, and hence the Fefechtz has to move, move, and when I say move – I mean move vertically downwards!!

SCHPRACHTZI: No, this isn't the great thinker I imagined,
This isn't the distinguished physicist I expected.

TCHARCHES: And don't you get fat, don't get cumbersome, because then how can I be seen with you in the cinema, after all I'm still a bit of a man, and I was an officer in the army and everything.

SCHPRACHTZI: With so much happiness, how can I not fatten up like a pig? But what do I care? I don't give a damn. I have everything I need, and if you don't like it, I'd happily give up the touch of your sweaty hands, and everything can go to hell, as long as I'm left in peace to lie on the sofa and nibble on my squeaky little biscuits. And you can go to the cinema with your friends. Go, go off to fart around with your army friends, twenty-seven-year-old man with a biography of farts.

TCHARCHES: Eating, eating, eating. Such hard work, chewing, grinding, wearing down your jaws, swallowing, shoving in chickens, pigs, watermelons, digesting and excreting and wiping, and the hunger inside never ends, and the craving sucks and sucks and sucks away…but what else can you throw to your soul other than chickens and pigs and watermelons? Here soul, want some Schnitzel?!

(The Acceptance Song.)

Swollen legs,
A bit of hair on her ankle,
And also on her chest,
Meet my wife,
All in all a good woman,
A woman who gets things, knows how to cook,
Takes the housework on herself,
What else can I say?
I'm an unhappy man,
But who's even born for happiness?
In general, a person sits at the table,
Beyond their plate they don't know, they don't see,
They forget there ever was, in their youth, something
more they had wanted to be.

SCHPRACHTZI: Sweaty hands,
Thinning hair, a tired gaze,
And short breath,
Meet my husband,
All in all a devoted man,
Loyal as a dog, although in the company of men,
He tries to put on a reckless air,
What else is there to say?
I have no expectations for the future,
But who lives for the future's sake?
In general, a person falls into bed,
Closes their eyes so they don't have to see,
And forgets that, in their youth, there was something more
they had hoped to be.

TCHARCHES: My wife, our love is facing
the back end of life.
If life were a character, and that character had a backside –
Then we're deep deep inside.

Wickedness will unite us,
sweat and mud will be the glue
and on the horizon of our lives the rot is gleaming.

(They hug.)

Tomorrow is a festival, we're invited to your parents'.
Help me.

SCHPRACHTZI: I've already decided: nothing will stand
between my father's money and my son's happiness.

TCHARCHES: In that case let's go. It's time. We'll put in the
final nail.
Tomorrow morning a coffin seals, if God willing, all goes
well.

SCENE 23

*A room in the Schitz household. Afternoon. FEFECHTZ, TSESCHA.
SCHPRACHTZI and TCHARCHES enter.*

SCHPRACHTZI: Hello, sick father and frail mother, we've
come.

TCHARCHES: We're hungry.

TSESCHA: What'll you eat?

TCHARCHES: Everything.

TSESCHA: Am I right in thinking you won't help me bring
things to the table?

SCHPRACHTZI: Correct.

(TSESCHA and SCHPRACHTZI exit.)

TCHARCHES: How's it with you? How's the appetite?
On my end business is going great, thank God.

And the dirt, Dad, the one you're getting closer to
like a warm fluffy blanket,
that dirt is giving me lots of satisfaction.
Tcharches Peltz – earthworks contractor.
Of course, with a bit more credit,
there would be much more momentum, eh?
Soon we'll be expanding into construction,
also for the army.
I'm sentimental about the army,
generous, an open hand,
they let a man make a living
and also feel like he's making a homeland.
All that, of course, with a bit more credit.
After that maybe ammunition. Importing equipment,
weapons,
and god knows what else.
Why not? I feel like it. America.
With a bit of credit…will you give me some?
You're staying silent. No, you wouldn't understand me.
You've always been a small-money man,
now go and rest with your pocket change.

(Lies down next to FEFECHTZ.)

Actually, you know, you've got it good. What are you
missing? Going to die, lying in bed, not lifting a finger,
being waited on, being given things. You don't have
any hopes to finance, ambitions to achieve. You don't
need credit, your legs are already out of business. Just
lying there indulgently in bed seeing the world from the
perspective of a calm person. What can you do – it's a law
of nature: The young have to make way for the dying old
people.

(Suffocates FEFECHTZ with a pillow. SCHPRACHTZI enters.)

SCHPRACHTZI: Oh, my orphaning,
>   my orphaning's near.
>   I can hear its footsteps.
>   Still it's a pity. My dad.
>   After all he carried me in his arms
>   and wiped me and everything. Anyway.
>   Thoughts like that harm the pregnancy,
>   I'll have time to be sorry later, right?
>   Little fetus in my stomach – justify
>   a terrible thing which I would do with pleasure!

TSESCHA: Will you eat…

TCHARCHES: Steak! I want a steak!

SCHPRACHTZI: With chips.

(TSESCHA exits. TCHARCHES removes the pillow, leans over FEFECHTZ, walks over to SCHPRACHTZI and pulls her to him. TSESCHA enters. Pulls her in too.)

SCENE 24

A room in the Schitz household. Afternoon. Everyone. The air raid siren sounds.

TCHARCHES: War again.

SCHPRACHTZI: War?

TSESCHA: War at lunchtime?

TCHARCHES: *(Takes SCHPRACHTZI aside.)*
>   Sort out the inheritance at the lawyer's.
>   You get half by law,
>   we'll take the other half by rights.
>   Start looking for an appropriate home for her.
>   And have her stop eating meat every day,

enough pigging out at my expense.

(Kisses her. Starts walking away.)

SCHPRACHTZI: Tcharches!...

TCHARCHES: Schprachtzi!…

FEFECHTZ: Sausage! Sausage!

TSESCHA: Fefechtz! Fefechtz! My Fefechtz!

TCHARCHES: *(Stops.)* What…?! What…?!

FEFECHTZ: Sausage, sausage!

TCHARCHES: Sausage…!

(Picks up the pillow, the air raid siren sounds again, puts down the pillow.)

All right, you've earned yourself a few more breaths.
Thank the wars. Those are your breathing breaks.
Breathe, breathe.
We're going to expand the business, see you later.
Next time, Dad, the end will be the end.

(To SCHPRACHTZI.)

And also a nice holiday in the fresh air
away from the stench of chewed meat.

(Starts leaving.)

SCHPRACHTZI: Tcharches!

TCHARCHES: Schprachtzi!

(Exits.)

TSESCHA: But who starts wars between two and four in
the afternoon? See, the World War itself started in the
morning, that's what I call European culture.

SCENE 25

On one side, a room in the SCHITZ household. Evening. FEFECHTZ in bed, watching television. On the other side, an office in the town hall. SCHPRACHTZI and TSESCHA.

TSESCHA: Tcharches Peltz, twenty-seven years old, officer,
    he sent a postcard from the front two days ago.
    Is there any news? No news.

SCHPRACHTZI: Happiness, happiness, don't go away,
    you belong only to me, don't mix up the address,
    and the husband I loaned to the army
    I want him back, I don't care about the rest.

FEFECHTZ: Ay, ay, the TV's full of burnt up tanks…It's not
    only Fefechtz who can't move, other people also can't
    move now…

TSESCHA: Tcharches Peltz, twenty-seven years old, officer,
    he sent a postcard from the front two weeks ago,
    Married for a year, pregnant wife,
    sole provider for his paralyzed father-in-law,
    Tcharches Peltz, twenty-seven years old, officer.
    Is there any news? No news.

SCHPRACHTZI: Death, death, go to a different city,
    go to the neighbours, go to a different place.
    I want to see my husband come back
    with two legs, two hands and a face.

FEFECHTZ: The TV's full of people without hands and
    without legs, and charred casualties and blinded eyes…
    more casualties, more scars, more cripples, more
    miserable people, a huge pile of chopped up meat, come
    on, more, more, more…

TSESCHA: Tcharches Peltz, twenty-seven years old, officer,

he sent a postcard from the front a month ago,
average height, charming smile,
eyes overflowing with love and kindness,
pregnant wife, married for a year,
a home filled with love and warmth,
Tcharches Peltz, twenty-seven years old, officer,
Tcharches Peltz, twenty-seven years old, officer,
Tcharches Peltz, twenty-seven years old, officer,
is there any news?...

SCHPRACHTZI: Tcharches!!! Tcharches, just now, when I
suddenly love you so much!

SCENE 26

*A room in the Schitz household. Dusk. SCHPRACHTZI, TSESCHA,
FEFECHTZ. In the middle of the song TCHARCHES enters.*

(The Song of the Messenger.)

TSESCHA: At six in the evening the messenger will come by,
At six in the evening the messenger will come by,
Not on a galloping horse or from the sky,
He'll come with the doctor in a small car one day,
He'll knock on the door and in a weak voice he'll say...

SCHPRACHTZI: At six in the evening the messenger will
come by,
And find me prepared for him
Like a bride all prepared in her dress,
And at six in the evening, at six in the evening, before the
sun finally sets,
A shout will ring out, a shout will ring out from one end of
the street to the next.

TCHARCHES: And the pointless words which I said to you

Take on a heavy new meaning.
And you will suddenly love me
As you have never loved me before,

But my face, and my words,
And the last smile on my lip,
From your life they're already passing away
As into memory they slip.

TSESCHA: At six in the evening the messenger will come by,
And at quarter past six the messenger will say goodbye,
And go to deliver messages at another house nearby,
And in another house a woman will wait that day
He'll knock on the door and in a weak voice he'll say…

SCHPRACHTZI: At quarter past six the messenger will say goodbye,
And leave me sitting on the edge of my mattress,
Like a tired bride after taking off her wedding dress,
And at seven in the evening, at seven in the evening, after the sun finally sets,
An empty silence will ring out from one end of the street to the next.

TCHARCHES: And the pointless words which I said to you
Take on a heavy new meaning.
And you will suddenly love me
As you have never loved me before,

But my face, and my words,
And the last smile on my lip,
From your life they're already passing away
As into memory they slip.

SCENE 27

A room in the Schitz household. Evening. SCHPRACHTZI.

SCHPRACHTZI: Tcharches, Tcharches, a living man,
    a few little swindles,
    here and there some quick little deceptions,
    weaknesses, stupidity, pettiness,
    a few loathsome smiles at each other
    but all with so much warmth.

    It takes so long to meet a man,
    to move into a flat, furnish it, get married,
    so long to get pregnant and make some plans
    going shopping in Europe…
    And now, again, everything from the beginning?!
    I don't have the strength. I don't.

    In the middle of this exhausting life,
    the State came to my house, reached out a coarse hand,
    and took my husband.
    Already under the chuppah I could see:
    there was another bride there with my husband and me.
    On his other side, sticking her nails into his arm,
    stood the State,
    and when we walked – she walked with us,
    she accompanied us day and night,
    she got into bed with us,
    sat at the dinner table with us.
    She came to us from every direction,
    trickled from the sky and from the ground,
    through the radio, the newspaper and the cinema,
    infiltrated through the water pipes,
    the cracks in the wall and the gaps in the blinds,
    she hid the sun and the stars from us,

she penetrated our eyes and our ears and our noses,
she penetrated the pores on our skin:
She with her coarse, sweaty palms,
with her dirty, blood-soaked fingernails,
she held my husband in a grip of death
and took him with her to the grave of her bed
to crumble him under my feet
and turn my life into memories,
fading dreams, hazy imagination, dust!

In the middle of this exhausting life,
the State came to my house, reached out a coarse hand,
and took my husband.
Now she also wants me to congratulate her on this death:
Welcome, death,
welcome, grave, welcome, coffin,
welcome, blood and burnt flesh and wounds:
Welcome!

(The Lament of Tcharches' Death.)

Tcharches, my dead husband,
A man who was my own,
I don't have any more strength to cry,
And these are the final tears in my eye.

Because dryness wipes away my tears on your grave.
And dryness crumbles the features of your dead face,
And yellows the photos in the family album
Which contain so few moments of grace.

SCENE 28

A room in the Schitz household. Evening. TSESCHA and SCHPRACHTZI. FEFECHTZ is lying in bed.

TSESCHA: Seventy-five lira for a kilo of steak. In the end I'll
fry my own
backside, that's cheaper and at least I'll know what I'm
eating.
Hard times,
Schprachtzi my girl,
all the time it took you to find a man,
and the man's gone.
Good luck trusting a man's word.
Knead your rump fillet well
so that you again have
something to offer
when your man finally arrives.

(Dead TCHARCHES enters.)

Who are you?

TCHARCHES: Tcharches.

TSESCHA: Tcharches?! Dead people don't show up at dinner
time. The dead have office hours in our dreams.

(TCHARCHES doesn't move.)

What do you want?

TCHARCHES: A Steak.

TSESCHA: A Steak?

TCHARCHES: A Steak.

TSESCHA: Seventy-five lira for a kilo of meat, and you want
us to feed the dead as well?!

TCHARCHES: I lie alone in the dark. I miss steak.
Schprachtzi, remember the lakerda,
Schprachtzi, remember the chips,
remember a bottle of wine at the beach.
remember a wedding cake.

SCHPRACHTZI: Go away, Tcharches,
and leave me with my sorrow over you.

TCHARCHES: Schprachtzi, remember the scheming,
Schprachtzi, remember the cheques,
remember warm breath and whispering,
remember wicked laughter in bed.

SCHPRACHTZI: Go away, Tcharches,
And leave me with my sorrow over you.

FEFECHTZ: Let him stay.

TSESCHA: No!

FEFECHTZ: Let him stay!

(Gets to his feet.)

TSESCHA: A miracle! Fefechtz! A miracle!
My husband's alive, healthy, in one piece,

(FEFECHTZ hits TSESCHA.)

And beating his wife!
I've got a man,
he'll take me to Los Angeles! A miracle!

FEFECHTZ: *(Approaches TCHARCHES.)*
Let him stay under the table,
between our shoes,
let him pick up the crumbs.
Let him crawl on his rotten stomach

and wipe the floor.
Let him push his bleeding cheeks
against the soles of my slippers.

TCHARCHES: I'm glad to be home, thank you.

(Gets under the table.)

FEFECHTZ: I've always been fond of you, boy,
down there, dead, on the floor, you're more precious to
me than ever.
And the business must, of course, keep going.
With a dead son-in-law under the table,
with a single daughter dressed in black and crying,
with my wife's graying hair,
we can get down to some serious work.

SCENE 29

A room in the Schitz household. Evening. Everyone. FEFECHTZ stands next to the table.

FEFECHTZ: You left me an earthworks company –
I'll continue in the earth, in the water and in the air,
I'll double the fortune, the number of tools,
I'll double the wars, I'll double the borders,
I'll double and triple the number of labouring hands,
And I will multiply the dead as the sand that is on the sea shore!
And to all the doubters, here you have it:
The answer's under the table!

(To TSESCHA.)

Food!

(TSESCHA exits, SCHPRACHTZI cries.)

And you, fill your mouth with food
and cry quietly,
like soft background music,
which just increases the appetite.

(Sits down.)

I've got dead people under the tables,
lots of dead people under the tables,
and under the chairs and the beds and the cupboards,
the whole house is full of dead people,
and I've got dead people in storage for the winter,
and a stock of dead people for next year,
and for the long term I've got dead people who are still alive,
and I've got dead people who haven't been born yet,
I'm counting on dead people, building on dead people,
I eat dead people, and breathe dead people,
dead people, dead people, dead people…

(TSESCHA enters with food.)

TSESCHA: If I didn't know that we were living through
    history,
    I wouldn't be able to hold on.

(They eat.)

END

THE TORMENTS OF JOB

Translated from the Hebrew by Naaman Tammuz

An epic play, recounting and interpreting the biblical story of Job, set in the Roman Empire, with elements taken from Christ's Passion. The question of God's existence goes a long way from its biblical source to become a drama of the individual facing a destiny ordained by brutal power and authority.

Cast of Characters

JOB
GUESTS
SERVANTS
BEGGARS
HERALDS
BAILIFFS
FRIENDS
SOLDIERS
ENTERTAINERS
DECEASED

Premiere	The Cameri Theatre, Tel Aviv, 1981
Director	Hanoch Levin
Costume and Stage Design	Ruth Dar
Lighting design	Avi Tzabari
Music composition	Foldi Shatzman
Musicians	Misha Blecherovitch, Beni Kadishzon, Avi Shilo, Dan Shwartzman, Itay Crispin,

Cast:

JOB	Yossef Carmon
ELIPAZ	Albert Cohen
BILDAD	Ilan Dar
TSOFAR	Yitshak Hizkia
OFFICER, BEGGAR, HERALD OF POVERTY	Sassi Sa'ad
HEAD BAILIFF, PATHETIC CLOWN	Dov Reizer
BEGGAR, HERALD OF POVERTY, HERALD OF DEATH, CYNICAL CLOWN	Mati Serri
BEGGAR, MIDGET	Reuven Sheffer
GUEST, STRIPPER	Rose Meshikhi
THE CIRCUS MANAGER	Yehuda Fuchs
THE BEGGARLY BEGGAR, HERALD OF DEATH	Ami Weinberg
HERALD OF POVERTY, HERALD OF DEATH, JESUS	Eli Glazer
BEGGAR, SERGEANT	Yirmi Amir

First Chapter – The Beggars

A feast in JOB's house. The gorging is over. The GUESTS are strewn around, stuffed and lethargic. Piles of scraps on the tables.

JOB: What is a sated man?
A sated man is a finished man, lost.
What's left for him to hope for?
Everything's full, blocked, sealed up,
lying there motionless, breathing laboured,
feeling like life itself is a heavy stone on his heart,
the greatest despair you can imagine!
After that kind of darkness the horizon can only get brighter.

But what happens two hours later?
Two hours later the despair's still despair,
although it's less absolute, the horizon brightens.
The man still isn't moving, the stomach's still aching,
but the breathing's easier.

And after four hours?
After four hours even the stomach
starts sensing some hope. Not the rumble
of an actual appetite yet, but some little thought sneaks in,
and the man, who an hour ago was lying on his back like
a turtle,
emitting agonized belches at the ceiling,
wakes up a little, rolls over onto his stomach,
hands the task of emission over to his backside:
Who said life was a heavy stone?

And after six hours?
After six hours has the stone turned into a bird?
Because life is now now life is light, colourful, wings spread,
the belly's full of gentle little chirps, and the man's once
again prancing around refreshed and awake,
gliding down towards the table with a wet mouth.

A new man is born every six hours!

GUEST: I've done well. In six hours
I usually get born at least twice.

B

SERVANT: Sir, the beggars are asking to approach the table.

JOB: Blessed art thou lord, who feeds every thing. Let them in.

(The BEGGARS enter, assail the table, gnaw at the bones.)

BEGGAR: Bones. Just chewed bones.
You think that's the end of the meal? Wrong!
There isn't a single bone that's been cracked and sucked
and which doesn't have something more hidden inside.

We don't suck like you,
you who have gorged yourself on meat
and tossed the bone aside with a careless lick;
We do it devotedly, diligently, very deliberately,
almost in tears. And you'd be surprised
how much fat and moisture's still in there.

It's true that some of the moisture
is the saliva you've left in there.
But all the more so, sucking on a bone
which has been in the mouth of a sated man –

that's not just the bone, it's also the pedigree.

(They finish and exit.)

C

SERVANT: Sir, the beggars' beggars are asking for permission
to approach the table.

JOB: What!! Another round on this pile of bones?!
Blessed art thou lord, who feeds every thing. Let them in.

(Weak crippled BEGGARS enter and launch themselves at the table.)

BEGGAR A: Twice-chewed bones. The leftovers
of leftovers. No matter,
what's been sucked and has sated twice
won't let us down the third time around either.
True, there's no marrow, no moisture,
but the bone, on the other hand, is already ground down,
soft and crumbly, really porridgy,
and ready to eat.

We wolf down warm bone porridge,
and the stomach takes care of all the rest.

BEGGAR B: And it even sometimes happens that a bone's
been forgotten,
with a bit of marrow and fat in it, after all, the top beggars,
over time,
develop the habits of true lords,
sucking carelessly here, skipping something there,
then we show up…

*(They suddenly find one of these overlooked bones, fight over it. One
of them wins out and chews on it. The others look at him. They
finish and exit.)*

D

SERVANT: Sir, the beggarly beggars' beggar of all beggars is
asking for permission to approach the table.

JOB: What's he going to eat, the table?!
Blessed art thou lord, who feeds every thing. Let him in.

*(The BEGGARLY BEGGAR enters, elderly, feeble and rickety,
collapses onto the table.)*

BEGGARLY BEGGAR: Empty. Not even a bone. But even if
there were,
how would I chew on it? I don't have any teeth.

My nourishment depends on one
of the middle class beggars occasionally
swallowing the bones too fast,
a bone gets stuck in his throat and he throws up.

I can swallow the vomit without chewing,
and also easily digest what's anyway
already half digested.
And if I get extra lucky, I find in the vomit
a piece of what used to be a potato or a beetroot.

True, that doesn't happen often, that's why I'm
always feeble, about to die of weakness.
Still – you get used to it. With a little patience
someone always ends up vomiting in the end.
Yes, somehow you stay alive. There is a God,
Pa-Ra-Pim-Pim-Pim, Pa-Ra-Pim-Pim-Pim,
Maybe someone'll vomit in my path, Pa-Ra-Pim-Pim-Pim.

(Exits.)

JOB: What have we just seen? A miracle? Or nature's course?
    A chicken bone fed an entire throng,
    The last one even sang a song.

    We've seen two things, that much is clear:
    Firstly, there is a God!

GUESTS: Blessed is he and blessed is his name!

JOB: Second, God giveth again and again!

GUESTS: Amen! Amen!

Second Chapter – The Heralds of Poverty

JOB and the GUESTS are napping. HERALD OF POVERTY A enters.

HERALD OF POVERTY A: Bad news, sir.

(Pause.)

Sir, bad news.

(But JOB is snoozing. The HERALD raises his voice.)

Sir, very bad news.
Very, very bad news.

(Shakes JOB.)

Excuse me, sir, for insisting, but that's how it is
with bad news – I didn't come up with it –
the person being informed is usually asleep, it always
happens at night,
and then they come and wake him so that god forbid he
spends
a single moment of his life unaware of the disaster.

(Shakes JOB harder.)

Sir, I have very bad news,
It's meant for your ears, it's yours,
I must deliver it to you, there's no two ways about it!

JOB: Don't shout, I'm digesting!

HERALD OF POVERTY A: And how will you digest this, sir?
Your iron mine in Lebanon

has totally collapsed in an earthquake.
A hundred and eighty slaves were buried alive.

JOB: *(Straightens up in his chair, stunned.)*
Say it isn't so! If you have a spark of humanity in you –
say it isn't so!

HERALD OF POVERTY A: And if I say it isn't so –
Will the stones in your mine jump up
and stack themselves on top of each other again?

JOB: My little iron mine!
My little mine in Lebanon!
This is how a man feels when his arm or leg
is suddenly ripped off. That iron mine is half of all I own.

(Gets up.)

HERALD OF POVERTY A: Where to, sir? What needs to be
done – has been done.
The police are investigating. Sir's bookkeepers
are balancing the accounts. Sir's attorneys
are wording the appropriate claims to the imperial
treasury in Rome.
The emperor does after all personally guarantee
investments intended for national development.

(Exits.)

JOB: What's happened to me is what always
happens to others.
The worst possible thing has happened to me.
It's impossible for anything worse to happen.
And if each of us is called upon to contribute
our fair share of suffering and torment –
I have hereby contributed my share.
Thank god, now I am clean.

B

HERALD OF POVERTY B enters.

HERALD OF POVERTY B: Bad news, sir.

JOB: They already informed me.

HERALD OF POVERTY B: Who? I thought I was the first…

JOB: Someone was already here before you.

HERALD OF POVERTY B: In any case, when new updates from Alexandria arrive, I'll inform you immediately.

JOB: Alexandria?!

HERALD OF POVERTY B: Alexandria, of course Alexandria.

JOB: What's happened in Alexandria?

HERALD OF POVERTY B: You said you'd been informed…

JOB: What's happened in Alexandria?! What's happened in Alexandria?!

HERALD OF POVERTY B: A huge storm. The port of Alexandria was flooded.
Your shipyards collapsed into the water, their ships shattered against the rocks.

JOB: What am I?! Some kind of joke?!
This is my life here! My life, my life!
Those shipyards and those ships that you've destroyed with your careless words
were the second half of my possessions! Now there's nothing!

(Pause.)

Everything?! Is there nothing left?! Are you sure?!

(Pause.)

My life's works, two beloved children
who I brought into the world and nurtured and raised.
Not just children! –
Me, my flesh and blood, my hands and my feet and my
milk and my blood! It's my very self I gave there, the best
years of my youth and my adulthood! They've killed me!
Slaughtered me! Sliced my corpse in two!
I'm buried; half of me's crushed in an iron mine in
Lebanon,
and half of me's in Alexandria, drowned in the port!

(Turns to leave.)

HERALD OF POVERTY B: Where to? What needs to be done –
has been done.
The police are investigating. Sir's bookkeepers
are balancing the accounts. Sir's attorneys
are wording the appropriate claims to the imperial
treasury in Rome.
The emperor does after all personally guarantee
investments intended for national development.

(Exits.)

JOB: Earlier I thought the worst had happened to me!
I was wrong, it's happened now.

(To the GUESTS.)

Excuse me, everything's collapsed.
I must go to my office.

(Turns to leave.)

C

HERALD OF POVERTY C enters.

JOB: Perhaps you have some bad news for me?

HERALD OF POVERTY C: Yes.

JOB: *(Scared.)*
    Excuse me, I was just joking.

HERALD OF POVERTY C: I wasn't.

JOB: Lebanon?

HERALD OF POVERTY C: No, sir.

JOB: So, Alexandria.

HERALD OF POVERTY C: No, sir.

JOB: Something else?

HERALD OF POVERTY C: Yes, sir.

JOB: *(Laughing.)*
    I don't have anything else, I don't
    have any more businesses. Go and give
    your news to someone else.

HERALD OF POVERTY C: No, to you.

JOB: To someone else.

HERALD OF POVERTY C: To you alone.

JOB: I have nothing. Two heralds before you
    already wiped it all away.

HERALD OF POVERTY C: Sir, listen...

JOB: Stop holding me up. I need to go to the attorneys
    in order to collect my payout from the emperor in Rome.

HERALD OF POVERTY C: That's exactly what the news is about.

JOB: Has something happened to the attorneys?

HERALD OF POVERTY C: The attorneys are fine.

JOB: So…what?

HERALD OF POVERTY C: Rome. A military coup.

JOB: Man! What are you talking about!
A coup in Rome?! The emperor won't have it!

HERALD OF POVERTY C: He's already had it.

JOB: Not as long as he's alive!

HERALD OF POVERTY C: That's true. Which is why he's dead.

JOB: Dead or alive – he won't have it!

(Pause.)

Dead?! The emperor of Rome?! There's no emperor?
The most eternal of all men in our world, two thirds
of the trade in iron and lead, eight tenths
of the iron and lead production, the empire's
steel cash register, the big, infinite fund, on which we
mortals are merely the interest – he's dead?!
If he's dead – who's alive?! Who's alive?!

(Pause.)

I've got one plot of land left which I bought once
in Jaffa, not far from the port…that's all that's left…

HERALD OF POVERTY C: The new emperor's also decided…

JOB: …I can set up a shop on it…

155

HERALD OF POVERTY C: ...with regards to all the strategically located land...

JOB: ...not a big shop...a kind of room...

HERALD OF POVERTY C: on complete confiscation...

JOB: ...even just a counter...

HERALD OF POVERTY C: ...with no financial compensation.

JOB: Well, not even a counter then.

(Pause.)

What do my attorneys say about this?

HERALD OF POVERTY C: You have no attorneys, sir.

JOB: What do the bookkeepers, the clerks say?

HERALD OF POVERTY C: You have no bookkeepers, you have no clerks.

JOB: I'll go to my office to find everything out for myself.

HERALD OF POVERTY C: You also have no office, sir.

JOB: This is my office! There's my chair,
my beloved work desk,
all my little toys...

HERALD OF POVERTY C: Not yours anymore.

JOB: Curse you! Don't tell me 'Not yours!'
Who do you think you are?! Who and what are you –
'Yours, not yours' – curse you!

HERALD OF POVERTY C: Sir also isn't a position to speak to me like that.

JOB: What?!

HERALD OF POVERTY C: And lower your tone.

JOB: *(Raises his hand to strike him.)*
   Servant! Dog!

HERALD OF POVERTY C: *(Pushes him back.)*
   You're a dog yourself. A dog made you.
   Your father is a dog. Your mother is a dog.
   You're a son of a dog. Tfu!

(Spits in his face and leaves.)

D

The GUESTS retreat slowly and leave.

JOB: You're leaving? Yes, it's late, good night to you.
   The trouble is that it's suddenly gotten late. Because otherwise
   we could still sit around, and casually reminisce:
   do you remember how once, five minutes ago, I was a rich man?
   It wasn't that long ago, five minutes, remember?
   I walked the earth like a lord. And once, five minutes ago,
   who'd have dreamt of calling me a dog or spitting in my face?!

(Suddenly he sobs. Stops.)

Yes – the trouble is that it's suddenly gotten very late.
Five minutes, remember? Those were the days.

(The last of the GUESTS slip away and leave. He's left alone.)

Third Chapter – the bailiffs

The BAILIFFS enter.

HEAD BAILIFF: We're the bailiff's clerks. You're bankrupt.
　　We've come to seize everything you have,
　　other than you yourself, body and soul,
　　and your undergarments.

　　(To the other BAILIFFS.)

　　Take the tables, take the chairs, take the mugs,
　　take the plates, take the cups, take the forks,
　　take the knives, take the spoons, take the bowls,
　　take the pots, take the jars, take the bottles,
　　take the corks, take the corkscrews, take the boxes
　　of the corkscrews, take take, take the candlesticks, take the
　　lamps,
　　take the maps, take the napkins, take the towels,
　　take the sofas, take the carpets, take the rugs,
　　take the vases, take the plant pots, take the decorations,
　　take the screens, take the curtains, take the windows,
　　take the blinds, take the glass, take the frames,
　　take the door bolts, take the locks, take the keys,
　　take the doors, take the tiles, take the ceiling, take the walls,
　　and if there's anything I've forgotten – then without
　　violating anyone's rights – take it as well.

　　*(The BAILIFFS empty the hall and strip JOB of his clothes, apart
　　from his undergarments.)*

JOB: You forgot the gold teeth!
　　I've also got gold teeth in my mouth!

(Opens his mouth.)

HEAD BAILIFF: Don't be ridiculous.

Don't try and make us out to be monsters. We're all only human,

We all come home to a wife, a pair of slippers and a bowl of hot soup.

(The BAILIFFS exit.)

B

JOB: I emerged naked from my mother's womb, and my mother emerged naked from her mother's womb,

and we each emerge one from the other with a shudder, in a long, naked line.

'What shall I wear?' my mother asked in the morning, but at day's end

I carried her naked into her grave. Now I too am naked.

(The HEAD BAILIFF sneaks back in, approaches JOB, grabs him by the throat, pulls out a pair of pliers.)

HEAD BAILIFF: Open your mouth and don't make a sound, else – you die!

(JOB opens his mouth wide, the HEAD BAILIFF pulls out the gold teeth. JOB is about to start screaming from the pain.)

One tooth, two, three…

No, not a sound! Swallow the scream!

Does it hurt? Is your mouth bleeding?

Bite your lip! Swallow the scream!

Help me finish up this job nice and smooth.

(Exits. JOB screams silently.)

JOB: My sons and daughters, my children,
Here is the hand daddy fed you from.
Like a magician he pulled from this very hand
an inexhaustible bounty, bread and honey and butter,
all the world's pleasures, all the abundant sweetness
we thought would never run out. And now it's run out.
The magic's run out, the hand is empty and now it's
reaching out to you:

My sons and daughters, congratulations! A new father's
been born to you!
Look at him, how heartwarming, like a baby,
he's naked, he's crying and wetting himself, helpless,
he doesn't have any teeth either. Take him in your arms,
rock him, feed him porridge and milk,
sing him a lullaby so he sleeps, he's in such need of love
and warmth.

Oh, my children, the hand is empty, the giving father is
no more,
A new father's been born to you – a taking father!
Congratulations!

Fourth Chapter – The Heralds of Death

HERALD OF DEATH A enters, stands silently in front of JOB.

JOB: The house is empty. You also don't have that brisk pace
of someone who's come to take something.
You're reaching your hands out towards me hesitantly,
you want to tell me something.

(Pause.)

If you had difficult news for me,
You'd have assumed a more unyielding stance.
Since you're trying very hard to be humane,
I can tell that the news isn't just, it's terrible.

(Approaches him.)

You'd be doing me more of a favour if you were just
staring at me coldly.
Eyes like those, saturated with compassion and
commiseration,
for someone in my situation, can mean only one thing...

(And suddenly a cry escapes from his throat.)

Which of them?!

HERALD OF DEATH A: The eldest. At lunch. Seated at the table.
A sudden and mighty gust of wind struck the house. Fire
quickly engulfed every corner and climbed upstairs.
From outside they heard the screams of fear and agony of
those trapped in the room;

By the time the fire died down, all the screams had died down too.

(Two stretcher-bearers enter, carrying a corpse covered in a blanket. They lay it on the ground and leave together with HERALD OF DEATH A.)

JOB: Here is my eldest son. The baby who used to fall asleep on my shoulder

serene and trusting. The baby who used to call out to me at night 'Daddy!'

and knew that I'd come, and fold him into my arms. And when he was running around in that room

and screaming, engulfed by smoke, all the years suddenly fell away from him

like a shell, and he was once again a frightened child,

and 'Where's Daddy!' he called out to me, 'Daddy, Daddy!' he shouted and didn't understand

how it could be that his flesh, which was so dear to his father, was going up in flames,

and 'where's Daddy?' he called out to me 'Daddy, Daddy!'

Here is my eldest son. His face is turned towards me, but is already looking at

something which is beyond me, as though, disappointed, he's turned his back

on me and walked away, leaving me to carry the weight of my guilt alone.

B

HERALD OF DEATH B enters.

JOB: I can't bear any more news.

I have two daughters and a son left. Have pity.

HERALD OF DEATH B: May the god who's also taken both of
  your daughters from you have pity on you.
  At the same lunch held by your eldest son,
  at the same table, to which, as it turns out,
  he invited all his brothers and sisters.

  *(Four stretcher-carriers enter with two stretchers on which lie two
  bodies covered in blankets, place them on the ground and exit with
  HERALD OF DEATH B.)*

JOB: My daughters, my girls, I'm only just starting to grieve
  for your older brother. Now you've arrived, two dead girls,
  and you're also silently and stubbornly demanding your
  share of grief. Like back when you used to jump onto
  my neck when I got back home, rejoicing, whooping,
  chattering incessantly, kissing my
  cheeks with warm lips, and your breath so fresh,
  and calling out: 'Daddy, look at our new dresses!'…
  'Daddy!' you call out to me now, 'See how we're lying
  here without moving! How we're not breathing! Daddy,
  do you think it'll pass like all the childhood illnesses?
  When, Daddy? When will we get up? When will we go
  out to the park? When will the doctor let us see the sun
  again? And if we don't get up, Daddy, weep for our lives!
  Weep for the golden days of our childhood,
  which were a preparation for the great happiness, and
  where is it, Daddy, the great happiness?!'

  But wait a minute, my daughters, wait, I'm not done with
  your older brother yet,
  How will I have enough grief for you all? I mean even if I
  transform
  into a burning torch of grief and anger, how long will I be
  able to burn for?
  How long will I be able to shout 'My eldest son and two
  daughters are dead, my eldest son and two daughters are

163

dead…!' The land is so big and the sky so far, and I have
only one throat to shout with, one throat!!

And I haven't yet forgotten the grief of losing all my
precious possessions,
And I loved my possessions too,
Oh my possessions and money, oh my children my
children, oh how much
grieving have I been given to do!

(Pause. And suddenly.)

He invited all his brothers and sisters to the meal?!
Was my youngest son there too, at the same table?!

C

HERALD OF DEATH C enters.

HERALD OF DEATH C: No. Your youngest wasn't there.
He arrived late…

JOB: I have a son!!

HERALD OF DEATH C: …and death was lying in wait for him
on the way. In an earthquake
a boulder detached from a mountaintop, rolled down onto
the path below
and crushed the people walking on it, one of whom was
your son.

*(Two stretcher-carriers enter with a stretcher on which lies a body
covered in a blanket. They place it on the ground and exit.)*

It might comfort you to know that death was instant.
There were no convulsions and no suffering.

(Pause.)

It might comfort you to know that the tragedy isn't yours
alone.

Other people were killed, including a bride and groom,
and several children.

(Pause.)

I don't have any more words of comfort for you.

(HERALD OF DEATH C exits.)

JOB: My youngest, the dearest of them all, the grief for each
    of you individually

    should have completely flooded me. The grief for all four
    of you

    is something I haven't the strength to bear.

    And so, my youngest, I am deferring the news of your death

    to a later date. God willing I will live to see the day

    when I have strength for the backbreaking labour of
    grieving for you.

    For now I'll just say this: Welcome.

    Everyone has returned. Here are all my children.

    My boys, my girls, you've come back home.

    And the house is full like it used to be. Welcome.

D

JOB sits silently in front of the bodies. The itch hits him, initially in one place, almost imperceptibly. He scratches himself absent-mindedly. The itch doesn't subside. He scratches himself again. He starts feeling itchy on different parts of his body. The pain of the itch intensifies. He scratches himself frantically. He rips his underwear off to make it easier for him to scratch himself. He rolls around naked on the bare earth, scratching and rubbing his body on the ground. Terrifying animal screams suddenly burst from his mouth. He rolls around and screams until he's completely exhausted. He remains on all fours, whimpering quietly, then collapses on the ground, curled up like a fetus and lying motionless. A spasm occasionally passes over his body.

Fifth Chapter – The Friends

JOB's FRIENDS enter, ELIPAZ, BILDAD and TSOFAR, and see him from far away

ELIPAZ: We're looking for a man called Job.

We're his best friends. We heard that a tragedy
had befallen him. We've come to console him.

(JOB doesn't respond.)

BILDAD: We're looking for a man called Job.
We're his best friends…

TSOFAR: Friends, this is our friend Job.

(The three of them stand in shock for a moment. Slowly approach him.)

ELIPAZ: Job, it's your friends, Elipaz, Bildad and Tsofar.

JOB: *(Groans from the pain of the itch.)*

The itch! The itch! All my skin's on fire!
The only thing preventing me from being a happy man –
is just the itch! Just the itch!
And let me tell you, my dear itchy animals,
were it not for itching – the whole world would look very
different.
Because what is there for anyone to complain about –
everything's perfect. Such a beautiful and balanced world,
we live, we die – that is the way of the world, only the itch
spoils the happiness. Do you know what caused
the fall of the emperor of Rome? Itching. The emperor of
Rome raised his hand

and scratched his nose and in doing so left his neck
exposed.
Listen to someone with experience:
Between mankind and happiness lies only the itch.

(The three FRIENDS cry quietly.)

B

JOB: Why are you crying? Are you also itchy?

ELIPAZ: Our good friend Job, don't admonish us
for not being afflicted by your terrible curse.
Like you, we too are subject to God's wrath
or his grace, and if God were to strike me,
then I'd be there naked and scratching in your place,
and you would be standing here
and commiserating with me, with your clothes on.

God chose you to suffer,
and us – to express our condolences.

Friends, now we'll also tear our clothes, put ash
on our heads, and pray in subservience to God.

(The three FRIENDS sit opposite JOB.)

JOB: What's God got to do with it?
What's the destruction of my life got to do with God? If
God did this,
what's his game? What are his rules? Why did he
send back my sons as corpses on a single day,
why did he collapse my mines in Lebanon, why did he sink
my ships in Alexandria, why did he topple the Roman
emperor from his throne?!
And why, maybe you can explain this to me, did he serve
me up this itch for dessert?!

What's he punishing me for, this God? Is this retribution, is this divine justice?! No, my friends, a world in which Job exists contains no God!

ELIPAZ: Dear friend Job, there is nothing further from us
than the desire to preach morals to you in your current situation.
We aren't forgetting for one moment that we currently have it good –
although who knows for how long – and that you have it bad.
We're also far from trying to insinuate
that God is punishing you for your sins. Who doesn't know
that Job is a righteous man? And nevertheless. There's a 'nevertheless' here:

Rummage around within yourself a little. Maybe you've sinned before? No?
Try to remember, now's the time. No? Not even many years ago?
Never? All right, let's suppose not. Maybe you were about to sin? No?
Not that either? All right, let's suppose not. But maybe you sinned in your thoughts?
Not even in your thoughts? Let's suppose not. Lots of 'supposing' going on here.
That really makes you a righteous man, and if you're righteous,
then perhaps God is just testing you, like he tested
another righteous man, Abraham, and like Abraham he'll reward you
afterwards seventy-seven times over?

Who can know the thoughts of the Lord? Because in the divine plan
we are the lines, and God, he alone,
sees the plan in its entirety.

Man keeps a small tally, one plus one, a plate and a handkerchief,
And God sits up above and sums up all the handkerchiefs, all the plates, the heavens and the earth.

Observe the world…don't tear off parts of it,
see it all. See how right, how just it is.
The great and beautiful world, all-embracing, into which
our lives flow like the water pouring out from the darkness of the jug
and bursting suddenly out into the open field, and here is soil, here is sky,
here are trees laden with fruit, and birds nesting in their branches,
a mighty and multifaceted world, a world full of ravages, but also full of remedies and consolations,
a world as familiar to us as home, but also full of mystery and secrets,
a world in which the darkness is encompassed within an enormous hoop of light.

Job, a a brave and noble soul is required in order to hold the entire world
in your gaze. If there is a brave, noble soul within you –
now is its hour. Rise up, lift yourself out of your torments and believe in God!

JOB: My good friend, you're torturing me!
You talk to me about justifying the divine,
first prove to me the justification for humanity,
don't torture me. Let me scratch myself in peace.
I don't know the grace of creation. I don't know God.

BILDAD: You knew him when you had it good.

JOB: When I had it good – I had it good. Now
    I've got it bad, I don't know God.

ELIPAZ: Does God exist when we're happy
    and disappear when our happiness disappears?
    Is God a soap bubble,
    With our words we inflate him,
    and with our little finger we burst him?
    People as tortured as you, even more than you,
    have called out to him in their anguish. They saw no
    contradiction between suffering and God.

    Because who are you with all your suffering?! From a
    hundred cubits away your cries can no longer be heard.
    From a thousand cubits away you look like
    an ant. Can you imagine what you look like
    from the stars?!

JOB: Then let the stars acknowledge God's existence! Let whoever
    can reconcile his concepts of justice and injustice
    acknowledge him! Whoever feels
    God's arms embracing him – let him embrace God back!

    I am small and blind, and groping around with my
    fingernails like a mole in a dark burrow.
    I live in the darkness, in the pitch black,
    and the light is something I only hear stories about!

ELIPAZ: The blind man doesn't know the sun,
    But knows that it exists.
    You are consumed by your itch, but know
    under your skin that God exists.

JOB: No! I exist! You exist!
    The difference between us exists! God does not exist!
    The itch on my skin exists! The death of my sons exists!

The loss of all my possessions exists! What I don't have –
that's what exists!

BILDAD: You're very arrogant, you know? Have some humility.
Don't presume that if you're suffering
and we express the utmost empathy with your suffering
that you're also correct.
There's the demagoguery of the sated man, but there's also
the demagoguery of the suffering and the tortured.
And you're not allowed everything, no, not everything
quite yet!
You think that if day and night you shout 'My itch exists!'
that invalidates God. Your world right now is the itch –
Fine. God has patience and benevolence. He's not angry.
You're not the first itchy person he's seen.
I don't have God's benevolence. I am a short-tempered man!
We won't let our Holy One be spat on!

JOB: I observe the world through my itch –
What do you observe it through?
Through your stomach? Your satisfaction? Your fat? Standing
on the sturdy foundation of your own lives,
feeling firm ground under your feet,
how will you realise that everything is fluid, built on water?
You need someone to guard your vaults,
and you've appointed God to do it:
I no longer have a vault – I've dismissed God from my world.

TSOFAR: My friends, a terrible cry is escaping
from our good friend Job's throat. The eyes of our good
friend Job are blurry with blood and tears, how could
he see God? Give him a day or two, the world will once
again become clearer to him, I'm sure of it, because
within a man's soul, as in a lake, the anger and the
hardship sink down,

and God's image is once again reflected in the clear waters.

Now let's go. Let's leave him
to seclude himself with his sorrow. We'll return tomorrow.

C

BILDAD: I'm not sure I'll return. Let's speak openly:
This philosophizing about God didn't start today.
The arguments for and against are known. But now I'm talking
not about philosophy, but only about life. The day-to-day life
which we mortals – with a vault, without a vault – lead
within a law-abiding society. Yes, law and order.
Who gives our life meaning? Who gives meaning to our laws?
In our society – God is the meaning. If God doesn't exist –
life has no meaning, the law is empty,
hollow, with no purpose and no meaning. If God doesn't exist –
stealing or not stealing, it's all the same.

JOB: You are scared of thieves. That's why you're placing
the burden of meaning on my suffering.
But what is the meaning other than suffering? I'm
scratching and scratching
and trying to dig around in my suffering to find meaning in it.
And I'm telling you: There's nothing hidden within the
suffering, just suffering!
And I can only see suffering filling the world!
And every lump of suffering, is made up of a thousand shards
of suffering, and every shard of suffering is in turn made up of
millions of molecules of suffering!
Suffering exists! I exist! You exist!
The difference between us exists! God does not exist!

BILDAD: You don't exist! You don't exist!

No person counting himself as a member of our society
will speak this obscenely, like a vile animal! Not even for
a moment!

Not as long as they count themselves part of our society!

JOB: 'Our society'?! Which society is 'our society'?!

(Points at the corpses.)

Here is my society. They are the ones I live and connect
with. They and I – our society – has no room for God!

BILDAD: Crowd together and find room! Four corpses
and a boil-infested beggar will neither crown
nor dismiss almighty God!

It's easy for you. You speak as someone with the benefit of
having nothing to lose.

I do. I haven't been afflicted like you have. I need to go
on living.

And it's not easy constantly holding the loose tension
of life in your hands. And I'm also tired; I also want to
fall to the ground pounding my chest with my fists and
screaming and crying. But I restrain myself.

I won't let you sit there and shout that there's no God! I
won't let you! Won't let you!

JOB: You won't let me?! What'll you do to me?! Cut
my tongue out? Kill me? Please, go ahead:
There's no God! There's no God! There's no God!

*(His shouts sound like dog barks, especially as he's kneeling on the
ground.)*

BILDAD: Look at God's dog, crouching on all fours
at God's feet and barking: 'There's no God!'
God raises his foot and kicks the dog in the face, but the dog
only sees the boot and howls: 'There's no God!'

JOB: How it befits you, that stance with the boot
　　ready to kick my face. You're at your best. You've never
　　looked so content with yourself. And all that talk
　　was nothing more than a preface to the boot.
　　You were born to kick – so kick!

D

TSOFAR: But my friends, what about compassion?
　　Not only is the letter of the law divine, but compassion
　　is also divine, have you forgotten? Who are we
　　to be harsher than God? Who are we to judge him?
　　The man is drowning, and we on the beach won't reach
　　out a hand to him?

　　(Approaches JOB.)

　　In this world in which we are all merely
　　frightened orphans searching for our father,
　　how could we forget the father's pity for his sons?
　　And you crouching beneath us
　　and scratching yourself on your pile of corpses,
　　how could we forget your father's pity for you?

　　(Kneels beside JOB.)

JOB: My father? Yes, I had a father once.

TSOFAR: And you called out to him at night when you'd had
　　a bad dream.
　　You'd wake up frightened and drenched in sweat in your
　　bed and call out: Daddy!

JOB: Daddy! I called out: Daddy!

TSOFAR: And he was always there, he came over to you and
　　stood over you,

and lifted you up in his arms, near his face,
and you felt his warm breath on your face.

JOB: *(Tears start flowing from his eyes.)*
Daddy…

TSOFAR: And you buried your frightened face in his neck
and a smile of relief spread across your lips,
and your breath became regular again, and you fell asleep.

JOB: *(Sobbing.)*
Daddy…Daddy…where is he, my father?

TSOFAR: *(Hugging JOB.)*
Up there.

JOB: I'm his little boy, and I'm miserable.
I had a nightmare in bed…

TSOFAR: He can hear you. You had
a bad dream, call out to him.

JOB: I had a bad dream, Daddy,
And I'm frightened and drenched in sweat…

TSOFAR: Reach your hand out to him.

JOB: *(Raising his hands in the air.)*
Lift me in your arms and I'll bury my face in your neck…

TSOFAR: He's reaching out his hands to you, can't you see?

JOB: My eyes are blurry with tears

TSOFAR: He's answering you, can't you hear?

JOB: Yes, I think I can hear. He's answering me.
And now I can also clearly see
his hands outstretched towards me.

TSOFAR: He'll never leave you.
    He's hugging you…

JOB: He's hugging me…I can feel
    that now he's hugging me…

(He suddenly bursts out crying.)

    Daddy, look what's happened to me, Daddy!
    Look what's happened to me in this world
    into which you happily brought me!
    Look what's happened to your son!
    Look what's happened to the happiness!

TSOFAR: You had a dream, I told you already, the world is a
    dream bubble.

JOB: *(Calms down very slowly.)*
    Yes, a dream. I just had a dream.

TSOFAR: And now you've woken up in your father's arms,
    And he's slowly rocking you,
    up, far above the world,
    stars here, moon there,
    serenely and silently, and your eyes are shut
    and you don't open them at all to see…

JOB: *(With his eyes shut.)*
    And I don't open them at all to see…

    (And silent happiness starts flooding him.)

    Daddy's alive, Daddy's not dead,
    my father's risen from his resting place,
    that's how my sons and daughters will also rise,
    because the world is a dream, just a dream bubble,
    and death, like snow, melts in the heat.

Goodbye to suffering, goodbye to torments,
Goodbye to my dead children's corpses,
I'm a baby again, curled up in my father's lap,
high above the world, carried on up,
serenely and silently, my eyes are shut,
and I don't open them at all to see...

(TSOFAR cradles him in his lap.)

Cradle me, Daddy, cradle me, like that...

TSOFAR: Call out to him, speak to him: Our father in heaven...

JOB: Our father in heaven...

TSOFAR: Who sits on high...

JOB: Who sits on high...

TSOFAR: I entrust my spirit into your hand...

JOB: I entrust my spirit into your hand...

TSOFAR: And take refuge in the shadow of your wings...

JOB: And take refuge in the shadow of your wings...

TSOFAR: Hear my voice...

JOB: Hear my voice...

TSOFAR: Let your ears hear my pleas...

JOB: Let your ears hear my pleas...

TSOFAR: For you are good, and forgiving and full of grace...

JOB: For you are good, and forgiving and full of grace...

TSOFAR: For the lord is supreme and above all else...

JOB: For the lord is supreme and above all else...

(Pause.)

ELIPAZ: My friends, look, the skies are opening.
　　See how great is his love for us.
　　For he named us the children of God.
　　My loved ones, we are indeed the children of God!
　　And the skies are opening.

Sixth Chapter – The Soldiers

A

A group of armed SOLDIERS enters, led by an OFFICER.

OFFICER: In the name of the new emperor, the emperor of
mighty Rome and its provinces,

This is the word of the emperor: I am God. That's to say
him, the emperor. There is no God other than me, the
emperor. All prayers, all sacrifices to other gods –
are forbidden. Religious rituals in the temple – are
forbidden. The image of the new God will replace all
other images. There are no priests, no Levites,
no Rabbis, no cantors, no synagogue managers. The new
God will send his own managers

For this is the word of the emperor: The God of the Jews
is null and void.
Anyone who believes in him is a heretic and a rebel
against the empire.
To strengthen the new faith and in order to clarify what
has come to pass:
Any believer in the god of the Jews will receive a skewer
in the arse.

B

OFFICER: *(To ELIPAZ.)*
You, come here.

(ELIPAZ approaches him.)

Does the god of the Jews exist, or not?

(Pause. To the SOLDIERS.)

This man is a rebel against the empire.
Sit him down on the skewer.

BILDAD: Esteemed soldiers, why are you jumping to
such hasty conclusions based on his silence,
which stemmed merely from his great excitement at the
ascendance of our new emperor,
to whom we are all the most loyal of servants?

OFFICER: *(Pointing at ELIPAZ.)*
Has his excitement passed yet? We're waiting for an answer.

BILDAD: Elipaz my friend, you no doubt recall how,
when we came here an hour ago and saw
the magnitude of the tragedy which has befallen our friend
Job, how you said to me: This world is packed so full of
suffering, devoid of God.

(Pause.)

Esteemed soldiers, everyone here will confirm it, he told
us: There is no God.

OFFICER: We want to hear it from his mouth.

BILDAD: *(To the OFFICER, quietly.)*
Let's step to one side. He'll say anything you like,
just not in front of everyone.

OFFICER: The confession is public, that's the emperor's
decision.

BILDAD: Elipaz my friend, the esteemed soldiers would like
you to repeat your previous statements.

(Pause. He hugs ELIPAZ.)

Elipaz my friend, when you're deeply contemplating this
issue,

think, not only about Job's dead children, think also
about your own children, they're alive. Think also about
your fields, they're waiting for the harvest.
We've had a wonderful crop in our fields this year, haven't
we? Think about your home,
think about your evening meal, a meal as wonderful as the
end of a hard day's work…
about your slippers and the glass of wine, the chatter with
friends around the table,
the lovely routine of our lives. The routine of the days, the
seasons,
the festivals. Have you already been swimming in the sea
this year? Have you already warmed your bones
in the sun on the soft sand this season? Elipaz my friend,
this evening will you eat your rich, wonderful dinner,
or will the rest of the world eat it – everyone but you?!

ELIPAZ: *(Cries with him.)*

Tell me more. Tell me about my children.

BILDAD: Like fruit on a tree, you are the mighty trunk
from which your children's red hearts hang. And
the rough skewer which will pierce your flesh will also
pass through their soft flesh.
That's why they'll wait for you. Elipaz, I am now the
mouth of your children,
The small sweet mouth, opening with eternal innocence
against the horrors of the world,
hear this mouth screaming! Will you allow the skewer to
be thrust in?

ELIPAZ: Oh my children, small sweet mouths!

BILDAD: Oh Daddy, hear the cries coming
from our small, sweet mouths. Unlike Job's

children who are frozen forever, our bodies are warm, it's still not too late,

the final step from which there's no going back hasn't been taken yet,

don't forsake us, Daddy!

Dying for your God, Daddy, is a big sacrifice,

now we're calling on you to make an even bigger sacrifice:

To live for the sake of your children!

ELIPAZ: *(Cries a bit more, wipes away his tears.)*

From the things you said, Bildad my friend, in such a tangible way,

my heart was touched by the call to make a sacrifice.

Not the sunshine, the crops, nor the evening meal, whose hour is indeed

approaching, that I can sense by my increasing appetite,

but the plea of those dear to me, on which I cannot turn my back,

it alone has brought me after deep thought to the inevitable conclusion:

(To the OFFICER.)

There is no God.

C

OFFICER: *(To BILDAD.)*

You. Come here.

(BILDAD approaches him.)

Does your God exist or not?

BILDAD: I have never hidden my thoughts from public view.

I have always stood, and I reiterate my stance, by the importance of the social law and order.

There's no doubt that the naïve attempt to place God at the heart of the social order
was necessary as a historical transitionary phase in mankind's development.
God was a rung on the ladder, a means by which to climb to a higher rung on which the emperor is sitting.
Miserable are those people stuck in the middle, on one of the rungs!
Joyful are those who have climbed up, to the top of the ladder, where I too now stand, peeking out from under the hem of the emperor's robe and calling out in gratitude:
There is no God!

D

OFFICER: *(To TSOFAR.)*
   You.

TSOFAR: *(Approaches him.)*
   There is a god...

OFFICER: *(To the SOLDIERS.)*
   Sit him down...

TSOFAR: ...up my arse.

OFFICER: Who?

TSOFAR: God.

   (Pause.)

OFFICER: You're complicating things for me a little bit.
   On one hand you're claiming that there is a god,

meaning, you're not renouncing his existence. On the other hand,

I'm not stupid enough to think that you actually believe in him if you shove him up your arse. On the other hand, if God exists everywhere, then he clearly also exists in the arse, meaning,

that you believe in him again. On the other hand, if you believe in him,

is there nowhere else you can represent him besides a filthy arsehole?

Basically, you're either mocking me, or you're trying to be funny in order to ingratiate yourself with the authorities.

But I have precise instructions, and I need from you a simple answer to a simple question: Does god exist or not?

TSOFAR: 'A simple answer to a simple question', ahh, what an eternally-military sense of humour...

(Pats the OFFICER's back in a friendly gesture. The OFFICER punches him in the face. TSOFAR drops to the ground, blood dripping from his nose. He gets up, still trying to be comical in order to preserve his dignity, wagging his finger humorously at the OFFICER.)

A rascal, eh? Rascal...

(Tries to pat the OFFICER's back again, who again punches him in the face, TSOFAR drops to the ground, gets up, approaches the OFFICER, struggles to stand up, wiggles his finger comically at him again.)

Listen, they'll start thinking
we have some kind of disagreement...

(The OFFICER punches him a third time, drops him to the ground.)

My friends, how vigorous today...

(The OFFICER lunges towards him to continue the punching. TSOFAR can't take it any more and bursts into tears while crying out.)

There is no God! There is no God!

I mean we can all see there's no God, can't we?!

E

The OFFICER turns to leave with his SOLDIERS. Suddenly notices JOB curled up on the floor. Approaches him.

OFFICER: You. Get up. Does your God exist or not?

JOB: You charming fool, can't you see he's
    reaching his arms out to hug me?

OFFICER: *(To the SOLDIERS.)*
    Sit him down on the skewer.

TSOFAR: *(To the OFFICER.)*
    Don't waste your precious time
    on this pile of human ruins.
    The man's lost his mind because of a terrible tragedy –
    he's not responsible for his actions or his words.

OFFICER: Joker, you've got a tendency to talk more than you
    should.
    And besides, since when is madness any excuse? One madman
    in a nearby village who claims to be the son of God
    already has twelve apostles. So what? Are they
    also mad? And so is the emperor's army supposed to sit
    on its arse
    and leave everyone in the world alone with the excuse
    that it's a madhouse?

    And in all honesty let me tell you something else: my men

186

are hungry for entertainment, they haven't seen any meat
on a skewer today:

and from the skewer's perspective, whether it's a sane arse
or a mad one is

neither here nor there.

TSOFAR: Job my friend, time to open your eyes.
We dreamt for a while that there was a god,
now wake up, face your suffering, the pain from yesterday.

Bark, bark at the empty skies,
bark like before 'There is no god!', because nothing's changed,
and remember the death, remember the poverty,
remember your rolling around in the dirt, the itching,
and most of all – remember the skewer!

JOB: But my loyal friend Tsofar, what are you
so excited about? What's happened?
Someone's four children have died and he's crying?

Do you know that from up above, from God's lap,
a crying man looks like he's sneezing? The shrouds –
like handkerchiefs? The grief, the happiness – all the motions
are similar, and quite ridiculous? From up above, my friend
everything's amusing.
Who'll separate me from my father?
Who'll bring me down
from God's lap?

OFFICER: He's right. Help him climb up to God's lap on the
skewer.

F

*(TSOFAR pulls some money out of his pocket, holds it out surreptitiously
to the OFFICER.)*

TSOFAR: Take fifty Dinars and let him go.

OFFICER: Are you trying to buy the army...on the cheap?

TSOFAR: *(Puts the money back in his pocket.)*
    I tried.

OFFICER: Try double the price. Maybe that'll work.

TSOFAR: *(Looks over at ELIPAZ and BILDAD. They don't react.)*
    No, it's not worth more than fifty to me.
    I tried as much as one does.
    My conscience is clear.

OFFICER: *(Angry, points at JOB.)*
    At long last sit him on the skewer!!

G

The SOLDIERS spread JOB's legs and move the skewer closer.

SERGEANT: Have you found the anus? Yes, in the middle.
    Good.
    The arsehole can even be found, as they say,
    by a blind man on a moonless night.

SOLDIER: You can't mistake the smell.

SERGEANT: And now to put it in, push, yes, like that.

JOB: Arrrgh! My arse! My arse! Oh, God!
    My arse, my arse! God, my arse!

OFFICER: This person's entire being
    is now focused on his backside.
    All the family ties, the urges,
    the emotions, the beliefs and the opinions
    are blending in his mind into a kind of amorphous paste,

a heavy fog, from within which flickers, like the beam of a lighthouse
the excruciating pain in his arse.

As the skewer climbs up within the stomach cavity
the pain in his arse will also fade into the fog,
and give way to new areas for his being to focus on.

JOB: Arrrgh! My intestines! My intestines! Oh, God!
My intestines! My intestines! God, my intestines!

OFFICER: Now, as mentioned, he's shifting God
from his backside to his intestines.

TSOFAR: *(Crying out.)*
Renounce God, Job!
Say that God doesn't exist!
Renounce God!

(The SOLDIERS lift the skewer on which JOB is impaled and plant its base in the ground.)

JOB: Father, they're carrying me towards you on a metal rod.
Over rods and crosses and spears and fires they're lifting us,
our arms outstretched, to our forefathers. I am going to my father,
riding on a knife! How horrible is the journey, but how great is the grace,
how sweet the rest waiting at the end of the journey, in my father's lap!

(He falls silent.)

H

The three friends stand and look at JOB on the skewer.

BILDAD: See how he's looking at me. His tormented eyes

piercing me with the rudeness of someone who's owed
something.
What? What have I done and what do I owe?
And does having a skewer in your stomach suddenly
make you into a saint?

And what are you looking at me for, from up on that skewer,
so proudly? God, who you believe in,
doesn't like those who are arrogant. God, who you believe in,
loves me, the inferior, the fearful, the lowest of the low,
the mud.
I am the soft human mud which gets molded into strong beliefs.

And if I were sitting up there instead of you
on the skewer and staring at you, what then?
Would you come and sit here instead of me? If so, what's
the difference?
And what's the point? And what would be different in the
world? And why
am I standing here justifying myself anyway? Does anyone
even owe you anything?

So wipe that pleading from your eyes!
I already told you: You're you and I'm – me!
You hear? You're you and I'm – me!
You're you and I'm – me!

Close your eyes already! Or lift them to the heavens,
swine! Search the heavens for your daddy,
shout to the heavens and cry to the heavens,
go and cry in God's lap that down here on earth
you lost your trousers!

(The three friends exit. JOB calls after them.)

JOB: Don't leave me alone with God!
My friends, don't leave me
alone with God!

Seventh Chapter – The Entertainers

A

The CIRCUS MANAGER enters.

CIRCUS MANAGER: Isn't it a crying shame about this man?
    Isn't it a crying shame
    that a performance like this is going to waste without an
    audience?
    A shame about all the potential tickets, calling out with no
    voice
    like the souls of unborn children?
    And I'm not even talking about the educational value of a
    show like this
    for a public which is still wondering whether God exists or not.

    I've directed musical circuses in Europe's
    most important capital cities.
    I wouldn't be exaggerating if I said I've directed all of Europe.
    I have a stripper, I have midgets,
    I have a French kitchen, drinks and music for dancing,
    what I'm missing is precisely a hot arse on a skewer.

    Five hundred Dinars to the emperor's coffers
    For the right to feature this man
    In my circus show.

OFFICER: Were the emperor to sell tickets himself,
    the emperor would make at least five thousand.

CIRCUS MANAGER: How? Are you kidding? We've already
    missed the part with the shoving of the skewer

with the pulling down of the trousers and the screams and
the fear and all the humiliation and the chuckling,
which is the juiciest bit.
The rod's deep in his stomach, he's got barely an hour of
silent agony left in him!
How many tickets, do you think, would you sell for one hour
of introverted suffering? And who's interested these days
in seeing a man suffering quietly? The audience, as you
know, pays
in order to hear a bit of singing.

OFFICER: This man's going to live for another six-seven hours,
and with singing too, maybe even until the morning.

CIRCUS MANAGER: Where's the singing now?

OFFICER: He's resting.

CIRCUS MANAGER: Resting? Really? And is anyone insuring
me against
a sudden hemorrhage or a stroke which might happen at
any moment?

OFFICER: A hemorrhage in the stomach cavity – yes:
But the time it'll take the rod to pass his diaphragm,
if at all, towards the heart...

CIRCUS MANAGER: I don't know much about anatomy.

OFFICER: Thirty percent of the ticket price goes to the circus,
thirty to the emperor.

CIRCUS MANAGER: And the remaining forty?

OFFICER: I'm also a person.

CIRCUS MANAGER: In that case, forty to the circus, forty to
the emperor,
and twenty to the person.

OFFICER: No less than forty to the person.

CIRCUS MANAGER: Listen, we're all people.

OFFICER: I don't know much about philosophy.

CIRCUS MANAGER: Enough, fifty percent to the circus, fifty to the person.

OFFICER: And the emperor?

CIRCUS MANAGER: The emperor doesn't profiteer from backsides.

OFFICER: You're right.
(They shake on it.)

CIRCUS MANAGER: *(Turns to the audience.)*
Dear audience, the sun has set, another
hard day's haggling has come to an end,
now, on your way home to the soup and the potatoes,
don't forget to throw a little potato to your soul.
Have you drawn the curtain? Turned off the lights?
Locked up the shop? –
Ladies and gentlemen, five minutes for art!

B

The circus actors enter and surround JOB. Amongst them are a MIDGET and a STRIPPER. The MIDGET courts the STRIPPER and sings.

MIDGET: Once, when I was three,
such a lovely age,
no one thought that I was small
or called me midget to my face.
We shared a future together,
Both of us equally,

Lots of happiness on your horizon,
And a similar happiness – for me.

But you grew up and left me far, far behind,
And today your face reaches the sky, and my face reaches
your behind.

Don't call me a midget,
call me an eternal child,
because my heart is so stormy and hot,
and beats with the passionate blood that I've got
and so much emotion, so much tenderness to unlock
and you might be happy to know, I also have a long cock

STRIPPER: I spent a good few years in Africa,
and I know what long is. I also know what
hard is. My hole, if I may say so,
is already adapted to African dimensions,
and I won't stick noodles into it.
And there, ladies and gentlemen, you have the most
important outcome
of living in Africa.

MIDGET: Don't judge us by Africa's standards.
We live in Asia. Judge us by Asia.

*(The STRIPPER dances and strips in front of the MIDGET. When
she's naked she inspects his erect member.)*

STRIPPER: Well, even by Asia's pathetic standards,
I hereby refute the common claim
that nature created you in the spirit of opposites:
A short body with a long cock. No, nature
screwed you all the way: A short body and a short cock
and a short life. And what do you have that's nevertheless
long?

The suffering, of course. Your suffering is very very long and hard.

(Looks at JOB, turns her attention to the skewer.)

Here I see something long which might actually fit me even by Africa's standards.

(The STRIPPER spreads her legs, puts her crotch against the skewer, rubs it and moans in pleasure, as though in response to the agonized moans of JOB impaled on top with his legs splayed out sideways. Their convulsions and moans give the appearance of intercourse, with the skewer acting as the man's member.)

JOB: *(In agony.)*
    Daddy...Daddy...

STRIPPER: *(In pleasure.)*
    Oh mama....Oh mama...

(And she sings as she rubs up against the pole.)

Between my legs I have a black hole,
between my legs I have a black hole,
who will come and plug my hole,
who'll light it up, it's dark as coal,
who'll shove it in from the front,
until it comes out of my arsehole.
Between my legs I have a black hole...

MIDGET: *(Masturbates and sings.)*
    Don't call me a midget...

(And the two songs merge into each other with great movement and fanfare.)

C

The skewer cuts through JOB's lungs. He has difficulty breathing.

JOB: Arrrgh! Air! Oh, God!
   Air! Air!

CIRCUS MANAGER: What are you standing around like oafs for?!
   Don't you have a spark of humanity?!
   Give him water – we need to prolong
   his death throes a bit longer,
   there's a sea of people still crowding the entrance!

OFFICER: Too late. The skewer's past the diaphragm
   and penetrated the lungs.

JOB: There is no God –
   Take me off the skewer! There is no God!

OFFICER: It's too late, my friend. Death
   has taken root in you. Go
   along with death!

JOB: Air…there is no God…
   I swear to you there is no God!!!

OFFICER: It's a shame. For the same price you could have died
   as a man with principles.

JOB: Take me off the skewer!
   There is no God – and that's final!

D

*Two CLOWNS climb up a ladder on either side of JOB, make him up
and decorate him like a CLOWN.*

PATHETIC CLOWN: 'That's final' he says, and there's no one
   to remind him

how many times he's finalised things in his life.

Because what is a man? Here's a man for you:
Once he said there was a god, and once he barked that
there wasn't a god,
Once he called out my son my son, once he called out my
arse my arse,
this evening his mouth was full of roast pigeon, by sunrise
he had a metal rod up his arse,
the one singing, is now the one crying, and will soon be
the one who's fallen silent.

So what is a man? Is he the things he said yesterday,
Or the things he's crying about now, or his upcoming
silence?
Is he his memories, is he his hopes,
is he the things he does, is he the things that are done to him,
is he the final cry he lets out on his deathbed,
or the very first cry between his mother's legs?
Is he the whole terrible and pathetic jumble that stretches out
between these two cries?
If so, where's the thread connecting it all,
where's the thread, and what's the meaning here?

So what is a man? And what is life?
And the thread, ladies and gentlemen, most of all: where's
the thread?

CYNICAL CLOWN: 'What is a man? What is life?'
What is a fly? What are haemorrhoids and strife?
Why do we care where the thread is?
Why do we care what a man is at all?
Why the hell do we care about the world as a whole?!
Ladies and gentlemen, you're now seeing
a man falling from the roof of a tall building.

His arms are spread, he's rolling and tumbling in the air,
his broken screams are echoing in space,
and so, taking a small step back to avoid blood splattering
on your clothes,
you stand transfixed and watch his fall,
your faces displaying a mix of passion and horror
in anticipation of the decisive and irreversible moment
when his body hits the ground.

Don't ask about the reason for the fall, the moral or the meaning,
just watch the play: A man is falling, and will soon be dead.

E

JOB lets out a death rattle.

CIRCUS MANAGER: *(To JOB.)*
>You're not going to leave me halfway through are you?
>You look like a decent person, you're my children's bread
>for tomorrow. Listen to them calling out to me: father….
>father…
>You're not going to take the bread from my children's
>mouths are you?

OFFICER: It's too late. It's death.

CIRCUS MANAGER: He can easily drag it out for another hour.

OFFICER: I don't tell you how to train elephants,
>so don't you tell me how to smell dead people.
>For ten years I've lived with death, like a small monkey,
>sitting on my shoulder and playing with my ear.
>Ladies and gentlemen, this is death.

>*(Reaches his hand out for money. The CIRCUS MANAGER hands
>him his share.)*

JOB: Death? Death itself? So this is the famous moment
I've heard so much about? It's arrived?

*(The OFFICER and the SOLDIERS exit. The CIRCUS MANAGER
tries to distract JOB and not let him sink to his death.)*

CIRCUS MANAGER: Hey! Man! What do you reckon now?
Is there a God? Can you see anything over there? Is there
one? Or just a black hole, adjusted to Africa's standards?
Eh? Man, tell us! Tell us! Tell us!

(He hits him desperately.)

PATHETIC CLOWN: This man is currently far away, above our
heads.
He already knows something we don't.

But he won't say a thing. He's now already
at that dizzying height at which you don't know anyone
any more, all the plains
and the hills are behind him, his life's story and his
actions, the people and the tools
which bound him to the world, are now all detached from
him,
he's even been released from the tight grip of his father's
arms, left them
far below, now it's just him alone, alone, wrapped like a
great priest
in the simple gown of the secret of his death, in which
every one of us, each in our own time, will also wrap
ourselves.

JOB: *(With the last of his strength.)*
What is a man on a skewer?
A man on a skewer is a finished man, a lost man.
It's impossible to describe a greater despair than this;

200

From a darkness like this, the horizon can only get
brighter.

(Vomit and blood burst from his mouth. He dies.)

CIRCUS MANAGER: *(Angrily.)*
'Get brighter!' Couldn't you have lived another hour?!
'Get brighter!' Tfu!

(Spits on JOB's corpse. The circus and the audience scatter and leave.)

Eighth Chapter – The Dead

A

The most beggarly of the BEGGARLY BEGGARS' BEGGARS enters. Licks JOB's vomit.

BEGGAR: Like I already said: With a little patience
    someone always ends up vomiting in the end. Yes,
    somehow you stay alive. There is a God.
    Pa-Ra-Pim-Pim-Pim, Pa-Ra-Pim-Pim-Pim,

    (Exits.)

B

THE DEAD sing.

THE DEAD: But there is mercy in the world.
    And we will rest one day.

    This is how the dead repose
    Silently, whiling time away.

    Weeds will grow above the flesh,
    The wind will carry the scream away;

    But there is mercy in the world.
    And we will rest one day.

END

A WINTER FUNERAL

A burlesque in eight acts

Translated from the Hebrew by Naaman Tammuz

'A funeral or a wedding – which comes first?' is the great question at the heart of this eight-act burlesque play by Levin. The death of an old aunt on the day of her cousin's wedding threatens to postpone the happy occasion. To avoid the bad news, the family embarks on a crazy escape journey that takes them to the end of the world and back. Will they be able to cheat time and destiny?

Cast of Characters

LAJCEK BOBIJCEK, *a bachelor, approximately forty years old*

ALTE BOBIJCEK, *his elderly mother*

SHRATZIA, *Lajcek's aunt, approximately fifty years old*

RASCHES, *her husband*

VELVETZIA, *their daughter, the bride*

TSITSKEIVA, *Shratzia's co-mother-in-law*

BARAGUNTSELEH, *her husband*

POPPOCHENKO, *their son, the groom*

PROFESSOR KIPPERNAI, *a middle-aged bachelor*

ROSENZWEIG, *an elderly exerciser on the beach*

LIECHTENSTEIN, *an elderly exerciser on the beach*

ANGEL SAMUELOV, *the angel of death*

SHAHMANDRINA, *a Buddhist monk, ageless*

PSHOSHITZIA, *a pretty, giggly girl*

WEDDING GUESTS, WAITERS, A GRAVEDIGGER

Premiere	The Cameri Theatre, Tel Aviv, 1978
Director	Hanoch Levin
Costume and Stage Design	Moshe Shternfeld
Lighting Design	Nathan Pantorin
Music Composition	Foldi Shatzman
Choreography	Boris Svidansly and Irit Golan

Cast:

LAJCEK BOBIJCEK	Shmuel Segal
ALTE BOBIJCEK,	Shoshana Douer
SHAHMANDRINA	Shoshana Douer
SHRATZIA	Lia Kenig
RASCHES	Avraham Ronai
VELVETZIA	Sandra Sa'de
TSITSKEIVA:	Shlomo Bar-Shavit
BARAGUNTSELE:	Mosko Elkalai
POPPOCHENKO	David Stern
PROFESSOR KIPPERNAI	Israel Becker
ROSENZWEIG	Pesach Gotmark
LIECHTENSTEIN	Nathan Volfovitch
ANGEL SAMUELOV	Gideon Zinger
PSHOSHITZIA	Meirav Geri

Act One: The mother's death

Night. The BOBIJCEK household. ALTE is on her deathbed. LAJCEK is beside her.

ALTE: I'm going to die. It's winter. Who's going to come to my funeral?

LAJCEK: People will come, Mum.

ALTE: Who? Who accompanies lonely old women to their graves in the winter?

LAJCEK: I do, Mum.

ALTE: Who else?

LAJCEK: Auntie Shratzia, and Uncle Rasches and their daughter Velvetzia.

ALTE: Tomorrow is Velvetzia's wedding. There you go, I've missed a wedding as well.

(Pause.)

If my funeral's tomorrow, will they come?

LAJCEK: Of course they'll come.

ALTE: And postpone the wedding they've been waiting for their whole life?

LAJCEK: The wedding will get postponed, Mum.

ALTE: And all for me?

LAJCEK: You're very dear to them.

ALTE: What are they saying on the radio about tomorrow's weather?

LAJCEK: Rainy.

ALTE: Rainy. Just my luck. They'll never skip a warm wedding with meat and cognac for some small elderly woman's funeral in the rain.

LAJCEK: They will, Mum. They'll skip it and come with black umbrellas.

ALTE: *(Sinks back into her bed.)* It's all nonsense.

LAJCEK: Yes, Mum.

ALTE: They will come, they won't come – what difference does it make.

LAJCEK: Yes, Mum.

ALTE: *(Waking up suddenly.)* But you said they'd come!

LAJCEK: They'll come, Mum, they'll come. They'll all come.

ALTE: *(Bursts into quiet, muffled tears.)* Because someone *has* to be there…

LAJCEK: *(Also on the verge of tears.)* They will, Mum, they will.

ALTE: Because I definitely existed. On the actual ground. I existed, didn't I? I took up some kind of space, I did, I breathed air, I spoke a bit, I made food, I existed. It's still *someone* they're burying here after all.

LAJCEK: Yes, Mum. You took up space, you existed. All of us will be at the funeral.

ALTE: *(Stops crying. Contemptuously.)* All of us! Big deal! Three people – all of us!

LAJCEK: Four.

ALTE: I can only see three.

LAJCEK: Auntie Shratzia, Uncle Rasches and Velvetzia –
that's three. Together with me – that's four.

ALTE: Together with you, eh?! Together with him! As though
he's also someone to be counted at funerals!

*(The angel of death SAMUELOV appears in the background. ALTE
lets out a heavy sigh and dies.)*

LAJCEK: Mum?

(Pause.)

Mum?

(Pause. Sees she's dead, covers her face with a blanket.)

We'll all be there, Mum. Auntie Shratzia, and Uncle
Rasches and Velvetzia. And me. And maybe, who knows,
maybe the groom's family will also come. And we'll stand
there, around your grave, a whole group of people, some
young, some old, one of them even very young and very
beautiful, and we'll think about you, and mention you
and talk about you in whispers out of a feeling of loss and
sadness.

(Crying.)

Because you really did exist in the world, Mum, we
all witnessed it, and your death, Mum, is the death of
someone who was definitely here, and now is definitely
not here.

Act Two: A knock at the door

Night. The entrance door to Aunt SHRATZIA's flat. The flat's entrance hall on one side and the staircase on the other. LAJCEK is standing in the staircase and knocks on the door. Knocks. Pause. More knocks. Pause. And more knocks. He occasionally puts his ear to the door, trying to hear voices inside. He can't hear anything and keeps knocking. Uncle RASCHES enters the hall in his pyjamas, walking in a daze towards the door. Aunt SHRATZIA in a night gown enters after him. Their conversation, like all the subsequent conversations inside the flat, takes place in whispers, with patient LAJCEK's knocking also mingling into them.

SHRATZIA: Where do you think you're going?!

RASCHES: To open the door. Someone's knocking.

SHRATZIA: Shhh! Did you find out who's knocking?!

RASCHES: How can I know who's knocking without opening the door?

SHRATZIA: So you just run off in the middle of the night to open the door for god knows who!

RASCHES: *(Thinks for a moment.)* I can ask from inside who it is.

(Prepares to go to the door. SHRATZIA grabs his arm and pulls him back.)

SHRATZIA: And why would you ask who it is?! Am I here inside?

RASCHES: You're inside.

SHRATZIA: Are you inside?

RASCHES: Huh? Yes, I'm inside.

SHRATZIA: Is Velvetzia inside?

RASCHES: Inside.

SHRATZIA: Is her fiancé Poppochenko inside?

RASCHES: Inside.

SHRATZIA: Is his mother Tsitskeiva inside?

RASCHES: Inside.

SHRATZIA: Is his father Baraguntseleh inside?

RASCHES: Inside.

SHRATZIA: Is everyone asleep?

RASCHES: They're asleep.

SHRATZIA: Is anyone else supposed to be inside?

RASCHES: No one.

SHRATZIA: So why would you ask who it is?! Why would you care who it is?! Why would you care about the entire rest of humanity?! Or maybe you're waiting for someone?

RASCHES: No.

SHRATZIA: Or maybe we want to see someone?

RASCHES: No.

SHRATZIA: In which case, what do we want?

RASCHES: To sleep.

SHRATZIA: And what else do we want?

RASCHES: To marry off our daughter Velvetzia tomorrow.

SHRATZIA: With what head?

RASCHES: With a clear head.

SHRATZIA: And why are we born?

RASCHES: To buy a flat.

SHRATZIA: And what's a flat for?

RASCHES: For a wall.

SHRATZIA: And what's a wall for?

RASCHES: For a door.

SHRATZIA: And what's a door for?

RASCHES: For a lock.

SHRATZIA: And what's a lock for?

RASCHES: For not opening.

SHRATZIA: So why are we born?

RASCHES: To not open.

SHRATZIA: Exactly! So I don't go looking for trouble and
I don't open doors! I want to marry off my daughter
Velvetzia tomorrow, that's all, four hundred guests and
eight hundred chickens are already waiting for tomorrow,
and I'm not going to risk the chuppah which has cost
me my entire life and all my savings, for whatever it
is which might be waiting to ambush me behind that
door! I don't want to see anyone and I don't want to
hear about anything which isn't to do with the wedding!
From now until the end of the wedding, the entire earth
can be destroyed for all I care – I'm lifting this chuppah
tomorrow! To sleep!

*(They both turn away from the door and start walking back, but
a louder knock than the previous ones stops them in their tracks.)*

He'll wake everyone up!

*(Pause. Silence again. They start walking again. Another knock,
and they stop. And with a sudden epiphany.)*

Lajcek Bobijcek!

RASCHES: Bobijcek?! At two in the morning?! But he's a
decent guy!

SHRATZIA: Him, him! Knocking and knocking and knocking
and knocking, knocking politely but not budging – it can
only be him!

*(RASCHES starts walking unquestioningly towards the door.
SHRATZIA grabs his arm.)*

Where are you going?!

RASCHES: To open it. It's Lajcek Bobijcek, your cousin.

SHRATZIA: Did you arrange a meeting with him?

RASCHES: No.

SHRATZIA: Is it really important for you to see him?

RASCHES: No.

SHRATZIA: But what *is* really important for you?

RASCHES: To sleep.

SHRATZIA: And what else is important?

RASCHES: Marrying off our daughter Velvetzia tomorrow.

SHRATZIA: And his mother, Alte Bobijcek, how old is she?

RASCHES: Almost eighty.

SHRATZIA: And her health?

RASCHES: So so.

SHRATZIA: And if her son, Lajcek, suddenly shows up at two
o'clock in the morning, what do you conclude from that?

RASCHES: What *do* I conclude from it?

SHRATZIA: Is it the same thing I conclude from it?

RASCHES: What do you conclude from it?

SHRATZIA: That if he suddenly shows up at two o'clock in the morning – oh no, if he suddenly shows up at two o'clock in the morning! – that means that…?

RASCHES: That…?

SHRATZIA: *(Nodding her head.)* That, that!

(Starts crying quietly.)

RASCHES: Why are you crying?

(Pause.)

If you explain it to me, maybe I'll cry too.

SHRATZIA: *(Carries on sobbing and nodding her head.)* Yes-yes! Why-why!

RASCHES: *(Confused.)* That, that, yes-yes, why-why, twee-twee, zoom-zoom, pish-pish, you're talking in Chinese twins!

SHRATZIA: Dead! Old Alte Bobijcek is dead! She's missed Velvetzia'le's wedding!

RASCHES: *(Shocked.)* Missed it?! Velvetzia's wedding?! Velvetzia's?! Missed it?!

SHRATZIA: Obviously! If she's dead, she's missed it! How would she come to the wedding?! She'll be buried six feet underground!

RASCHES: Yes, and even if she comes, how would she eat?

(Suddenly lets out a short laugh.)

I wouldn't have died two days before Velvetzia's wedding! Madness! Dying two days before Velvetzia's wedding!

Gah! Dying's one thing! But two days before Velvetzia's wedding?!

(More knocks at the door. RASCHES, unquestioningly, turns to go to the door.)

SHRATZIA: Where are you going?

RASCHES: To open the door for him. It's Lajcek Bobijcek, his mother's dead and he's come to tell us.

SHRATZIA: Yes?

RASCHES: Yes. No?

SHRATZIA: And if we open the door for him, then what happens?

RASCHES: He comes in.

SHRATZIA: And then?

RASCHES: He tells us.

SHRATZIA: And then?

RASCHES: We cry with him a bit, maybe.

SHRATZIA: And when a person dies – what do you give them?

(Pause.)

What celebration do you have for someone who's died?

RASCHES: A funeral.

SHRATZIA: That takes place when?

RASCHES: Tomorrow.

SHRATZIA: And what have we got tomorrow?

RASCHES: Velvetzia'le's wedding

SHRATZIA: A funeral and a wedding – what comes first?

RASCHES: What do you mean?

SHRATZIA: We'd need to postpone it, postpone it! You open the door for him now – and Velvetzia'le's wedding gets postponed!

RASCHES: Postponing Velvetzia's wedding? How could something like that even happen?! Velvetzia's wedding has a date!

SHRATZIA: We open the door – we're at old Alte Bobijcek's funeral!

We're at Alte Bobijcek's funeral – there's no Velvetzia'le's wedding! Nothing! Four hundred guests, eight hundred chickens – into the bin!

(Sobs.)

RASCHES: *(Stunned.)* I've never heard of anything like this before. Postponing Velvetzia'le's wedding! I mean, Velvetzia's wedding most definitely has a date! There's a date! A date! I've heard lots of strange things in my life, but being able to postpone Velvetzia's wedding, that's something I've never heard of.

(Shudders with horror.)

Postponing Velvetzia's wedding! Really! Velvetzia! Postponing! Velvetzia's wedding!

(As he continues talking the idea amazes him more and more.)

Really! Postponing! And postponing what? – Velvetzia's wedding! Velvetzia's! Velvetzia's! I mean really! Velvetzia's wedding! Velvetzia!

SHRATZIA: Shhh!

RASCHES: Velvetzia's! Velvetzia's!

(Falls silent.)

SHRATZIA: *(Crying.)* I was fond of the old lady, I really was!
I would have been the first one to show up to the funeral!
Finally, an aunt! But she died at a bad time for me! She
knew that I've been waiting my whole life for Velvetzia's
wedding, that Velvetzia's wedding is a part of me, of my
flesh. Take Velvetzia'le's wedding away from me and
what's left?

*(A long series of knocks at the door. SHRATZIA cowers as though
trying to escape. She whispers to herself while crying.)*

Have mercy, Bobijcek, have mercy! Understand me! I
understand you, and everything, but understand my side
as well! I can't open the door for you, I just can't! Have
mercy, Bobijcek! A bit of humanity, Bobijcek! Don't you
have a heart, Bobijcek?! Your own mother wouldn't nag
people so much about her own funeral, you murderer!!

(RASCHES starts walking towards the door.)

Where are you going?

RASCHES: To break his hands.

(SHRATZIA grabs his arm to stop him.)

SHRATZIA: Stand still!

(Locks her arm with his and leans on him sobbing.)

Just as god finally wants to give someone a wedding, a
funeral ends up slipping out of his sleeve.

(The knocking doesn't stop.)

We need to go and tell everyone not to get up or turn the
light on.

(TSITSKEIVA and BARAGUNTSELEH enter in their pyjamas.)

TSITSKEIVA: What's going on, in-laws?

SHRATZIA: Shhh!

TSITSKEIVA: Shhh! On the eve of my son Poppochenko's wedding? shhh?! We don't get people knocking like that on our doors in the middle of the night, scum!

SHRATZIA: Must be a drunk.

RASCHES: A crazy drunk.

SHRATZIA: Go to bed, in-laws, he'll leave in a minute.

(TSITSKEIVA and BARAGUNTSELEH keep standing there.)

TSITSKEIVA: You won't find crazy drunks at our place.

LAJCEK: *(Certain he's heard a noise inside.)* Auntie Shratzia?

TSITSKEIVA: *(Looks at SHRATZIA suspiciously.)* Auntie?

SHRATZIA: *(Tries to laugh.)* He's calling me 'Auntie', the drunk.

TSITSKEIVA: Do you know him?

RASCHES: No!

LAJCEK: Uncle Rasches?

RASCHES: *(Embarrassed.)* Barely.

SHRATZIA: Some distant acquaintance.

RASCHES: Very, very distant. Siberia.

SHRATZIA: Suddenly showed up. Weird creature.

RASCHES: A cat.

LAJCEK: Auntie Shratzia, Uncle Rasches, open up, I have bad news to tell you!

SHRATZIA: We know him, he's an exaggerator.

RASCHES: An exaggerator and a wholesaler.

TSITSKEIVA: You won't find a...

LAJCEK: Mum's dead!

(SHRATZIA can't keep up the pretence, starts sobbing quietly and breaks.)

SHRATZIA: What can I tell you, mother-in-law, you be the judge: My aunt died, and her son's come over in the middle of the night to share the news! How can I bring myself to open the door and receive the message?! If there's a funeral tomorrow then we need to postpone the wedding, Velvetzia'le's wedding...

TSITSKEIVA: And Poppochenko's.

SHRATZIA: ...because otherwise what sort of human face do we have?! This way, I was thinking, I don't open the door, I don't know anything, we marry Velvetzia'le off...

TSITSKEIVA: And Poppochenko.

SHRATZIA: ...and then tomorrow at midnight, after the reception, I'm open to receiving the message, after all death's not running away anywhere! Now you tell me, mother-in-law, what would you do if you were in my shoes, same thing right?! Wouldn't you approve my policy?

(Falls into TSITSKEIVA's arms and continues crying.)

TSITSKEIVA: God knows what it is with you lot, strange uninteresting people. Your family worries me a great deal.

SHRATZIA: And the policy? I was asking about the policy!

TSITSKEIVA: The policy. What do I know? It's a policy!

BARAGUNTSELEH: I also dreamed a political dream just now. I dreamed I was sitting on the toilet one morning, and just then the president of the United States shows up and knocks on the door. I don't know that it's the president of the United States, so I shout 'What's the matter, Tsitskeiva, did you forget your keys?!' And just like that, with my trousers down I run to the door to open it and give her a piece of my mind, and suddenly – it's the president of the United States with his whole entourage, and I don't have any trousers on, and I even called him Tsitskeiva! And then I wake up, and my heart relaxes straight away, it was just a dream, but someone actually is knocking on the door, and suddenly there's this death, and a funeral, which means that even outside the dream, real life's also bad.

TSITSKEIVA: That's how it is with us, the president of the United States, no less, and no announcements about death at two in the morning.

(Another long string of knocks. SHRATZIA recoils into TSITSKEIVA's arms.)

SHRATZIA: He'll wake the children! We need to go over and warn them!

(POPPOCHENKO enters in pyjamas.)

POPPOCHENKO: I woke up.

SHRATZIA: Shhh!

TSITSKEIVA: Go back to sleep Poppochenko! You need all your strength tomorrow to get through a wedding.

SHRATZIA: Go, go dream, bride-groom.

POPPOCHENKO: I don't dream.

TSITSKEIVA: He doesn't dream. He's like me, a realist.

RASCHES: He's also not asking what those knocks are. *(To POPPOCHENKO.)* Aren't you curious what those knocks are?

(POPPOCHENKO looks at him in bewilderment.)

TSITSKEIVA: Why would that interest him? He's an educated man, he's not curious. He's not interested in anything. Go to sleep Poppochenko.

(VELVETZIA enters in a night gown.)

VELVETZIA: Is Daddy dead?!

SHRATZIA: Shhh!

RASCHES: What do you mean dead? He's alive, and why is it immediately Daddy? Is Daddy the only one here? Is Daddy sicker than everyone else? Has Daddy been complaining chest pains? And if someone's going to die then why not, for example…Auntie Alte?

SHRATZIA: *(Falls into VELVETZIA's arms and sobs.)* Auntie Alte Bobijcek has died and her son Lajcek Bobijcek has come to deliver the news! How can I possibly open the door?! How can I possibly hear the news, because if there's news – there's a funeral, and if there's a funeral – there's mourning – we're closely related after all – and if there's mourning, then where's the wedding, where are the four hundred guests, the eight hundred chickens? In the bin! So how can I possibly open the door! As a matter of fact, let's hear what the young generation has to say. Velvetzia, you tell me, who have I prepared all this for if not for you, you tell me, is Mum's policy right?!

(POPPOCHENKO who's been feeling for VELVETZIA's hand in the dark has found it and is stroking it softly.)

POPPOCHENKO: Velvetzia.

VELVETZIA: Poppochenko.

SHRATZIA: Lost in their pure love. Why would they be concerned with matters of policy now.

TSITSKEIVA: *(Laughing bitterly.)* Pure love! It's lust they've got! Lust and passion!

(The knocking stops. Pause.)

Has he gone?

RASCHES: Who?

SHRATZIA: Even if he's gone, he'll be back. We know those people. You want to sleep – he's at the door. You get into the bath – he's at the door. You sit down to eat – he's at the door. Spends half his life in front of doors. Even she, the old woman may, she be resting in heaven, wouldn't miss a knock on the door, god forbid.

(Pause. SHRATZIA walks on her tiptoes towards the door in order to look through the keyhole. She walks silently, slowly, tensed up, holding her breath, and everyone follows her the same way, a dense tense clump. SHRATZIA bends over to look through the keyhole at exactly the moment when LAJCEK on the other side of the door bends over to look through the keyhole as well. They both peer into each other's eye, but because of the dark don't see anything. They both straighten up at the same time. Pause.)

LAJCEK: Auntie Shratzia, Uncle Rasches…

(A shudder runs through the group.)

…my mother died two hours ago and I really want to tell someone how it happened, and I don't have anyone else, just you.

(Pause.)

I wouldn't disturb you in the middle of the night, especially the night before Velvetzia's wedding, had something really important not happened to me. I believe, as did my mother in her final moments, that something important has happened to her. What do you think?

(Long pause. LAJCEK exits. SHRATZIA cries harder, but in total silence, while the rest of the group start backing away slowly.)

SHRATZIA: Yes, this is all very human, but we have to get over it, we have a long hard day ahead of us, a historic biographic once-in-a-lifetime day, a day we need to invest all of our energy, senses and intelligence in, a day which will warm our bones in our old age, it's the day our daughter Velvetzia's getting married!

TSITSKEIVA: To our son Poppochenko!

(SHRATZIA bends over again to look through the keyhole and everyone bends down along with her. At that moment LAJCEK, who's climbed up a ladder outside the building, sticks his head through a small window behind them. He looks for a moment at the group bent over with their backsides pointed at him, and then.)

LAJCEK: There you all are, all ready with your heads bowed for my mother's funeral which will be taking place tomorrow at four o'clock in the afternoon.

(All the people in the group turn their heads in complete surprise, see LAJCEK's head in the window, and swiftly turn their heads back to the door, they're not giving up that easily, they carry on standing frozen in their hunched positions, trying to hide their faces between their shoulders and shutting their eyes. After a long pause.)

But I can see you.

SHRATZIA: *(Whispers through her teeth, as though under a spell.)* But we totally can't hear you. We're asleep. We're sleepwalking in our dreams. And now, asleep and dreaming we're going back to bed.

(They all hold hands with each other, and in a strange kind of part-procession, part-dance, they start walking along softly.)

LAJCEK: And when, if I may ask, will you wake up?

SHRATZIA: It'll take a long long time.

RASCHES: If at all.

(They exit right in front of LAJCEK's astonished eyes. Pause. A light comes on in a neighbouring flat. Professor KIPPERNAI appears on his flat's balcony.)

KIPPERNAI: Hello. I am Professor Kippernai. I live here, in the flat next to your aunt Shratzia. I heard everything you said. I heard your mother had died. My condolences.

LAJCEK: Thank you. They're at home, but they're asleep and dreaming. They have a wedding tomorrow.

KIPPERNAI: I know. They're sleeping deeply ahead of their big celebration.

LAJCEK: But at the same time I have an internal obligation to inform them of my bad news. Do you understand? My mother's died. My mother. She was my mother, the woman without whom I wouldn't have been born. Do you understand? Maybe it doesn't matter to the rest of the world whether I was born or whether I wasn't born, but for me, being born or not being born makes a big difference, enormous, you understand? And her funeral's tomorrow at four o'clock, and they need to be there, nothing will change that: My mother was here in the world, very definitely, she was, I saw her.

KIPPERNAI: I understand and I offer my condolences.

LAJCEK: The group for the funeral is quite small as it is, but still…

KIPPERNAI: Yes, no one wants to die on the moon.

LAJCEK: That's why I can't give up, you understand? I'll go over to the obituary printer now to get the obituary notices printed and then come straight back here. I'll wait here until the morning if that's what it takes.

KIPPERNAI: Why don't you leave them a note?

LAJCEK: You don't always see a note.

KIPPERNAI: That's true. I remember one young lady who I left note after note for. Very large ones. Posters basically.

(Lets out a short laugh.)

She didn't see them. Forgive me for laughing in your time of mourning.

LAJCEK: No, you're a professor, you need to unwind sometimes.

(Turns to leave.)

KIPPERNAI: Mr...

LAJCEK: Lajcek Bobijcek.

KIPPERNAI: Mr Bobijcek, I would gladly take it upon myself to inform them of the bad news first thing in the morning, but they...they just don't speak to me.

LAJCEK: Don't speak? Why?

KIPPERNAI: I don't know. It's been a few years already. I'd sometimes go to their place to sit, to chat. One day I sat down...

(Lets out a short laugh.)

...and they just stopped talking and went to sleep.

LAJCEK: When you sat down?

KIPPERNAI: Right when I was sitting down.

LAJCEK: But why?

KIPPERNAI: And why do people die?

LAJCEK: You're right. I'm going to the obituary printer and coming straight back here afterwards.

KIPPERNAI: I'll be up, Mr Bobijcek, you can come in and wait at my place.

LAJCEK: And take up a professor's research time?

KIPPERNAI: I'm asking you to come in. Even a professor's heart sometimes goes out to others.

LAJCEK: Thank you, I'll come gladly.

(Exits. KIPPERNAI continues standing on the balcony and looking at SHRATZIA's flat. SHRATZIA, RASCHES, TSITSKEIVA, BARAGUNTSELEH, POPPOCHENKO and VELVETZIA sneak out of the building into the street, wearing heavy coats, clutching umbrellas and shawls.)

TSITSKEIVA: But can someone finally tell me where we're running to?

SHRATZIA: Shhh…we'll find something, we'll find somewhere.

TSITSKEIVA: Everything's shut now.

SHRATZIA: It'll be okay, the main thing is to hurry up.

RASCHES: And I've got a place.

(Everyone turns to him and waits for his next utterance.)

End of December, a storm's raging, three in the morning, the eve of our daughter Velvetzia's wedding…

TSITSKEIVA: To our son Poppochenko.

RASCHES: And where's the last place Bobijcek would think of looking for us?

(Excitedly, while pointing at his forehead.)

The beach.

TSITSKEIVA: The beach?! Did I hear you say 'the beach'?!

RASCHES: I've got a brain, eh?! And in my brain – there's a devil! And the devil – he's got a brain too!

SHRATZIA: Yes, we'll light a bonfire, why not, a picnic, a picnic on the beach. Come, come.

(Pulls RASCHES and exits with him.)

TSITSKEIVA: Three in the morning, rain, storms, everything's shut, everyone's asleep, everyone's under their blankets dreaming it's summer, and only us, us, all night, *psiakrew cholera[1]*, like wet dogs, we're going to run around in the streets, goddammit, what a shitty life, and what's this on your side of the family, people dying the day before a wedding, and in the winter, and in the middle of the night, your family really worries me, goddammit, what a strange and uninteresting life, I wish a hydrogen bomb would annihilate this universe already, I wish it with all my heart, *jasna cholera[2]*, who said there was no god, there is a god, but he's Turkish.

BARAGUNTSELEH: A German walks into a Chinese restaurant, the waiter asks him…

(TSITSKEIVA grabs him forcefully, they both exit. VELVETZIA turns to leave as well, POPPOCHENKO stops her.)

POPPOCHENKO: Velvetzia.

---

1   [Polish] Goddammit
2   [Polish] Goddammit

VELVETZIA: *(Turns to him.)* Poppochenko.

(They both exit. From above, from the balcony of his flat, Professor KIPPERNAI watches the line of people leaving the house. It's apparent that he wants to say something to them, but the words don't come out. The whole line disappears down the street. Pause. LAJCEK comes back in a rush and is about to enter the staircase. KIPPERNAI calls to him from above.)

KIPPERNAI: Mr Bobijcek, they've gone.

LAJCEK: *(Agitated.)* Gone?! In the middle of the night?! Maybe they were sleepwalking?

KIPPERNAI: With their eyes wide open. With coats and umbrellas. And to tell you the truth, it looked like they were running away from something.

LAJCEK: What have they got to run away from?! The last time I saw them they were dancing in their dreams.

(Starts running around in the street.)

Which direction? Where can I look for them?

KIPPERNAI: I don't know.

LAJCEK: *(Turns to leave in a rush, comes back.)* Thank you for the information, Professor Kippernai. You've sacrificed a lot of your research time for me.

KIPPERNAI: What's more, in light of what's happened, and although I didn't know your dearly departed mother, I've decided to attend her funeral.

LAJCEK: *(To himself.)* That's already five, six with the gravedigger, half a dozen. Oh, Mum! There will also be a professor!

(To KIPPERNAI.)

228

Who would have imagined such a scholarly and contemplative man at my mother's funeral! Professor Kippernai, your generosity of spirit and your human emotions know no bounds. But if the world experiences a sudden scientific regression, won't I then be blamed for it?

KIPPERNAI: All the responsibility's mine.

LAJCEK: You are a noble figure. You have come to us like something out of the pages of a classical novel.

KIPPERNAI: Thank you. You can come up to my place now and sit for a little while if you like.

LAJCEK: No, that's a bit too much.

KIPPERNAI: On the contrary.

LAJCEK: And I still need to find Auntie Shratzia and tell her the bad news.

KIPPERNAI: Where will you look for them now in the dark, in the rain, in the early hours of the morning?!

LAJCEK: Maybe I'll go to the beach to think about it. On the beach your thoughts are fresh and it's easy to concentrate. Goodbye.

(Starts walking away.)

KIPPERNAI: *(Calls after him.)* What time is the funeral, Mr Bobijcek?

LAJCEK: At four o'clock.

(Exits.)

KIPPERNAI: *(Continues calling after him.)* Where do we meet? Which cemetery? Or are we leaving from the hospital? Which hospital? Four o'clock at the exit of the hospital or the entrance of the cemetery? Will there be organised transportation? Will there be room for me as well? I don't have a car! Should I take the bus straight to the cemetery? Which bus? Where does it leave from? From the central station? How often does one leave? And where exactly should I wait for you? Next to the gate or next to the grave? Where's the grave? Is it next to the gate? Is there only one gate? Or next to the fence? Next to which side of the fence? Will the funeral still take place if there's pouring rain? If not, how will I know? Will I be waiting out there in the rain? Is there even a pavilion there? How long should I wait for? Or maybe you'll phone the place to let me know about the cancellation? Is there a phone there? Will the cemetery office be open at four o'clock? Or maybe you'll call a public phone? Or maybe instead of calling me I'll call you? But where should I call? The mortuary at the hospital? Which hospital? Is there a phone in the mortuary there? Will you be there next to the phone? Will they let you wait next to the phone? Won't you be in the way? Will you even be able to answer phone calls? Or will you be busy grieving? Maybe there'll be someone next to you to answer the phone? But who? Do you have contacts at the hospital? Who'll answer the phone on your behalf if your aunt Shratzia and the whole family aren't there? Or maybe I'll come with you? Maybe I'll answer the phone? But if I'm there next to you in the hospital, how will I also be in the cemetery? And if I'm not in the cemetery and I don't call from the cemetery, why would I need to wait for my own call at the hospital? So which side of the phone would you rather I was on? On the cemetery side? Or on the hospital side? Or maybe the phone's actually broken?

(Pause. His head disappears from the balcony, he goes back to his room.)

Act Three: The picnic on the beach

Dawn of a gloomy day at the beach. Wind, rain, storm. The clash of waves breaking on the shore. The entire fugitive wedding band enters. The six of them, bundled up in their coats and holding open umbrellas fight the intense wind and the rain. They crowd together, stamp their feet to keep warm, shiver, groan and cough.

SHRATZIA: This is it, dear friends, our dawn picnic on the beach. Here we're really safe from Bobijcek.

TSITSKEIVA: Really some picnic, eh? A picnic to remember.

SHRATZIA: In ten years' time, believe me, it'll all just become an experience. 'Remember how we stood there, at dawn, on the beach, in the rain…?' Yes, yes, it's all just an experience.

RASCHES: Why don't we light a bonfire and dance on the sand?

TSITSKEIVA: *(Dryly.)* Why don't you go ahead and dance a bit, father-in-law.

(Pause. No one moves.)

RASCHES: Or at least sing a bit?

TSITSKEIVA: Why don't you go ahead and sing a bit, father-in-law. You haven't sung in a long time.

(Pause. No one opens their mouth, and suddenly BARAGUNTSELEH bursts out in a sad song.)

BARAGUNTSELEH: Then came the Tatars,
And slaughtered my mum:
The Tatar rode by on the hunt
Stuck a spear up into her…with a grunt.

(He waits for people to laugh. No one laughs.)

Then came…

SHRATZIA: Look, look what's rising, the sun, the sun's rising on our daughter Velvetzia's wedding day.

TSITSKEIVA: And our son Poppochenko's.

SHRATZIA: Today the sunlight is only ours, just like the hall, and like the band, and like the flowers and the guests and the chickens, today the sunlight is ours, it's coming from us, anyone who enjoys the sunlight today is getting a gift from us.

RASCHES: The light, and also the shade.

BARAGUNTSELEH: Anyway, a German walks into a Chinese restaurant, the waiter asks him…

(ROSENZWEIG and LIECHTENSTEIN, two elderly exercisers in swimming trunks and swimming caps, enter in a light jog. They see the group and stop, jogging on the spot. To the group.)

ROSENZWEIG: Rosenzweig. The healthy one.

LIECHTENSTEIN: Liechtenstein. Also healthy.

ROSENZWEIG: Exercising or committing suicide?

SHRATZIA: Celebrating.

ROSENZWEIG: Congratulations! What are you celebrating?

SHRATZIA: A dawn picnic in honour of our daughter Velvetzia's wedding.

TSITSKEIVA: And our son Poppochenko's.

ROSENZWEIG: To your health. Me on the other hand – I jog and exercise every morning, I look ten years younger than I am. How old do I look?

TSITSKEIVA: Seventy.

ROSENZWEIG: Madam, I'm surprised at you. I'm sixty years old and look fifty.

LIECHTENSTEIN: I'm turning sixty-three in February, and in February I'll look fifty-three.

ROSENZWEIG: I'm going to die ten years later than the date I was originally allocated. Let's say I die in five years' time, that means I'm now supposed to have been lying in the ground for the last five years, but here I am alive and well, breathing and jogging on the beach. Net profit. And all this how? From a seemingly little thing, from jogging. I highly recommend it. It's true that getting married is also good, but don't skip going for a jog every morning, in any weather, under any circumstance – that's even better.

RASCHES: Under any circumstance?! Really?! And if the sun doesn't rise tomorrow?!

ROSENZWEIG: Silly people, do I go by the sun? I go by my watch!

LIECHTENSTEIN: And why don't they all join us right now, and enjoy their longevity based on December's terms and conditions?

ROSENZWEIG: Liechtenstein's right, today's jog alone will add a week to your lives, because then all of December gets counted for you.

RASCHES: An extra week of life wouldn't hurt at all.

(He starts jogging alongside them, but when he realises that no one apart from him is joining in he stops and goes back to his place.).

Never mind, one less week of suffering.

ROSENZWEIG: So what, you'd rather die ten years sooner? You're reducing your chances of reaching the end of the century, and it's a shame, because the end of this century is also the end of the second millennium and they're going to be bringing out a special series of stamps to mark the start of the third millennium and we've already signed up for them. Goodbye and good luck.

LIECHTENSTEIN: But mainly – it's a shame.

(The two of them leave the group and carry on jogging down the beach. Everyone looks at them, shivering in the cold.)

RASCHES: Maybe we should have gone jogging with them after all?

SHRATZIA: What are we, at war?!

RASCHES: No.

SHRATZIA: What are we at?

RASCHES: A picnic.

(His teeth chattering.)

At a picnic. Still it's cold. I'll end up sneezing in the middle of the chuppah.

TSITSKEIVA: You'll sneeze?...

RASCHES: I'm not as immune as I look.

TSITSKEIVA: ...it's meningitis you'll get.

RASCHES: Why me?! Am I the only one who's cold here?! Straight away me!

SHRATZIA: Think about what's waiting for us this evening.

TSITSKEIVA: *(Groans.)* Evening, oh evening, who'll be lucky enough to see this evening, who?

SHRATZIA: *(Tries to cheer them up.)* And when we're sitting around the tables, my dear friends, and eating fish and drinking cognac, what will the Bobijcek be eating and drinking?

RASCHES: A salty bagel and a salty tear!

SHRATZIA: *(Tries to laugh.)* Ay, Bobijcek, Bobijcek, think about how he's busy looking for us all over town, running around to police stations, to hospitals, to hotels!

(Tries to laugh.)

Come on, dear friends, come on, imagine him running around, the Bobijcek, with his piece of news making his heart heavy, running, running, but with no one to deliver it to…and there are freshly-printed obituary notices already hanging at the entrance of his house, and the rain's probably washing them off, and he's picking them up out of the mud and sticking them back on, and they fall off again, and he's fighting the rain, trying to figure out where we are, where we are, and Alte Bobijcek's notices are already turning into soggy porridge, and Alte herself is frozen like a…

(She suddenly stops herself, has a change of heart, bursts out crying.)

Oh, Alte, Alte, may you be resting in heaven, forgive me, I don't know what I'm talking about any more… we want to warm up and there's nothing to warm up with…

(Falls silent. Pause.)

TSITSKEIVA: How strange life is, and at the same time how pointless and stupid. Even its strangeness isn't interesting. Here, we set out on a cold December evening from a warm bed, and came here to stand and freeze on the beach – how strange, and how uninteresting. And that's also how we're born, for example, we come into the world, and we see that there's black, and there's red, and there's black pepper, and there's vinegar, and there's

a moon and a sun and men and women: how strange
everything is, you think you're going to stop breathing,
like in the first second when you see an ambulance,
and then despite everything, the ambulance just passes,
and you don't stop breathing, and how stupid, and
uninteresting, and pointless.

BARAGUNTSELEH: Including your marriage to me?

TSITSKEIVA: Including everything.

SHRATZIA: But what kind of talk is this on the wedding day,
mother-in-law?! Are you from India by any chance?

TSITSKEIVA: I'm not from India, I'm from life.

SHRATZIA: In that case, we're from the same place. So why
would you say that it's stupid?! Just because it's easy to say?!

*(In the meantime ROSENZWEIG and LIECHTENSTEIN continue
their jog and some distance away bump into LAJCEK walking along
the beach bundled up in a raincoat with his head wrapped in a
wool scarf. ROSENZWEIG and LIECHTENSTEIN jog on the spot
alongside him.)*

ROSENZWEIG: Big crowd today.

LIECHTENSTEIN: Maybe they've heard of us?

ROSENZWEIG: *(To LAJCEK.)* Rosenzweig. The healthy one.

LIECHTENSTEIN: Liechtenstein. Also healthy.

LAJCEK: Lajcek Bobijcek.

ROSENZWEIG: Exercising or committing suicide?

LAJCEK: Grieving. My mother died and now I'm looking
for my aunt who disappeared in the night with the entire
family, so that I can tell her the bad news and the time of
the funeral. I have no idea where they might be. I came

here to watch the waves, and to concentrate and get some good ideas.

ROSENZWEIG: Did your mother, may she rest in peace, use to jog?

LAJCEK: Never.

ROSENZWEIG: That's a shame. She should have jogged. Your heart looks completely different after a jog, that's well known. Shame.

LIECHTENSTEIN: You could still have had a mother now.

ROSENZWEIG: Why don't you jog?

LIECHTENSTEIN: Do you want to make the same mistake as your mother?

ROSENZWEIG: Are you urgently trying to join her?

LAJCEK: What will jogging do for me?

ROSENZWEIG: Ten years.

LAJCEK: What'll I do with them?

ROSENZWEIG: You'll jog.

LAJCEK: Jog, you say. And if I run for a thousand years, will the jogging get me any closer to Auntie Shratzia, and will it improve my chances of giving her the terrible news about my mother's death and the time of the funeral, and will the jogging make my mother's funeral into a meaningful event for more than one person on this earth?

ROSENZWEIG: The answers are all 'yes'. The jogging will speed up your circulation and your respiration, it will supply new blood with fresh oxygen to your brain, improve your memory and cognitive ability, prevent sclerosis and give you countless new ideas regarding the whereabouts of your Auntie Shoshana...

LAJCEK: Auntie Shratzia.

ROSENZWEIG: Exactly. And lots of other people, who'll all come to your mother's birthday.

LAJCEK: To her funeral.

ROSENZWEIG: Exactly.

LAJCEK: *(On the verge of tears.)* Because she nevertheless took up some kind of space in the world...

LIECHTENSTEIN: The world is a world.

ROSENZWEIG: Onwards to a healthier world!

LIECHTENSTEIN: And ten years longer!

(LAJCEK joins them and jogs behind the other two. The three of them run in single file. At a certain point they turn and start jogging back towards the picnic group.)

TSITSKEIVA: There they are again, the two healthy ones.

SHRATZIA: I can see a third healthy one with them.

(And suddenly SHRATZIA lets out a shriek.)

And who's that third one?

RASCHES: Lajcek Bobijcek!

(They all freeze and watch in dread as the disaster approaches.)

TSITSKEIVA: Picnic, eh? Some picnic!

LAJCEK: *(From a distance, shouts.)* Auntie Shratzia! Uncle Rasches! Mum's dead!

SHRATZIA: *(Looks to the sky.)* Oh, Alte, Alte, may you be resting in heaven, you'll pay dearly for this, Alte!

(To the group.)

Dear friends, we have no choice, we're going to run!

TSITSKEIVA: Bah! Running too! Not just a picnic – a picnic with some running!

(In a threatening tone.)

The beach, eh?! I'd like to know who it was who decided 'to the beach'?!

POPPOCHENKO: The father-in-law, the father-in-law decided.

RASCHES: I didn't decide.

POPPOCHENKO: You decided, you decided.

RASCHES: 'You decided, you decided'! I didn't decide – I suggested.

TSITSKEIVA: A brain, eh?!

RASCHES: And what are you, physicists?!

SHRATZIA: He's getting closer, let's get a move on and run!

TSITSKEIVA: Me with my backside! Me at my age, on the day of my son's wedding, with this backside – goddammit – *psiakrew cholera!* – every time I sit on the toilet my bum cheeks reach down to the water.

SHRATZIA: Now's not the time for scorekeeping, mother-in-law, and I can't see what choice we have, no one here has a small bum, even Velvetzia's packing there, packing plenty, a serious piece of popo…

POPPOCHENKO: *(Elated.)* …chenko. That's right, I'm there!

SHRATZIA: …so every one of us, as they say, is carrying their whole world in their trousers, no one here has feathers, and when we need to get our backsides into gear there are no excuses, because if we don't get them into gear we'll be staring at a black car today instead of a white dress. Follow me!

(She starts running. The others still hesitate. She runs on the spot with her backside towards RASCHES.)

Come, Rasches'le come! Remember how many years I made you run after this backside?

(RASCHES starts running and the others follow them.)

POPPOCHENKO: *(In the direction of VELVETZIA's backside.)* A genius created this! A genius! And they say: it's descended from the ape! The head maybe, the head is descended from the ape, but this – only from God.

(They sing while running.)

MEN:

Bum, bum, bum,

Little globe of mine;

America, The Alps, the Southern Front,

Everything the heart could possibly want,

All in this little bed of mine.

WOMEN:

I have no America, I have no Alps.

And there's nothing here to want:

I have a dress, and in the dress a bum.

That's all I have on the southern front.

LAJCEK: *(From a distance.)* Auntie Shratzia! Mum's dead!

SHRATZIA: Run, dear friends, run! Now's not the time to lose yourself in thought, run, run!

BARAGUNTSELEH: *(Out of breath.)* A German walks into…a German walks into…I can't breathe…

(He stumbles and falls to the ground, TSITSKEIVA stops.)

SHRATZIA: Don't stop! Don't pick him up! Or we're all lost!

(TSITSKEIVA deliberates for a second, then carries on running with everyone. They exit.)

BARAGUNTSELEH: Tsitskeiva! Poppochenko! In-laws! Without me?! Without Baraguntseleh?! A wedding without Baraguntseleh?! Life without Baraguntseleh?!

(In wonderment, as though hearing his name for the first time.)

Baraguntseleh?! Does that sort of thing even exist?!

(The pursuers, the two exercisers ROSENZWEIG and LIECHTENSTEIN and with them LAJCEK, reach him.)

ROSENZWEIG: *(To BARAGUNTSELEH.)* Why on your stomach? Not like that – like this!

(Demonstrates proper jogging form to him.)

LIECHTENSTEIN: *(Dismissively.)* He thought jogging was the same as eating lettuce.

(To BARAGUNTSELEH.)

Jogging isn't eating lettuce, sir. You need to know how to jog.

LAJCEK: Is sir from the wedding family?

BARAGUNTSELEH: I am Baraguntseleh, the groom's father. And you are the terrible Bobijcek.

LAJCEK: Yes.

BARAGUNTSELEH: Have you heard this one? A German walks into a Chinese restaurant...

LAJCEK: *(Points at him ceremoniously.)* Mr Baraguntseleh, in the presence of these two witnesses I hereby inform you that my mother has died and that the funeral is today at four o'clock in the afternoon, and I officially give you power of attorney to pass this information on to anyone you see, in any place you encounter them and at any hour of the day or the night. Goodbye and see you at the funeral.

ROSENZWEIG: See you out jogging.

LIECHTENSTEIN: Not simple, not simple.

(The three of them carry on jogging and exit. BARAGUNTSELEH lies on the sand moaning and writhing from the sharp pain in his chest. He tries to get up but the pain doesn't subside.)

BARAGUNTSELEH: I think I'm having a heart attack. I think I'm going to die. How strange, as Tsitskeiva says, and how uninteresting. But she'll be at the wedding, and I won't. And then she'll say about this: 'How strange, and how uninteresting'. And she'll carry on living.

(The angel SAMUELOV enters.)

Have you heard this one? A German walks into a Chinese restaurant. The waiter asks him: 'What will you have today?' The German answers: 'What I'll be shitting out tomorrow'. The waiter says: 'You can only get that the day after tomorrow'. The German answers: 'I'm not here the day after tomorrow, I'm in Holland'.

(Laughs. Pause.)

You're the only one who's listened until the end. Who are you?

SAMUELOV: Angel Samuelov. The angel of death. I've come to take your soul.

BARAGUNTSELEH: Today's my son's wedding.

SAMUELOV: We take people from weddings, cinemas, lavatories, bathtubs, love-making, even in the middle of the news on TV.

(Pause.)

BARAGUNTSELEH: I also haven't lived at all yet. I'm still a child.

SAMUELOV: We also take babies.

(Pause.)

BARAGUNTSELEH: Will it hurt?

SAMUELOV: Have you ever passed gas?

BARAGUNTSELEH: Why?

SAMUELOV: You just pass gas. Same as you've always done.

BARAGUNTSELEH: From behind?

SAMUELOV: From behind, of course. Only this time, not just one round or two, you just start releasing and don't stop. And that way, very slowly but without stopping, in a silent evacuation, thin and continuous, you let out your soul until you're completely empty. And there's nothing left inside but a hollow space. That's death.

BARAGUNTSELEH: That should feel nice. A great relief.

SAMUELOV: Yes. And now start letting out gas. And don't stop.

(BARAGUNTSELEH breaks wind.)

BARAGUNTSELEH: *(While fading out of consciousness.)* And that's all the soul is?

SAMUELOV: That's all the soul is.

BARAGUNTSELEH: And the whole life spirit?

SAMUELOV: The whole life spirit.

BARAGUNTSELEH: I never knew the foundations our lives are built on were so simple.

SAMUELOV: Yes, there's no mysticism in it. You let it out, you empty yourself, that's it.

BARAGUNTSELEH: I mean if I was a child and I'd done this in class during a lesson they'd have thrown me out.

SAMUELOV: No one at school's interested in your soul. They're interested in it in the afterlife.

BARAGUNTSELEH: In that case you must have, over there in the afterlife, quite a collection of farts…!

SAMUELOV: Yes.

BARAGUNTSELEH: What do you do with them?

SAMUELOV: That hasn't been decided yet.

(Pause. BARAGUNTSELEH's soul very slowly leaves him. SAMUELOV watches it.)

Yes, like that, Mr Baraguntseleh, well done. Like that. Floosssss…Floosssss…you're letting it out very nicely. You had a big soul.

BARAGUNTSELEH: *(With the last of his strength.)* If you'd taken me after the wedding reception, I'd have had an even bigger soul.

(He dies.)

SAMUELOV: *(Guides the soul as it flies.)* Come, come, soul, don't be shy, you smelly little butterfly, upwards, like that, lovely…

(He exits. BARAGUNTSELEH's corpse remains on the beach. The two exercisers enter, chatting as they jog.)

244

ROSENZWEIG: Have you ever seen anything like it?! They suddenly all flew off, the entire bunch of them! They saw him, the shouty one, they lurched forward like boiling lava, one moment they were still on the ground and suddenly – floating upwards, rising and rising!...

LIECHTENSTEIN: Him too, the shouty one, when he saw them flying off, he let out this terrible shout, spread his arms out to his sides, jumped into the air and started flying after them 'Auntie Kratzia!' or 'Auntie Pratzia!' God knows, and then disappeared after them into the clouds!

ROSENZWEIG: Although to tell you the truth, I'm not really a big fan of flying, in flight you don't activate your circulation and your lungs like you do when you're jogging.

LIECHTENSTEIN: That's for sure, no doubt.

ROSENZWEIG: Also not the leg muscles.

LIECHTENSTEIN: That's also true.

ROSENZWEIG: You know what the proof is: How long does a bird live?!

LIECHTENSTEIN: Nothing. Two tweet-tweets and we're done.

ROSENZWEIG: Show me one bird that'll make it to the third millennium!

LIECHTENSTEIN: *(Full of contempt.)* To the third millennium?! – She won't make it to the third dustbin!

(They see BARAGUNTSELEH's corpse.)

ROSENZWEIG: And who do we have here?

LIECHTENSTEIN: The one who fell earlier.

ROSENZWEIG: He looks dead to me.

LIECHTENSTEIN: He's not going to be doing any more jogging.

ROSENZWEIG: Let's jog and call the police.

(They both jog out and bump into Professor KIPPERNAI who's running towards them.)

ROSENZWEIG: *(To LIECHTENSTEIN.)* Listen, it's getting crowded here.

(They turn around. KIPPERNAI runs after them.)

KIPPERNAI: Excuse me, perhaps you happen to have seen an orphan...

ROSENZWEIG: He flew off.

KIPPERNAI: Flew off?!

ROSENZWEIG: Into the clouds.

KIPPERNAI: He was looking for an aunt...

ROSENZWEIG: She flew off.

KIPPERNAI: Her too?

ROSENZWEIG: Into the clouds.

KIPPERNAI: Did they all fly off?

ROSENZWEIG: One died.

LIECHTENSTEIN: He thought jogging was like eating lettuce.

ROSENZWEIG: Do you jog regularly?

KIPPERNAI: No, I'm just here by coincidence...I'm looking for...I'm Professor Kippernai...

ROSENZWEIG: Professor? And how do you get a steady supply of oxygen to your brain if you don't jog?

LIECHTENSTEIN: He has a bicycle pump, he connects it to his ear.

KIPPERNAI: But how could that…into the clouds?! Did they really fly?!

ROSENZWEIG: They flew off, flew off! Flew off! Flew off, flew off!

LIECHTENSTEIN: He can't comprehend it, he doesn't have enough oxygen in his brain.

(To KIPPERNAI.)

They flew off, flew off!

ROSENZWEIG: And it's obviously silly to fly instead of jogging.

(And KIPPERNAI spreads his arms and tries to glide while running, but doesn't succeed. He calls up to the sky.)

KIPPERNAI: Mr Bobijcek! Mr Bobijcek! I already started worrying, I was already worried, Mr Bobijcek! Mr Bobijcek! This is Professor Kippernai!

(He carries on shouting again and again while ROSENZWEIG and LIECHTENSTEIN continue jogging alongside him.)

ROSENZWEIG: Do you see this beach? I'm the one that brought jogging here. All the jogging you see on this beach for ten kilometres up and down, it's all me, I brought it, including the circulation and the breathing, heart, lungs, arteries, veins, the chemical structure of blood, blood cells, oxygen absorption, all that, along the ten kilometres of this beach and also further away, it's absolutely all me, I brought, and I invented. Anyone who jogged took it from me, and thanks to me, and I taught, and I gave, and I organised, and I did, it's all me, me, me, me…

(Breathes heavily. The three of them jog out. The angel of death SAMUELOV jogs behind them.)

Act Four: Himalayas

In the early hours of the morning, on a snow-capped mountaintop in Tibet, the wedding party is climbing: SHRATZIA, RASCHES, VELVETZIA, TSITSKEIVA and POPPOCHENKO. They approach the summit.

SHRATZIA: Does anybody know where we've landed?

RASCHES: We flew north, we were in the air for ten minutes, we're somewhere around Herzliya.

TSITSKEIVA: Is there a tall snow-capped mountain somewhere around Herzliya?

RASCHES: *(Angrily. He's suffering badly from the cold.)* We flew north, we were in the air for ten minutes, we're somewhere around Herzliya.

(They reach the summit where the Buddhist monk SHAHMANDRINA is sitting motionless in a yoga pose.)

And here's a Yemeni bagel seller.

SHRATZIA: We really must be in Herzliya.

(To SHAHMANDRINA.)

Do you have five bagels?

SHAHMANDRINA: *(It's clear that the unexpected visit is upsetting him very much and disturbing his focussed tranquillity.)* Forty years…alone…not a bird…not a sound…me…God…no bagels.

(Shrinks away and tries to remain focussed on his meditations.)

SHRATZIA: *(To the rest of the group.)* I can't quite understand what he's saying. But I think he doesn't have any bagels.

TSITSKEIVA: And I don't think this is Herzliya either.

RASCHES: *(Already not so sure of himself.)* I said somewhere around Herzliya.

SHRATZIA: *(To SHAHMANDRINA.)* You really must excuse us for the interruption, we fell here completely by chance without having any breakfast. So you don't have any bagels, eh?

(Pause.)

My name's Shratzia.

RASCHES: Rasches.

TSITSKEIVA: Tsitskeiva.

VELVETZIA: Velvetzia.

POPPOCHENKO: Poppochenko.

TSITSKEIVA: My husband Baraguntseleh should be arriving any minute now.

SHAHMANDRINA: Shahmandrina…monk…Buddha…

SHRATZIA: It's a pleasure. And if I may ask, how does a Buddhist gentleman like you end up around Herzliya?

SHAHMANDRINA: Forty years…here…Himalaya…not move…

SHRATZIA: Himalaya?

(Everyone looks at RASCHES.)

TSITSKEIVA: Himalaya, eh?! Who was it who said 'Herzliya', I'd like to know!

POPPOCHENKO: Him. He said it. The in-law.

RASCHES: I didn't say it.

POPPOCHENKO: You said it, you said it.

RASCHES: 'You said it, you said it!' You snitch! I didn't say it – I asked! Am I supposed to guess our flight speed?!

TSITSKEIVA: A brain, eh?! And in the brain – there's a little devil! And the devil – he's got a brain too!

RASCHES: Well, so what?! What are you looking at?! At me looking stupid?! So I'm stupid, so what?! So it's not Herzliya, so it's Tibet, so there's no brain, and there's no devil, so it's empty, empty space, clean and pleasant emptiness, so what?! But most importantly, have I done well in life?! I've managed to raise a family, get a flat and arrange a wedding for my daughter, while being stupid. Fact. And I've seen cleverer people who haven't even managed that, with all their wisdom. Here, look at me and look at him, the Yemeni, sitting here for forty years alone like a dog with his arse in the snow between heaven and earth. No family, no flat, no daughter to marry off! So who's the stupid one here?!

SHRATZIA: What are you getting so jumpy about. Tibet, so it's Tibet. The main thing is that we get back in time for the wedding, the first guests won't arrive before six.

TSITSKEIVA: We have an appointment at three o'clock at the French-International Bridal Salon in Givatayim!

SHRATZIA: So, we'll fly straight to Givatayim!

TSITSKEIVA: And who says we'll be able to fly again?! Miracles twice a day?! And if we do fly, who knows how long it'll take?!

RASCHES: Ten minutes from there to here – ten minutes from here to there.

(Points at his brain.)

TSITSKEIVA: And if we go against the wind?! A brain, eh?!

RASCHES: *(Out of patience, shouts at the top of his lungs.)* Yes, a brain! Us – on the bride's side – a brain! You – the entire family – on the groom's side – an arse!

TSITSKEIVA: Kidneys! Piss!

SHRATZIA: Enough, enough, hush!

TSITSKEIVA: Hush in the grave! Catheters!

SHRATZIA: Enough, mother-in-law! Save your strength! We've still got to fly the Himalaya-Givatayim line today! Let's relax, rest for fifteen minutes, take a deep breath and fly back.

POPPOCHENKO: It's a shame I didn't bring a camera.

SHRATZIA: What's there to photograph here? It's just Asia!

POPPOCHENKO: I'd photograph Velvetzia.

(To VELVETZIA, with glistening eyes.)

Velvetzia.

VELVETZIA: Poppochenko.

SHRATZIA: The most important thing is to get some rest before this evening. The Bobijcek, thank God, won't find us here. And let's not stop Shahmandrina from becoming at one with his nonsense.

(They all crowd together due to the cold.)

RASCHES: It's cold. Colder than the picnic on the beach.

TSITSKEIVA: Ay, ay, ay, where's that lovely warm picnic on the beach!

SHRATZIA: Excuse me for interrupting you again, Mr Shahmandrina, but it's just that we left home today without having any breakfast. I understand you don't have any bagels, but maybe something else?

(Pause.)

Maybe something else?

SHAHMANDRINA: Forty years...no food...

SHRATZIA: Forty years?! And what does a Buddhist gentleman like you live on for forty years?

SHAHMANDRINA: Air...

(Breathes deeply.)

SHRATZIA: *(Draws a deep breath once, twice, with a sour smile.)* Air, eh? Still, after forty years I wouldn't say no to a piece of pickled herring, eh?

(To TSITSKEIVA.)

You think I believe him, the Persian? He'll wait until the afternoon, and when we're really hungry he'll offer us something for double the price.

(To SHAHMANDRINA.)

That trick won't work Shahmandruleh, not with us. In the afternoon we won't buy anything from you. It'll make more sense for us to wait until the wedding reception in the evening, so you won't be doing any business with us.

(Pause.)

So if you do happen to have something, you're better off getting it out now.

(Pause.)

Fine. We're here, and our eyes are open. And if you don't mind, we'll hang around here until two o'clock, we won't interrupt, we'll be quiet, you can carry on...

(Winks to RASCHES.)

...fasting, you don't need to mind us, thank you, we have a wedding today, we have business of our own.

(Everyone huddles together and shivers.)

RASCHES: I'm cold. I'm freezing.

TSITSKEIVA: Ay, ay, ay, that lovely warm picnic on the beach, it was really summer there!

RASCHES: Maybe we can light a bonfire?

SHRATZIA: Rasches, Poppochenko! Wood for the bonfire!

RASCHES: I can't see any trees.

POPPOCHENKO: No trees and no newspapers. Total desolation. Snow. And in the snow – Velvetzia.

SHRATZIA: What can we set fire to?

(To SHAHMANDRINA.)

A real gem, this Tibet of yours.

TSITSKEIVA: I read somewhere that they sometimes set fire to themselves, these Buddhist monks, as a protest.

(Pause. SHRATZIA glances at SHAHMANDRINA as though assessing him. Approaches him.)

SHRATZIA: Excuse me, another small question: Were you thinking of killing yourself today?

(Pause.)

No?

(Pause.)

Because in fact there's some kind of war going on in Asia right now.

RASCHES: A very brutal war.

SHRATZIA: Terrible bloodshed.

RASCHES: We must protest.

SHRATZIA: So we thought that you, a man with a conscience…no?

(Pause.)

Anyway, if you happen to decide to do it, call us and we'll gather round you.

(To the group.)

So, turns out he wants to go on living, the Shahmandruleh. All right, dear friends, ten minutes and we're off. Don't move too much so you don't waste energy, let's sit close together for warmth, and without moving, just like the Shahmandrulik, and let's focus our thoughts on a single point, maybe that'll help.

(They all sit crowded closely together in a yoga position. Since the summit is very narrow, they're forced to sit up against each other and against SHAHMANDRINA, who gets nudged and pushed out of his spot, and who feels extremely uncomfortable. From the look in his eyes and his body language it's apparent that they're stopping him from concentrating. They all look like they're focussing on a single point.)

RASCHES: I'm cold.

SHRATZIA: Are you focussing on a single point?

RASCHES: *(Sobbing.)* I'm focussing on loads of points, but I'm cold, I'm cold, I'm cold…

SHRATZIA: *(To TSITSKEIVA.)* We need a bonfire.

TSITSKEIVA: There's no choice, we'll light Shahmandrulik.

SHRATZIA: What do you mean 'light'?! He's a human being after all.

TSITSKEIVA: *(Laughs.)* A human being! Is that a human being?!

SHRATZIA: Isn't it?

TSITSKEIVA: Where does it say that? That's an Indian or a Persian, or a parrot or God knows what, is that a human being? Am I going to let us freeze in Tibet because of him?! And what's Poppochenko, a cat?!

SHRATZIA: Still, we're in the Tibetan mountains after all, and over here everyone's Persian like this, and to light him, who knows, they won't understand that this is a matter of self-preservation…

TSITSKEIVA: How is it even relevant who understands? Is anyone going to see? Is anyone going to know? We're at the top of the Himalayas, you heard it yourself, even birds don't make it here. We'll light him, we'll warm up, we'll thaw out our limbs, and in ten minutes – hop! – they can try and come looking for us in the sky! Do you have matches, mother-in-law?

SHRATZIA: *(Takes a box of matches out of her purse and hands it to TSITSKEIVA.)* I for one didn't see anything and didn't hear anything.

(TSITSKEIVA lights a match and touches it to the hem of SHAHMANDRINA's robe. The robe doesn't catch. She tries in other places on the robe but to no avail.)

TSITSKEIVA: Everything here's frozen. If only we had some petrol or kerosene…

(She lights another match and tries to light SHAHMANDRINA's ear. The ear doesn't light.)

SHAHMANDRINA: *(Turns to her.)* Forty years…!

TSITSKEIVA: Sit still and shut up!

(She swivels his head back. To SHRATZIA.)

The ear's frozen as well.

SHRATZIA: Rub it a bit, maybe it'll thaw out. I didn't say anything.

(TSITSKEIVA massages SHAHMANDRINA's ear. He tries to pull his head away, but she's stronger than him and grips his head tightly.)

TSITSKEIVA: Sit still and shut up, fatso, before I throw you off! We're not from Tibet, and you're not impressing us with that patchwork blanket of yours, you bum!

(She finishes massaging his ear and tries to light it again, unsuccessfully.)

It's thawed, but it won't light.

SHRATZIA: There's no fat, that's the problem. There's nothing to light.

TSITSKEIVA: *(To SHAHMANDRINA.)* Why don't you eat anything?! Don't you have a house?! Don't you have a mother?! Are you a street urchin?! Go and get a job, you parasite! Fasting at our expense!

SHRATZIA: Maybe he's got other parts of his body, fatter ones. Maybe the arse.

TSITSKEIVA: Give me a hand, mother-in-law, let's turn him over, try the arse. Our last chance, Shahmandrulik's arse.

(SHRATZIA hesitates for a moment. Glances from side to side and finally, with a 'Screw it, what's the worst that could happen!' motion she goes over and helps TSITSKEIVA. They both grab SHAHMANDRINA under his armpits and turn him over so that his head is pointing down and his feet are pointing up.)

SHAHMANDRINA: Forty years...not a bird...!!

SHRATZIA: *(To SHAHMANDRINA.)* This is yoga, it's healthy for the brain. Ask Rosenzweig.

(TSITSKEIVA squeezes SHAHMANDRINA's backside.)

TSITSKEIVA: Nothing. It's all bones. Oh, these Indians these Indians, where will it end with these Indians. You tell me, Shmendrel, what kind of shape do you call that?! Is that a bum?! Is that a human being?! A cockroach! A spider! You've got no front, you've got no back, you've got no down and you've got no up! Where do you even start?! You'll never find yourself a bride! Never! You need an arse! An arse! Poppochenko simply had an arse, and that's the only reason he's achieved what he has!

(They both turn him back over. To the rest of the group.)

SHRATZIA: My dear friends, move away from him. Not only is he not warming us, we're actually warming him.

(They all move away from SHAHMANDRINA as best they can.)

RASCHES: I'm cold...I'm freezing...I can't feel my knees...I won't get to attend the wedding...I won't get to...

(And suddenly SHRATZIA lets out a scream.)

VELVETZIA: Has Daddy died?

SHRATZIA: The Bobijcek! The Bobijcek's arrived! The Bobijcek's here! Run and hide behind the summit!

(Everyone runs and hides behind the summit, with SHRATZIA dragging RASCHES who can barely move his limbs. SHAHMANDRINA remains sitting at the summit. LAJCEK arrives at the summit from the other side.)

LAJCEK: *(Urgently, to SHAHMANDRINA.)* Where are they? They're here, I know it! I saw them land! Where are they? Don't sit there like a Buddhist monk, just tell me where they are! Or are you already in cahoots with them! Where are they? My mother died! The funeral's at four o'clock! You're also invited! Where are they?

(On the other side of the summit, the group whisper to each other.)

TSITSKEIVA: We've got to fly away from here, mother-in-law! He'll find us in a second!

SHRATZIA: Rasches can't fly!

TSITSKEIVA: When Baraguntseleh tripped on the beach, did I say 'Baraguntseleh can't run'?!

SHRATZIA: Baraguntseleh didn't trip over in the Himalayas.

TSITSKEIVA: I'm flying off!

SHRATZIA: Shhh…I've got an idea, you wait for me here a minute until I get back.

(She sobs.)

It'll be okay, my friends! I'll lead you to the wedding, no matter what!

(She wraps herself in a white shawl and uses it to also wrap her face such that she's unrecognisable, a little similar in appearance to SHAHMANDRINA. She climbs up to the summit and stands in front of LAJCEK.)

LAJCEK: *(To himself.)* Everyone's dressing up as Buddhist monks today! Are they going to turn the day of my mother's funeral into a carnival?!

SHRATZIA: *(Changes her voice so that it's unrecognisable.)* Mr Bobijcek?

LAJCEK: Where are they?! They're here, I know it!

SHRATZIA: There are people, people you seek...

LAJCEK: Where are they?! Where are they?!

SHRATZIA: ...and who would be willing to conduct informal talks with you, and without any preconditions.

LAJCEK: Informal? What does that mean?!

SHRATZIA: Off the record.

LAJCEK: I don't understand! I'm looking for Auntie Shratzia! Just tell them that my mother, Alte Bobijcek, has died and that the funeral's today at four o'clock.

SHRATZIA: Only informally.

LAJCEK: Let it be informally! My mother's dead!

SHRATZIA: And any message you deliver during the informal talks, it's as though it wasn't actually delivered.

LAJCEK: I accept everything! I want to see Auntie Shratzia!

(SHRATZIA removes the shawl from her face.)

LAJCEK: Auntie Shratzia! I knew that was a costume! Mum's dead! The funeral's at four o'clock!

(Points at SHAHMANDRINA.)

And I bet that's Uncle Rasches!

(Jumps towards SHAHMANDRINA.)

Uncle Rasches! Mum's dead! The funeral's at four o'clock!

(Tries to rip SHAHMANDRINA's robe off. SHAHMANDRINA resists. They struggle while LAJCEK continues shouting.)

The funeral's at four o'clock! You've lost weight, Uncle Rasches! Mum's dead!

(The robe tears, SHAHMANDRINA falls flat on his face.)

SHAHMANDRINA: Forty years...not a bird...!

LAJCEK: You've gotten weak, Uncle Rasches! Mum's dead! The funeral's at four o'clock!

(SHAHMANDRINA stays lying on the ground. To SHRATZIA.)

What's up with Uncle Rasches?

SHRATZIA: That's not Rasches.

LAJCEK: Not Rasches anymore?!

SHRATZIA: No. That's Shmerl-Mendl, a Buddhist monk from Tibet.

LAJCEK: How did a Buddhist monk from Tibet reach us all the way over here?

SHRATZIA: He didn't reach us, we reached him.

LAJCEK: In Tibet?!

SHRATZIA: *(Contemptuously.)* Where else, Herzliya?! Have you ever seen a snow-capped mountain in Herzliya?!

LAJCEK: But the funeral's at four o'clock! From Tibet...! How will we make it...all of us...the funeral's at four o'clock!

(He falls into SHRATZIA's arms while calling out.)

Auntie Shratzia! Mum's dead! The funeral's at four o'clock! The funeral's at four o'clock! Mum's dead! Mum's dead!

(He starts prancing around in a mixture of grief and joy.)

Oh, Auntie Shratzia, Auntie Shratzia, I thought I'd never catch up with you, never! I started imagining that I'd never be able to unburden myself of the terrible news that Mum's dead! Mum's dead, dead! The funeral's at four o'clock, at four o'clock, at four o'clock! There is a god – the funeral's at four o'clock! Mum's dead – there is a god!

SHRATZIA: Lajcek, these are informal talks anyway, so why wear out your throat?

(LAJCEK calms down, but occasionally still lets out a small silent sob.)

And now I suggest we get straight to the point. Lajcek, we're tired of running away, we're tired of you pursuing us, and I'm sure you're also fed up of chasing us.

LAJCEK: I'm fed up, Auntie Shratzia, fed up, so fed up, I mean all I wanted…

SHRATZIA: Slow down, Lajcek. You know that my daughter Velvetzia'le…

TSITSKEIVA: *(From the hiding place.)* And my son Poppochenko.

SHRATZIA: …is getting married today…

LAJCEK: Mum's dead, Auntie Shratzia, the funeral's at four o'clock…

SHRATZIA: I said slow down. Otherwise I'm calling off the informal talks and we're all flying away.

(LAJCEK calms down. SHRATZIA tries the pleasant approach.)

You know that my daughter Velvetzia is getting married today, and I don't know whether you can even imagine how much we've all been waiting for this day.

LAJCEK: I can imagine…

SHRATZIA: No, you can't. You don't know what family is, what children are. I wouldn't be exaggerating if I said that this was the day we were born for. Yes, yes. It was already obvious to me when I was five or six! The reason I came into this world is to get to see my daughter's wedding day.

LAJCEK: Oh, Auntie Shratzia, Auntie Shratzia, who knows as well as I do what a wedding is, and I agree with you that a person is born to get married, and my own wedding is still waiting for me over there on the horizon, in the fog, and calling me…oh, Auntie Shratzia, my mother and I wanted so much to be guests at your daughter Velvetzia's wedding, we spent so many lonely evenings at home, not a living soul, no joy, no life for the spirit, but we knew that somewhere out there was an aunt, and that the aunt had a daughter, and that the daughter was growing and developing, and that the day would arrive when she'd get married, and there'd be a big celebration, and we'd be invited, and we'd wear our nicest clothes, and we'd leave the house in the evening to go somewhere where we'd see people, and real happiness…oh, Auntie Shratzia, who could have planned and who could have imagined that Mum would die the day before Velvetzia's wedding – because maybe you don't know yet, Auntie Shratzia, but Mum died tonight, Mum died! And now that what's happened has happened and Mum's dead and we need to bury her, how could I not inform you, Auntie Shratzia, because if you don't come to the funeral, who will?

SHRATZIA: Lajcek, I'll answer you openly and candidly, because this discussion is off the record and formally

speaking I don't actually know anything about your
mother's death…

LAJCEK: What do you mean you don't know?! Here I am,
telling you!

SHRATZIA: Bobijcek, I'm here for an informal conversation
with you, and you agreed! If I officially knew that Auntie
Alte, rest her soul, had passed away, wouldn't I run
straight to her funeral? Wouldn't I postpone Velvetzia's
wedding without thinking twice? How could I do anything
else? However, since me and my family don't know
anything about the death – and I'm going to make sure we
carry on not knowing – then Velvetzia's wedding is going
to go ahead as planned.

LAJCEK: And when will you agree to know that Mum's dead?

SHRATZIA: As far as I'm concerned, if it's really urgent
for you, then immediately after the wedding today at
midnight, but even better tomorrow morning, preferably
not before ten.

(Short pause.)

LAJCEK: But still Mum's dead.

SHRATZIA: Yes, it's a shame.

(Starts sobbing.)

LAJCEK: *(Pounces on the opportunity.)* Auntie Shratzia, it still
feels pressing for me to tell you the news about my
mother's death.

SHRATZIA: I understand, I'm an aunt after all.

LAJCEK: Just your participation in the funeral, an entire
family of happy people, including a beautiful young girl,
would give my mother's death a dramatic validity and
meaning and would prove that she took up space in the

world and that her life also had some kind of purpose.
Mum talked about it herself before her death. And if you
had – oh, Auntie Shratzia! – if on top of that you had also
postponed Velvetzia's wedding, what a festive air you'd be
giving to Mum's funeral, what an aura would envelope the
coffin as it was being lowered into the grave! A thousand
bouquets and a golden gravestone wouldn't have the same
effect on Mum as Velvetzia's wedding being postponed!
What joy, what warmth, what a bright light of formal
recognition inside Mum's dark grave! Auntie Shratzia, for
Mum's sake, for me, for all the dead who are facing their
final happiness, the happiness of their funeral, formally
acknowledge my mother's death! Acknowledge my
mother's death, Auntie Shratzia, and come with everyone
to the funeral!

(Sobs.)

SHRATZIA: No acknowledgment, no funeral, no wedding
postponement.

LAJCEK: *(Crying.)* And there's something else I haven't said…

(Pause. He hesitates.)

…The main thing is that I don't' want to miss Velvetzia's
wedding. I've been dreaming about attending Velvetzia's
wedding my whole life, first as a groom and afterwards,
when it became clear that Velvetzia wasn't created for
me, as a guest. But always, always at Velvetzia's wedding.
And now what? Am I going to drag along like an idiot in
the rain behind my mother's coffin knowing full well that
in another part of town that coveted wedding is roaring
along without me?!

SHRATZIA: *(Tries to calm him down, to win him over.)* We'll
invite you over to see Velvetzia after the wedding. And
more than once.

LAJCEK: That's not the same as the wedding!

SHRATZIA: It's even more than the wedding, it's more intimate, fewer people.

LAJCEK: I want people! Lots of people! To the wedding!

SHRATZIA: All right, we'll have another big party, no less big, especially for you.

LAJCEK: That's not the same as a wedding. What about my mother's funeral?

SHRATZIA: We'll send a representative. You'll share the news with him and he'll come to the funeral.

LAJCEK: Who?

SHRATZIA: We have a neighbour, a professor...

LAJCEK: He's not even a relative! And he's not married! He's alone! A professor, but alone! And besides, he's coming anyway! He's coming anyway! What good is a professor to me, he's also, like me, coming anyway! Anyway!

SHRATZIA: The professor is totally fine for funerals!

LAJCEK: Mum wanted you! You're her real relatives! Mum wanted you!

SHRATZIA: We're not available, Bobijcek! You hear?! Not available!

LAJCEK: You! Only you!

SHRATZIA: The professor!

LAJCEK: You!

SHRATZIA: No acknowledgement, no funeral, no wedding postponement!

LAJCEK: *(Wipes his tears away.)* In that case, Auntie Shratzia, I have no choice but to carry on chasing you until I catch you and give you the news.

SHRATZIA: You can chase us, orphan, but you won't catch us.

LAJCEK: I'll catch you, Auntie, I'll catch you. By the end of the day I'll get to see you walking slowly behind a coffin with your heads bowed!

SHRATZIA: Goodbye, Bobijcek.

LAJCEK: Goodbye, Auntie Shratzia.

SHRATZIA: And my regards to your mother.

LAJCEK: She's dead.

SHRATZIA: I don't know anything about that. I'm sending her my regards, you do with them as you see fit.

(They both turn to go, each their own way. Suddenly TSITSKEIVA leaps out, runs over behind LAJCEK and shoves him off the summit. With a terrible scream, gradually fades, he falls into the abyss. SHRATZIA and TSITSKEIVA look down after him, and when he disappears from view they sigh, SHRATZIA lifts her eyes skywards and says in a teary voice.)

Dear Alte, may you be resting in heaven, I'm sending you your son, so that you can carry on happily up there too, and so that you can advocate in favour of my daughter Velvetzia to he who sits on high…

TSITSKEIVA: And my son, Poppochenko.

SHRATZIA: Who's finally going to stand under the chuppah today, Amen.

(And they turn to the group's hiding place.)

We've been saved! We've been saved! Velvetzia's…

TSITSKEIVA: and Poppochenko's.

SHRATZIA: ...wedding is going ahead! We've been saved! There's a wedding! There's no Lajcek! There's no Lajcek! All the Bobijceks in the world are gone! They're gone! We've been saved!

(The rest of the group come out of their hiding place, RASCHES is crawling with difficulty.)

And now, my dear friends, to fly! To fly, to fly, it's two o'clock soon, let's fly to the French-International Bridal Salon in Givatayim!

(Everyone starts flapping their arms and flying, apart from RASCHES and SHRATZIA. RASCHES makes a few attempts to fly but his body's frozen and doesn't cooperate.)

VELVETZIA: *(Calling down from above, from the clouds.)* Is Daddy dead?

SHRATZIA: Fly away, fly away, I'm coming in a second!

(She goes down behind the summit where RASCHES is lying and kneels beside him.)

RASCHES: I thought you'd already abandoned me in the Tibetan snow.

SHRATZIA: *(Stroking his head.)* How could you think that, Rasches.

RASCHES: Yes, I thought you'd flown away...

SHRATZIA: ...and what's Rasches for?

RASCHES: To buy a flat.

SHRATZIA: And what's a flat for?

RASCHES: For Velvetzia.

SHRATZIA: And what's Velvetzia for?

RASCHES: For a wedding.

SHRATZIA: And what's a wedding for?

RASCHES: For a grandson.

SHRATZIA: And what's the grandson called?

RASCHES: Rasches.

SHRATZIA: So what's Rasches for?

RASCHES: For Rasches.

SHRATZIA: I'll never leave you, Rasches…

RASCHES: Because we can't have Velvetzia's wedding without me, right?

SHRATZIA: Absolutely not, you'll always be with us…

RASCHES: Because we've built our whole lives just for this moment, it's this moment we've been waiting and wishing for all these years…

SHRATZIA: Wherever I am and wherever Velvetzia is, you'll always be with us, deep deep in our hearts…

(She gets up and starts walking away very slowly choking back tears.)

Always with us, Rasches…always…your image will follow us in everything we do…in the chuppah and during the meal and the dancing…and also for a long time afterwards…you'll be in our heart…forever…your memory won't fade…Rasches, you're always with us…

(She exits crying quietly and flies away. SHAHMANDRINA sits down, makes himself comfortable again and takes a deep breath.)

RASCHES: *(Doesn't realise SHRATZIA is gone. Continues talking to her.)* My back's completely frozen. Do you remember the

day the fridge arrived? I plugged it in and stood in front
of it with you for the first time. A film of ice covered the
walls of the freezer like the down on a baby chick's back.
The engine hummed quietly and pleasantly. I wouldn't
swap that experience for a holiday in the Alps.

(His voice weakens.)

I stood there with you, hand in hand, as though we were
on honeymoon. I wouldn't swap that…

(The angel SAMUELOV enters.)

SAMUELOV: Angel Samuelov. The angel of death. I've come
to take your soul.

RASCHES: Today is my daughter Velvetzia's wedding.

SAMUELOV: You're all marrying something off today. A plague.

RASCHES: But there's a date. The wedding has a date!

SAMUELOV: So does your death.

RASCHES: *(Sobbing.)* Let me marry my daughter off this
evening! My entire life's been aimed at this date!

(Pause.)

SAMUELOV: All right, Mr Rasches, I'll let you live for the
wedding. You'll just do me a small favour as well.

(Stands over him.)

Let out some gas.

RASCHES: Gas?

SAMUELOV: From behind, you know. The way you all like
doing.

RASCHES: Is that all you want? Gladly. That thing – even
without anyone asking. That thing – always, happily. In

the morning, in the afternoon, in the evening, especially if I find myself sitting in a lecture…here you go.

(Starts breaking wind.)

SAMUELOV: That's it. And don't stop. Let it go. Like that. Lovely.

RASCHES: *(Pleased with himself.)* Yes. There, like that. I managed to get a fridge, I'll make it to Velvetzia's wedding, I let out a massive fart on top of the Himalayas…I've lived, I've lived, there's no doubt about that…a full and exceptional life…yes, there's no regretting this life, it's been. It's been…definitely been…this has been a life…and what's Rasches for…?

(He dies. SAMUELOV guides the soul in its flight.)

SAMUELOV: Come, come, soul, come fly, foul smelling little butterfly, upwards, like that, lovely…

(Turns to leave. Stops, turns to SHAHMANDRINA.)

And what about you Mr Shahmandrina?

SHAHMANDRINA: Forty years…to the sky…ready…take…

(SAMUELOV approaches him, looks him over dismissively, then, in a swift but strong movement, he lifts him in the air by the nape of his neck, and sees that he's as light as a feather.)

SAMUELOV: Go on, let out some gas.

(SHAHMANDRINA strains to break wind, unsuccessfully. SAMUELOV, contemptuously.)

Oich mir a mensch, afilu koyekh tsu machen a forts habt ihr nicht[3]

---

3 [Yiddish] Ha, this is a man, he doesn't even have the strength to let out a fart.

(Lets go of him. SHAHMANDRINA drops onto the snow. SAMUELOV exits. SHAHMANDRINA returns to his yoga pose.)

SHAHMANDRINA: To the sky…ready…take…

Act Five: A tile roof

The sloping tiled roof of a tall building. The survivors of the wedding group – SHRATZIA, TSITSKEIVA, POPPOCHENKO and VELVETZIA – are holding on to the slippery tiles of the sloped roof with their fingernails in order to not plummet to the ground. The delicate predicament obliges them to speak quietly, slowly, without moving, and they try to restrain their anger.

TSITSKEIVA: And who was it who shouted 'we'll drop down straight onto the roof of the French-International Bridal Salon!' I'd like to know who it was!

POPPOCHENKO: The mother-in-law...

SHRATZIA: Shut up! Shut up, you snake! So what! Who's supposed to know in advance that it's a tiled roof? Let alone a slopey one.

TSITSKEIVA: Brains! You, all of you – brains!

SHRATZIA: So we've has some experiences today, this is just another small one.

TSITSKEIVA: What an experience, eh?! In a second we're going to fall down and smash into little pieces, with blood, *cholera psiakrew*![4]

SHRATZIA: And you, criticism, criticism, all day nothing but criticism, what are you jumping up and down and moaning about, you had a son who managed to make it all the way to Velvetzia! So what?! Who do you think you are?!

TSITSKEIVA: And who, if you don't mind me asking, is Velvetzia exactly, who?!

---

4 [Polish] Goddammit

SHRATZIA: Velvetzia is who's standing on two feet while Poppochenko's in front of her on all fours!

TSITSKEIVA: When Poppochenko's in front of her on all fours, mother-in-law, Velvetzia's underneath with her legs spread open!

SHRATZIA: When Velvetzia's underneath with her legs spread open, Poppochenko's even further down, taking out the rubbish!

TSITSKEIVA: When Poppochenko's even further down, taking out the rubbish, Velvetzia and all of you, together with your aunt Alte Shmatte, are even further further down – in the grave!

SHRATZIA: When Velvetzia and all of us are even further further down, in the grave, Poppochenko and all of you are even further further further down – in Australia!

TSITSKEIVA: Kidneys! Piss! Catheters!

(In all the mutual shouting and punching one of them slips, pulling the entire group with her. They all fall and slip on the wet tiles, slide down and at the last second manage to grab hold of the edge of the roof with their fingers, shrieking in terror. They're scared to move or talk lest they drop and crash to the ground. And then, suddenly, from above the apex of the tiled roof, LAJCEK's blood-splattered face appears.)

LAJCEK: And there you all are, ready for my mother's funeral with your heads bowed.

(Everyone in the group shrivels up, lowers their head and avoids looking in LAJCEK's direction. He carries on climbing, sits up on the rooftop and continues announcing in a loud clear voice.)

I hereby give you formal notice: My mother is dead, the funeral is today at four o'clock!

(Pause. No one moves.)

274

KIPPERNAI: *(Calls from outside below.)* Mr Bobijcek, are you up there? This is Professor Kippernai, how do I get up?

Act Six: The sycamore-lined avenue

Early evening, a sycamore-lined avenue near the cemetery. A lone bench. The storm has subsided. A wintery sun is breaking through the clouds. The wedding group, SHRATZIA, TSITSKEIVA, VELVETZIA and POPPOCHENKO enter in single file hunched and dejected like hostages on their way to prison. LAJCEK is walking next to them, suppressing his victorious joy and supervising them. He stops and commands:

LAJCEK: Stop!

(They all stop. LAJCEK counts them. He's satisfied, rubs his hands happily.)

It's a pity about Uncle Rasches. I'd already imagined him at Mum's funeral. It's also a pity about the other in-law. In general, I feel pity for any person, for the whole world, so many people won't be at Mum's funeral. What a waste!

(A gravedigger enters, pulling a cart behind him and behind the cart is LIECHTENSTEIN. He turns to the others and points to the coffin.)

LIECHTENSTEIN: Rosenzweig. The healthy one. He was still jogging this morning. Sixty years old. Was supposed to have died at fifty. Ten years net profit.

(To those gathered.)

Will you join?

LAJCEK: *(Roars.)* They're already taken!!

(LIECHTENSTEIN carries on walking by himself behind the coffin, stops suddenly.)

LIECHTENSTEIN: And maybe we were wrong. Maybe we were jogging in vain. And maybe we should have swum, not jogged. If it ever turns out I was wrong – what a shame…in vain…

(The gravedigger exits with the cart, and behind him LIECHTENSTEIN. Everyone silently watches the sad funeral go by, and then SHRATZIA and TSITSKEIVA stand on either side of LAJCEK and support him.)

LAJCEK: Thank you, but our funeral's only in an hour.

SHRATZIA: *(Starts sobbing.)* Oh, Lajcek, Lajcek…

TSITSKEIVA: *(Joins the sobbing.)* An exceptional person…

(They both address an imaginary LAJCEK who's ostensibly lying at their feet.)

Your altruism…

SHRATZIA: The manly stubbornness with which you chased us and didn't give up until you caught us…

TSITSKEIVA: A real man…

SHRATZIA: It's such a shame about him…

TSITSKEIVA: That he was wasted like that…

SHRATZIA: Without a woman…without experiencing a bit of happiness in this world…

TSITSKEIVA: Living that way like a dog…

SHRATZIA: All those years just devoted to his mother…

TSITSKEIVA: Allowing himself to be taken advantage of…

SHRATZIA: He dedicated his whole life to her: For himself – nothing…

TSITSKEIVA: He never asked 'What about me?', 'When will I get to live?'

SHRATZIA: He never said to himself 'What's this, everyone's going off to dance and I'm going off by myself to escort dead people in the rain?' No, a saint, a total saint, kept on

277

giving in to his exploiter, even after her death he let her ruin a rare once-in-a-lifetime chance to find a beautiful rich pampered girl who would love him and calm him and accompany him through life…

TSITSKEIVA: Because they say he did once get the chance…

SHRATZIA: Yes, at his cousin Velvetzia's wedding…

TSITSKEIVA: To Poppochenko…

SHRATZIA: There were so many fantastic single girls there…

TSITSKEIVA: Waiting just for him…

SHRATZIA: But he missed it…and there weren't any others… and he died lonely…

TSITSKEIVA: Like a dog…

(LAJCEK also starts crying in self pity and his crying gets louder as the conversation progresses.)

While she, his mother, how would she have acted in his place? Would she also have given up on it if she were in his situation, the exploiter-murderer?!

SHRATZIA: No way! I knew her, I'm family! Before she had him, didn't she take her sweet time looking around for a man at banquets and weddings?! Didn't she look out for herself very, very well?!

TSITSKEIVA: And anyway, didn't she give birth to him as a result of intense pleasure in bed, the same pleasure she wanted to deny him when he was running off to her funeral instead of going to the wedding?!

SHRATZIA: And in the end, while she's resting quietly, sweetly…

278

TSITSKEIVA: And even resting in two places, both up above and down below…

SHRATZIA: Only he, the son, isn't resting and isn't at peace, he has convulsed and agonised…

TSITSKEIVA: And never stopped being cruel to himself… never spared or took pity on his own strength…

SHRATZIA: And never found peace for himself to his dying day…

TSITSKEIVA: May he rest in peace…

BOTH OF THEM: Amen!

(LAJCEK cries bitterly for himself.)

LAJCEK: What was I supposed to do?! What was I supposed to do in order to live a little…when my Mum's funeral suddenly landed…the mother who brought me into the world…my mother…

SHRATZIA: *(Strokes LAJCEK's head, who's sobbing in her arms.)* 'Mummy, Mummy!' Yes, there are always excuses for dropping out of life.

TSITSKEIVA: Scared of living. Not manly.

SHRATZIA: No, Lajcek, you're leaving the funeral, leaving all the nonsense and coming with us to the wedding, it's decided. I won't let your life be ruined!

LAJCEK: The funeral…

SHRATZIA: You're coming with us, it's decided!

LAJCEK: Even if I wanted to, what would people say if they saw me at the wedding today?

TSITSKEIVA: Who even knows? Who even sees you?!

LAJCEK: What would Velvetzia think of me, and her groom?!

SHRATZIA: Velvetzia?

(Laughs contemptuously.)

Come on, Velvetzia doesn't have anything or anyone to think about anymore!

LAJCEK: What would you think of me yourself?

SHRATZIA: You have nothing to hide from me, Lajcek…I'm your auntie…

TSITSKEIVA: Family is family…

LAJCEK: What will I tell myself?! How will I explain it to myself?!

SHRATZIA: Yourself?! You're scared of yourself?! You are you, everything stays inside, what's even the problem!

LAJCEK: And Mum?! What about Mum?! Will she get buried alone?! Alone?!

SHRATZIA: *(Laughs forgivingly.)* Come on, Mum, Mum won't know. Mum's dead. She died feeling that you'd participate in the funeral, that we'd all participate in the funeral, and that's the main thing.

TSITSKEIVA: *(In his ear, as though imparting a secret.)* And by the way, how would she even know that we didn't participate? Can she hear us? Can she see us? Does she know? On the contrary, she'll lie there in her grave, peacefully and quietly feeling that everyone was at her funeral, everyone, even a million people, the president, the army, cannons, a whole celebration, what's wrong, why not, is someone going to tell her otherwise?!

(Pause. LAJCEK falls silent. SHRATZIA strokes his head. He starts sobbing again, this time silently.)

SHRATZIA: Well yes, and you'll find a way to get along with yourself somehow. Believe me, that's the easiest thing. Come.

LAJCEK: *(Lets them drag him along. Crying.)* Are you making me leave Mum and come with you to the wedding?

SHRATZIA: Yes, Lajcek. We're making you.

LAJCEK: Are you forcing me?

SHRATZIA: Yes, Lajcek. We're forcing you.

LAJCEK: *(Stops for a moment. Cries harder.)* And is that all the force you have?

SHRATZIA: No, Lajcek. Here.

(Her and TSITSKEIVA hoist him in the air and walk out with him, followed by VELVETZIA and POPPOCHENKO.)

KIPPERNAI: *(His voice heard from outside.)* Mr Bobijcek, this is Professor Kippernai, we have less than an hour!

Act Seven: The wedding

Evening. The lavish wedding venue in the centre of town. Food, drink, music, dancing. In the midst of the festivities a guest enters the party. He sits down in the corner of the hall and finds himself something to eat and drink without drawing attention.

TSITSKEIVA: *(Chatting to one of the guests.)* How, you ask?

(Pointing at POPPOCHENKO's backside.)

Very simple. Poppochenko had an arse, and he sat on his arse, and that's how he made it, that's the whole secret.

POPPOCHENKO: *(Drunk, engaged in manly talk with one of the guests.)* Women. Bah. Shove a steak in them, mix it with a bit of wine, and they're yours from the front, from the back, from underneath and from on top and they even go cock-a-doodle-doo. *(Laughs an idiotic laugh.)* Women.

(Gets slapped in the face by VELVETZIA. Laughs despondently, returns to himself.)

Poppochenko.

(In the meantime, without being noticed, the guest approaches PSHOSHITZIA, a pretty, giggly girl who he's been looking at the whole time, and sits beside her.)

PSHOSHITZIA: You've been looking at me this whole time. Who are you? Why are you wearing a mask? Who are you hiding from? This isn't a masquerade ball, this is a wedding.

MASK-WEARER: *(In a strange voice.)* You're interested in me because I'm wearing a mask. Would you still be interested in me if I take the mask off? If you see my real face, can I trust that you'll love me?

PSHOSHITZIA: Love you?!

(Laughs.)

What are you talking about?

MASK-WEARER: As long I'm in the mask there's a chance, right? Admit there's a chance.

(PSHOSHITZIA laughs again. She has a pleasant, kind-hearted laugh.)

And if I take it off, maybe there won't be a chance any more. Maybe the chance will evaporate, or perhaps…it'll materialise. Why not? We'll dance and you won't want to leave my arms. And you'll be mine. And you'll marry me. And you'll give me great joy and solace.

I'll be the happiest of men. What do think about Memorial Days? How do you think you'd like to spend them? How about we head to the cemetery on the outskirts of town, you, me and the boy, yes, we'll take sandwiches, we'll drive there, we'll stroll with the little one between the white gravestones and the trees, we'll show him: your uncle's lying here, another uncle's lying here, they all worked hard, they got tired and now they're resting.

PSHOSHITZIA: *(Laughs.)* And now take off the mask, because I'm really starting to get curious.

MASK-WEARER: No, not yet. I need to leave myself a few more moments with a chance. The wonderful chance! The eternal chance! What do think about an intimate dinner by the light of a memorial candle? Just you and me, a white tablecloth, wine, the light of a little memorial candle flickering across our faces, casting sweet romantic shadows on the walls…

(He stands up, shaking and sweating.)

See how I'm shaking and sweating, shaking in fear of the moment when I'll have to take off the mask! I know that if I take it off you won't want to see me! I'm a despicable person! No! Why despicable?! How am I different to anyone else? I want exactly the same thing they want, are they all dancing now? Shall we dance?

(Reaches his arms out to her.)

PSHOSHITZIA: Not before you take the mask off your face.

(The mask-wearer raises his hands to his face, removes the mask. Underneath it is another mask, a little sadder than the first one. PSHOSHITZIA laughs.)

MASK-WEARER: I just want you to know that the face under this mask isn't my real one either. Underneath it there's another face, and under that one another face and as you peel off one face after another they get more beautiful, more pure. And the last face is only light. A bright pure light.

(He lifts his hands to his face, removes the mask. Underneath it is another mask, sadder than the last.)

And now shall we dance?

PSHOSHITZIA: *(Laughing and enjoying herself.)* I want the last face. I want the last face.

MASK-WEARER: *(Kneels at her feet.)* Give me just this one dance while there's a tiny shadow of a chance!!

(PSHOSHITZIA laughs and extends her arms towards him. He stands up, shaking from excitement and reaches his hands out to her. At that moment Professor KIPPERNAI storms into the hall. His dramatic entrance brings the dancing and music to an abrupt stop. Everyone freezes in their places. Silence.)

KIPPERNAI: I am Professor Kippernai. I haven't come as a
guest – I'm not invited, although I am a neighbour, the
bride's family hasn't spoken to me for years and I have
no idea why – no, no I haven't come on the strength of
an invitation! I've come on the strength of higher moral
forces which sent me here despite the fact that I wasn't
invited! Ladies and gentlemen, I have every reason to
believe that in our midst is a man who has snuck out of
his departed mother's funeral who only died last night,
who chose to go and frolic at weddings instead of paying
the debt of grief to his mother, and because of whom his
mother has been lying in a black coffin since four o'clock
in the afternoon and hasn't been escorted to her eternal
resting place! Ladies and gentlemen, higher moral powers
command me to find this man and bring him to his
mother's coffin, and I obey them!

*(He begins roaming between the guests looking for LAJCEK. The guest
in the mask retreats slowly and surreptitiously towards a distant
corner and folds himself up, trying to hide. Since he knows that his
moments of happiness are numbered, he gorges and drinks and fills
his mouth with anything he can. KIPPERNAI walks past all the
guests and inspects them with the demeanour of an angel of destiny.
He reaches the guest in the mask, who tries to shrink even more and
hide his face, but suddenly KIPPERNAI's accusing hand is pointed at
him, and KIPPERNAI announces in a loud and ceremonious voice.)*

Here is the man who betrayed his mother's death! His
name is Lajcek Bobijcek, and he sold his mother's funeral
for the price of a quarter of a roast chicken!

*(Pause. The cheery PSHOSHITZIA approaches the masked guest who's
huddled in the corner with his face lowered and rips the third and
final mask from his face. LAJCEK BOBIJCEK's face is revealed. She
laughs kind-heartedly. Pause.)*

SHRATZIA: *(Seeing that the happy atmosphere is on the verge of being annihilated, shouts.)* Bobijcek! Out, to where you belong, to the dark, the rain, to your lonesome mother's funeral!

(LAJCEK gets up very slowly, hunched over, starts walking towards the exit, stops in front of KIPPERNAI.)

LAJCEK: And you, what are you chasing for? What business is it of yours? And then you're surprised that people stop talking to you?!

(Continues walking towards the exit, stops, retraces his steps, approaches PSHOSHITZIA. Points at his face.)

Is this what you meant when you said 'I want to see the last face?'

(PSHOSHITZIA laughs.)

Here it is. Would you have fallen in love with me?

PSHOSHITZIA: No.

LAJCEK: Thank you, that's a relief.

(Grabs another piece of food from the table, shoves it in his mouth and leaves with his mouth full.)

KIPPERNAI: *(To all the guests.)* I have done my duty. I am also going to the funeral, because I promised I would, and Professor Kippernai keeps his word. Good evening.

(Starts to leave.)

SHRATZIA: *(Mockingly, as though to herself, but so that he hears.)* Professor!

(KIPPERNAI stops as though he'd been struck on his back.)

The man's a tailor!

KIPPERNAI: *(Turns to the guests.)* I taught for three years at an Italian girls' college near Milan, in the faculty for cutting and sewing. Goodbye.

(Turns and leaves.)

SHRATZIA: And the dancing continues, dear guests! The dancing continues! You're dancing on my finest hour!

(The band strikes up again, the dancing restarts, POPPOCHENKO takes VELVETZIA's hand and invites her to the dance floor.)

POPPOCHENKO: *(Delicately.)* Velvetzia.

VELVETZIA: *(Softly.)* Poppochenko.

TSITSKEIVA: *(Disgustedly.)* Ay, how stupid and pointless your love is compared to all the agony and suffering that this wedding caused us.

SHRATZIA: *(Looks at the guests dancing, tears in her eyes.)* Yes, the finest hour of our lives is coming to an end, the hour we spent so many long years preparing for. And what's next? What'll we prepare for from now on?

(The music and the dancing continue. The ghosts of RASCHES and BARAGUNTSELEH, and with them the angel of death SAMUELOV, appear at the ball without any of those present seeing them. The ghosts laugh.)

RASCHES: Look, a wedding.

(RASCHES and BARAGUNTSELEH exit laughing, SAMUELOV lingers for a moment next to TSITSKEIVA.)

SAMUELOV: Mrs Tsitskeiva?

TSITSKEIVA: *(Sticks her chest out at him.)* Me.

SAMUELOV: Angel Samuelov. Angel of death...I've come to take your soul.

(For a moment she doesn't move, as though digesting his words, and suddenly she attacks him, lifts him up by his shirt collar.)

Jasnapsiakrew cholera[5], tfu!!

(And with a mighty kick to his backside she throws him out.)

BARAGUNTSELEH: A bride and a groom smiling at a cake.

---

5 [Polish] Goddammit

Act Eight: A winter funeral

Dawn the following day, in the street, in town. A bleak day, wind blowing and rain falling. A gravedigger pulls the cart on which lies ALTE BOBIJCEK's corpse. LAJCEK walks behind the cart, looking like a man with a hangover. The ghosts of ALTE and ROSENZWEIG appear arm in arm in the street without anyone noticing them.)

ALTE: Look. A funeral. Someone running after a black coffin in the rain.

(They laugh and exit.)

LAJCEK: All my life I've dreamed of walking arm in arm with a beautiful loving wife behind my mother's coffin. Someone who would support me, who would add her pleasant feminine crying to my hoarse ugly crying, someone who'd come home with me after it all, and make me some tea, and stroke my forehead, and tell me in a soft, soporific voice: 'This is how life passes. These ones go, and these ones come. This is how life passes'. That's what she'd tell me in her soft, pleasant voice which would hold within it the great promise of life.

KIPPERNAI: *(Enters at the back, walks behind LAJCEK and the coffin, rubs his hands in satisfaction, but with some fear of LAJCEK.)* And here I am at the place to which, as I recall, I was invited yesterday.

(END.)

THE CHILD DREAMS

A Play in Four Parts

Translated from the Hebrew by Jessica Cohen
and Evan Fallenberg

A tragic drama following a group of refugees aboard a ship
and their futile search for a safe-haven. Inspired by the story
of Jewish refugees on the *SS Saint Louis* in 1939, Levin wrote
a play whose universal theme and impact have sadly become
relevant in our time.

Cast of Characters

THE FATHER
THE MOTHER
THE CHILD
PERSECUTED PEOPLE
BLEEDING MAN
SPECTATOR STARTLED BY DEATH
SOLDIERS
COMMANDER
WOMAN BORN FOR LOVE
WHIMPERING WOMAN
HUNCHED SOLDIER
OPTIMISTIC NEIGHBOR
SKIPPER
SAILORS
SHIP PASSENGERS
THOSE WHO REMAIN ON SHORE
MAN JEALOUS OF THE LIVING
LOGICAL MAN
COMFORTING PASSENGER
IMPASSIONED PASSENGER
DISAPPOINTED PASSENGER
WISE SAILOR
PORT GUARDS
LAME BOY
IMMIGRATION OFFICIAL
ISLAND RESIDENTS
TOOTHLESS RIDICULER
HUNGRY CHILDREN
TRUSTING PASSENGER

FEARFUL PASSENGER
ISLAND GOVERNOR
GOVERNOR'S WIFE
GOVERNOR'S ENTOURAGE
REPORTERS AND PHOTOGRAPHERS
LOAFER
DEAD CHILDREN
PROPHESYING DEAD CHILD
SENSITIVE DEAD CHILD
ARGUMENTATIVE DEAD CHILD
IMPATIENT DEAD CHILD
OBSERVANT DEAD CHILD
'MESSIAH'
DARING SOLDIER
CHILD WHO CRUMBLED TO DUST

Premiere	Habimah National Theatre, 1993
Director	Hanoch Levin
Costume and Stage Design	Roni Toren
Lighting Design	Ben-Tzion Munitz
Music Composition	Foldi Shatzman
Corpetitor/Piano	Haim Grinshpan
Synthesizer	Miki Naronsky
Choreography	The Cast
Soprano singers	Ema Zaslevsky, Shosh Lagil, Shimrit Carmi
Alto singers	Dafna Ben-David, Hani Shapira

Cast:

THE FATHER	Dudu Ben-Ze'ev
THE MOTHER	Geta Munte
THE CHILD	Dina Blei
PERSECUTED PEOPLE	Debby Giovanni,

Eliezer Apelboim, Alex Cohen, Ora Meirson, Assi Hanegbi, Yonat Matan, Yoram Meged, Yasmin Gera, Michael Coresh, Michal Rubin, Noa Goldberg, Sassi Sa'ad, T'khia Danon, Livia Hachman, Florence Bloch, Shmuel Volf.

BLEEDING MAN	Halifa Natur
SPECTATOR STARTLED BY DEATH	Ilan Hazan.
SOLDIERS	Asher Rinsky,

Dobrabov Melnik, Avital Livni, Yehonatan Enosh

COMMANDER	Haim Hova
WOMAN BORN FOR LOVE	Tali Atzmon/ Carmit Ben-Israel
WHIMPERING WOMAN	Amira Polan
HUNCHED SOLDIER	Emanuel Hanun
OPTIMISTIC NEIGHBOR	Lilian Barretto

SKIPPER	Yossef Shiloah
SAILORS	Yoram Meged,
	Melnik Dobrabov
SHIP PASSENGERS	Eliezer Apelboim,

Debby Giovanni, Noa Goldberg, Yasmin Gera, T'khia Danon, Shmuel Volf, Yonat Matan, Emuna Tzvi, Shimon Mimran

THOSE WHO REMAIN ON SHORE	Florence Bloch,

Michael Coresh, Yael Amitai

MAN JEALOUS OF THE LIVING	Michael Coresh
LOGICAL WOMAN	Yael Amitai
COMFORTING PASSENGER	T'khia Danon
IMPASSIONED PASSENGER	Shimon Mimran
DISAPPOINTED PASSENGER	Eliezer Apelboim
WISE SAILOR	Yoram Meged
PORT GUARD	Assi Hanegbi
LAME BOY	Ora Meirson
IMMIGRATION OFFICIAL	Alex Cohen
TOOTHLESS RIDICULER	Florence Bloch
TRUSTING PASSENGER	Eliezer Apelboim
FEARFUL PASSENGER	T'khia Danon
ISLAND GOVERNOR	Sassi Sa'ad
GOVERNOR'S WIFE	Livia Hachman
GOVERNOR'S ENTOURAGE	Yehonatan Enosh,
	Asher Rinsky
LOAFER	Assi Hanegbi
DEAD CHILDREN	Lilian Barretto, Debbi

Giovanni, Noa Goldberg, Yasmin Gera, Yonat Matan, Amira Polan, Emuna Tzvi, Michal Rubin, Shmuel Volf, Yael Amitai

'MESSIAH'	Shmuel Volf

Part One: The Father

THE CHILD's Room. Night

A

THE FATHER and THE MOTHER are leaning over THE CHILD, who is asleep in bed.

THE FATHER: When he falls asleep, the child becomes
    infinitely beloved to us.
    Quiet, his mouth open helplessly,
    reminding us: this is how he will look if he dies.
    A moment earlier we were still angry
    at his ruckus and chatter,
    a moment later almost weeping
    with longing for the sweet noise
    from the lips of the boy breathing steadily,
    lost in himself.

THE MOTHER: Let time stop now, at the height of happiness,
    for better than this, it will never be;
    let the three of us become a still life:
    'Parents watching a dreaming child.'

B

Strange noises can be heard from outside, increasing in volume. A man bursts into the room, followed by others, families, all alarmed, clearly being chased, murmuring under their breath. They dart back and forth. THE FATHER and THE MOTHER shelter THE CHILD who continues to sleep peacefully. An injured, BLEEDING MAN bursts in, stops, watches in astonishment as his blood trickles out. Everyone moves away from him, clusters together and watches him.

BLEEDING MAN: They made a hole in me… How could…
They punctured me… Like a box…
Look: I'm oozing onto my trousers… Leaking – drip-drop
– from the world…
Forty years of violin-playing are pooling
into a little puddle by my shoes…

(Falls to his knees, weakening.)

Where am I? – There, outside…
How could… I leaked, Mother…
I fell and I broke and I leaked…

(Falls on his face; the people gather around him.)

Ladies and gentlemen, either I was wrong about the violin,
or else the error is here…
Listen, music appreciation has suffered a serious blow here…
I shall protest…. I shall certainly protest…

SPECTATOR STARTLED BY DEATH: But to whom? To whom
shall you protest your death?!
That, after all, is the question of all questions: To whom
shall you protest?!

BLEEDING MAN: *(Growing weaker.)*
I shall protest… I tell you I shall protest…

(Falls silent and motionless. There is a moment of silence.)

SPECTATOR STARTLED BY DEATH: This is a great man, here.
That which is most important is behind him,
all that casts a shadow on our lives –
he is free of that, unburdened and happy,
a first-rate philosopher, he's solved the riddle,
he knows something even King Solomon
didn't in his lifetime.

C

Armed SOLDIERS enter and block the exits, followed by the COMMANDER and the WOMAN BORN FOR LOVE. She sees BLEEDING MAN and is horrified.

WOMAN BORN FOR LOVE: A dead man? A real one? Good
God, my first corpse!
So what they talk about – so much – does happen!

(Drawing near him, eyeing him.)

And thus he will lie, cold, austere,
the sac of his testicles shrivelled forever
like a dead mouse?
We have entered a terrible world!
How stifling it is here!

(Noticing the group of people huddled on the other side of the stage.)

Good God, it's the smell of their fear-juices being excreted!
How all their eyes are pinned on me!
I raise my finger – meaning!
I take a step – interpretation!
And what a tremor in the air, you are almost
tempted to call it the electricity
of savage love.

BLEEDING MAN: *(Suddenly coming to, with his last remaining
strength.)* Stop... Please...

WOMAN BORN FOR LOVE: Good God, still alive!
My first dying man!
Give him water! Will there be death rattles, too?

BLEEDING MAN: Stop, please... The blood... I'm a violinist...
Ask...

COMMANDER: A violinist? Well here's a shoe, made by a cobbler.

(He sticks the tip of his shoe in the BLEEDING MAN's wound. BLEEDING MAN dies.)

WOMAN BORN FOR LOVE: Good God, real military cruelty! D'you enjoy being outrageous?

COMMANDER: D'you enjoy being horrified?

D

COMMANDER: *(To group of PERSECUTED PEOPLE.)*
Take nothing, come with us.

WHIMPERING WOMAN: They'll kill us all!

THE MOTHER: We cannot go.

COMMANDER: Just like that!

THE MOTHER: Yes. Our child is sleeping.

(The COMMANDER, the WOMAN BORN FOR LOVE, and the SOLDIERS notice THE CHILD, asleep in his bed, for the first time. They stand mesmerized by the idyllic little tableau within the nightmarish scene.)

You mustn't wake him.

COMMANDER: Just like that!

THE MOTHER: Yes. He is a child. He must sleep at night. He dreams. They say children grow at night. At night their personality is formed, their soul opens up. My son, in particular, needs sleep, he was ill all winter, he is sensitive, the slightest breeze might impair his development. Such is my son.

(They all slowly gather around the bed as if witnessing a miracle. THE FATHER and THE MOTHER shelter him on either side.)

COMMANDER: A child. The essence of our lives. The pith.
Asleep, eh? Worlds collapsing around him and he
is submerged, enfolded in the bubble of his dreams,
breathing steadily, as though with his breath he bestows a
certain order and meaning upon the chaos of our lives.

(Putting his face close to THE CHILD's.)

Look, he breathes with such serenity, he has no
knowledge of my existence.
The wonder of sleep.
Hey, children, how is it that you sleep like that,
as if the world were a place for sleep?
After all, if we think things through,
you should be cowering, crawling on all fours,
howling with fear and beating your fists
on the walls –
that is how a wise man must live!

THE MOTHER: I beg you: Do not wake the child.
Above all – the child must not be woken.

THE COMMANDER: *(Mesmerized by the sleeping CHILD, repeats THE MOTHER's words.)*
Above all – the child must not be woken.
That is clear – the child, the child.
But how can he keep sleeping, if we must go?

WHIMPERING WOMAN: They'll kill us all!

THE COMMANDER: Shhh, softly, gently, we will peel the
sleep off him
as one peels the wrapping off a precious gift.
We will turn the world into a continuation of his dream.

THE COMMANDER: Hide your rifles behind your backs.
Remove your helmets.

(He and the SOLDIERS remove their weapons. They dress up with whatever they can find. An atmosphere of playfulness and mischief prevails. The tension dissipates. They cover BLEEDING MAN's body with a blanket and move the body aside. To THE MOTHER.)

Wake him, the clowns have come to town.

THE MOTHER: *(Waking THE CHILD gently.)*
My sweet child, wake up, look who's come to visit you.
A big circus, full of clowns and magicians, has arrived in town.
They have come to you, my little prince, to entertain you.

(THE CHILD tosses about gently in bed a little longer, stretching and curling up, then, opening his eyes, he looks for a moment at those present, squints at the light, smiles. At first he is slightly reserved, but he is slowly flooded with joy.)

THE CHILD: I love to wake up at night from a deep sleep
and discover that everything is in its place, that my father
and mother and the room, and all the books and toys –
everything is there, and life is ordinary, the smell of fish
cooking in the kitchen, the radio still playing, and the
simple serenity on my mother's face is stronger than the
tangle of dreams.

But more than anything, I love surprises. Oh, surprises –
the breath of life, the first snow on a tree in the window,
or a new toy on the chair, or, for example, like now,
nocturnal guests who fill every room of the house.

And who are these guests – who? Oh, the soul takes flight
with joy! Circus clowns and magicians come to our town,
bringing with them lights and colors, and the flavor of
marvelous adventures.

Oh, delight that brims over in me – I must roll around a little to calm myself.

(He jumps and rolls on the bed; slightly calmer.)

The world is a good and cheerful place, I recommend it to everyone, I recommend to those yet unborn to hurry up and be born: you won't regret it!

Father, Mother, thank you for the birth! Thank you, thank you!

(He jumps on his MOTHER and FATHER and kisses them.)

F

WOMAN BORN FOR LOVE: Good God, how I love a child! A man-puppy, with an empty testicle-sac, running after a ball in the sun! But what I love most about a seven-year-old child is arranging to meet in ten years' time.

(Caressing THE CHILD's head.)

Sweet, sweet. *Too* sweet, no? An oily sort of goodness that slides down your throat until it's disgusting, eh? Childhood. I know it well. Deep in our hearts we sense that this sweetness is not really life, that there's something else…

(Whispering in his ear.)

The nightmares – perhaps *they* were telling us the truth.

(Smiling, very close to his face.)

Remember me? You've surely dreamt of me before. The dreams were right. It was all in the dreams. And there is one dream from which one does not awaken.

What are you looking at? Haven't you ever seen teeth? Who is your father?

THE CHILD: Him.

WOMAN BORN FOR LOVE: Good God, that's a man to have conversations with about art until daybreak, or even a little longer!

(Wrapping her arms around THE FATHER's neck.)

Have we met? Not yet? First times are my favorite. Ah, if only I could live just the first times!

(Caressing his face.)

Undoubtedly you once looked like your son, and one day *he* will look like *you*: a bursting-full sac of testicles, a foolish grin spreading wider above a hanging pipe growing harder...

THE FATHER: *(Straining to laugh it off.)*

We give you a hard time, don't we?

WOMAN BORN FOR LOVE: Almost as hard as this?

(She quickly draws the pistol from the COMMANDER's holster, holding it between her legs with the barrel aimed at THE FATHER.)

Tonight we switch costumes: On your knees! Open your mouth!

THE MOTHER: No!!

(THE FATHER, trembling, kneels before WOMAN BORN FOR LOVE, putting his head close to her crotch.)

THE CHILD: Father! Father! That's my father! Forgive him! Forgive him! Forgive him, Miss! That's my father! You can't do that to him!

WOMAN BORN FOR LOVE: *(Putting the barrel of the pistol into THE FATHER's mouth.)*

Suck it nicely! The child! Above all – the child! We will make the child's heart rejoice!

(THE FATHER sucks on the barrel.)

Sing something nice about life for the boy! The sucking anthem!

THE FATHER: mm…mm…mm…!

WOMAN BORN FOR LOVE: All that's left of life for him is his final *mm*!

THE FATHER: mm…mm…mm…!

THE CHILD: Father! My big father! Get up, Father, get up!

WOMAN BORN FOR LOVE: *(To THE CHILD.)* You told us before that you love to wake up in the middle of the night and discover that everything is in its place. But there comes a night, where nothing is in its place anymore; the world that was solid, child, has melted, trickled through your fingers, and beneath your sturdy bed – the earth trembles.

And there is one dream from which one does not awaken.

THE MOTHER: *(Pushing THE CHILD.)*

Ask for mercy for your father! You're a child, she'll listen to *you*!

(The WOMAN BORN FOR LOVE thrusts the pistol deeper into THE FATHER's mouth.)

THE FATHER: mm… mm… mm…!

THE MOTHER: *(To THE CHILD, hysterically.)*

Ask for mercy! Sing her a song! Your voice has got to soften her heart!

THE CHILD: *(Straining to control his voice, singing.)*
The sweet days of summer are here,
Awash in joy we await,
The day is long, the night is far,

305

But already we start to fret:
Will summer be time enough? Will life be time enough?

WOMAN BORN FOR LOVE: *(Removes the pistol from THE*
FATHER's mouth, draws THE CHILD into her arms with
great emotion.) Ah, childhood, irresistible childhood! My
childhood, gone forever!

(With THE CHILD in her arms and THE FATHER rising to his feet
with a cry of relief, she takes a step in THE FATHER's direction and
shoots him in the face. He falls dead.)

Good God, it really happens!

COMMANDER: That was good. And it was right. After you
squeezed out all the terror from the man, you had to
restore his belief that he would live, and then, when he
believed – boom! In the face! All the filth! Hasn't yet sunk
in that he'll live – and then: he won't! How right! How
sly! Woman!

G

COMMANDER: *(Watching THE CHILD, as if for the first time.)*
But again, and always – the child!

(Approaching THE CHILD, gently.)

Ah, the child's ability to reach the most secret place inside
us. As if children were our thinnest, most painful inner
fibers. As if there, in childhood, was the purpose, and it
was lost.

(To THE MOTHER.) Go, you're both free now. You've bought
your lives at a high price.

(THE MOTHER falls on THE FATHER's body. A HUNCHED
SOLDIER approaches her. Quietly.)

HUNCHED SOLDIER: If your life and your child's life are dear to you – go!

THE MOTHER: I want to say goodbye to my husband!

HUNCHED SOLDIER: Don't indulge yourself. Goodbyes are a luxury from a bygone era.

THE MOTHER: What a world this is, where there's time to die, but to cry is a luxury?!

OPTIMISTIC NEIGHBOR: Oh, we'll cry! Happy days will come, and we'll cry – we'll cry our hearts out about everything!

(THE MOTHER takes THE CHILD by his hand, runs with him to the exit, returns, stands next to THE FATHER's body again, shuts her eyes, murmurs a requiem of sorts, as if trying to convince herself.)

THE MOTHER: There was a time when I didn't know this man who became my husband. When I was a little girl, did I know who he was? If someone had pointed him out to me on the street – 'that'll be your groom one day,' 'one day you will love him' – I would have laughed.

I will call out to that time: Come back! Come back! Come back, happy childhood in which I did not know of my future-love. Come back, childhood brimming with sunshine and joy and complete indifference to this man, the dead love of my life. Come, emptiness, fill up my heart!

H (REQUIEM)

WOMAN BORN FOR LOVE: *(Watching THE FATHER's body.)*

The second corpse you see is no longer your first corpse. Something virginal has been lost. The sweet horror has faded. And your heart twinges. And it's sad. Like the start of autumn. The first taste of a grape will never return. Farewell, youth: summer is over.

Part Two: The Mother

The pier, the ship. Evening.

A

Onboard the ship are those who were able to board. Beneath them, on the rickety pier, are those who were not. On the gangplank – SKIPPER, smoking a pipe. A sailor or two prepare the ship to sail. THE MOTHER and THE CHILD rush in, pushing their way to the gangplank. Among those left on the pier is MAN JEALOUS OF THE LIVING, pointing to those who were able to board.

MAN JEALOUS OF THE LIVING: Here is the pain: there will be some who live.

(Noticing THE MOTHER and THE CHILD.) And even a child: not only will he live, but a long time. *(Grabbing THE CHILD, feverishly prodding him.)* Let me give a farewell prod to flesh that will live after mine!

THE CHILD: *(Squirming out of his grip in terror.)* I don't know what you want!

MAN JEALOUS OF THE LIVING: I will die. Do you understand me? *(Demonstrating for THE CHILD as he speaks.)* I will lie down: like this. I will not be able to move, I will not feel. I will not be. But the main problem isn't that – it's not *my* life, I had a bad life anyway, I spit on my filthy life. The main problem is that *you* will live.

You understand me? You get the depth of the matter? I'll lie still: like this. And you'll dance with women: like this. And I'll lie with my mouth agape: like this. And you up above, you'll embrace them and laugh: like this. That's what makes the heart cry. And when you remember me, oh, then you'll laugh even harder: like this. And the women will laugh with you: like this. And me: like this. And they even harder: like this. And me: like this. And they're rolling on the floor laughing: like this. And me: like this. And like this. And like this. And like this. And they're peeing their pants laughing: like this. *(Cries out in desperation.)* God, they're peeing on the same earth I'm lying in with my mouth agape, decomposing! *(Weeping.)* I won't be able to bear it! I tell you: I will not accept it! Under no circumstance will I agree!

LOGICAL MAN: You think women are going to start peeing upward? It won't do you any good, it's physics.

MAN JEALOUS OF THE LIVING: *(Hysterically.)* I spit on physics! I will not accept it! *I'm* the child here! *(Points to THE CHILD.)* There: that's me. *(He grabs THE CHILD, tries to pull him against himself forcefully, as if to be absorbed into him. THE CHILD extricates himself with the help of THE MOTHER, who violently shoves MAN JEALOUS OF THE LIVING away. He continues to shout.)*

My father must come and make sure women pee upwards when I'm dead! *I'm* the child here! Me! *(Running out with a bitter cry.)* I'm the child! I'm the child! Me!

B

THE MOTHER and THE CHILD walk up the gangplank. THE SKIPPER blocks their path.

SKIPPER: The child.

MOTHER: Mine. You were paid for two.

SKIPPER: No one mentioned a child.

MOTHER: He's my son.

SKIPPER: This is a small, old ship, and the child poses special problems. I'm risking my life by sneaking over the border. We can expect to be searched on our way out of the port. He's liable to make noise, lose control. I'll be risking everything with the child.

THE MOTHER: He's a clever boy. He's in control of himself. He saw his father murdered yesterday right before his eyes, and he kept silent.

SKIPPER: He won't keep silent when danger touches his life.

THE MOTHER: Listen, this is not possible. I gave everything I had for this passage. You know that if we stay here – we will die. Put yourself in our place for a moment...

SKIPPER: Why should I? I'm not you, and you don't interest me.

THE MOTHER: You must have children of your own.

SKIPPER: Two. And there was another one who died.

THE MOTHER: The youngest one?

SKIPPER: She was three. I mourned her deeply at the time. I thought that life would not continue after her death. It did. I myself do not know how.

THE MOTHER: Think of her again and look at my child.

SKIPPER: I cannot think about my dead child at will, when it's convenient for someone else. There are times to remember her, there's the anniversary of her death, holidays and memorial days. Now I have work. I'm busy. But tell me, it's bothering me: Why should my daughter die, and your son live? And where were you when she died? I didn't hear you crying out or praying then. You were copulating with your husband and drinking wine while my child was dying in my arms!

THE MOTHER: Be kind. You're tormenting yourself and me for nothing.

SKIPPER: And why for nothing? Those who are alive should at least be tormented! Admit that you were copulating with your husband and drinking wine when my child was dying!

THE MOTHER: I didn't know her!

SKIPPER: She was copulating with her husband and drinking wine when my daughter was dying!

THE MOTHER: And if I was copulating? Your daughter is gone, nothing will help her, it's my son on the line now! Why should he have to pay for your daughter's death?

SKIPPER: Why should I be kind, tell me, give me a reason – a reason!

THE MOTHER: I have a child – and I want him to live!

SKIPPER: I'll tell you honestly: I loved my daughter, but I don't love your son. Simple as that.

THE MOTHER: If your daughter were alive, you would not understand my pain. And now that your daughter is dead – you want me to be in pain as well. Either way – you won't help.

SKIPPER: I won't. You were copulating while my daughter was dying.

THE MOTHER: Forgive me.

SKIPPER: I will not. She was three – the whole world to her parents; nothing to everyone else. And another thing. Tell me, I need to know: Could you without your son? Could you live without him?

THE MOTHER: *(Crying.)* I couldn't live for a moment without him!

SKIPPER: No, answer seriously, I'm asking, it's really bothering me: Could you live without him? Could you live without your son?

THE MOTHER: *(Shouting.)* No! No! I couldn't live without my son!

SKIPPER: But you could! You will carry on living even if he dies! You will breathe and eat and bathe and excrete! You will live without your son, you will! And that's the whole matter, that's what is so humiliating: that we can keep on living without that which is dearest of all.

C

SAILOR: Captain, we've finished loading the barrels of fuel.

SKIPPER: Set sail. *(He boards the ship. THE MOTHER, holding THE CHILD's hand, tries to force her way up the gangplank.)*

THE MOTHER: You can't stop us from boarding! Help me, people!

SKIPPER: *(Blocking her path, pinning her in his arms.)* The hysterics of women is not something we get worked up about. Our eyes have seen a great deal. *(THE MOTHER tries to free herself from his grip. He does not let go.)* And fiery, hah? So this is the body that copulated while my daughter was dying! Somewhere out there a child is dying – copulate with me!

THE CHILD: *(Beating SKIPPER with his fists.)* Help! My mother is being beaten!

SKIPPER: Hugged! She's only being hugged, the beauty! *(To THE MOTHER, overcome with desire, in her ear.)* I'll take him, you just give me a little something in return.

THE MOTHER: First you tormented us, now you're joking around!

SKIPPER: I've been at sea for two months, haven't touched a woman.

THE MOTHER: My husband, whom I loved, was murdered only yesterday.

SKIPPER: Yesterday was yesterday.

THE MOTHER: Here, on my dress, a blood stain, still wet.

SKIPPER: We'll take the dress off.

THE MOTHER: And you don't care, as you enter me, who I will see with my eyes closed?

SKIPPER: You'll see with your eyes closed whatever you see, I'll see with my eyes open what I see. Put yourself in my shoes. I'm old, I have no more opportunities. Frigid whores here and there. You're beautiful. The tears, the anger – they ignite your body. You are what I need. Sleep with me and I'll take the child. There are more loathsome deals.

(THE MOTHER looks at him for a moment as if weighing his offer, looks at THE CHILD, then takes THE CHILD's hand and walks down the gangplank with him.)

D

THE MOTHER: *(To THE CHILD.)* Come, let us sit.

THE CHILD: What will we do now?

THE MOTHER: Nothing. Just sit.

SKIPPER: *(To the SAILORS.)* Start the engines!

(THE MOTHER and THE CHILD sit on the dock facing the ship, watching the final preparations.)

THE MOTHER: There is great relief when you stop begging for your life, when you give up the struggle. Have you seen a beggar sleeping on the sidewalk, with a tin cup at his head? Drop a coin in, or don't, he lies there as if the whole business has nothing to do with him. That is life!

THE CHILD: But if no one drops anything in, the hunger will eventually rouse him to struggle.

THE MOTHER: And that is precisely the matter: struggle for what? For the life of a beggar? It's not worth his trouble.

THE CHILD: Will we die?

(Silence. He begins to whimper.)

THE MOTHER: That's the trouble, that you're a child, and you haven't yet exhausted your capacity for self-humiliation. How much more wallowing you will do, until you are finally crushed!

THE CHILD: *(Crying louder.)* I'm frightened!

THE MOTHER: *(Falling on him, cuddling him.)* Never, ever will I leave you! We will never part! You know that, don't you? *(THE CHILD nods as he cries.)* And if there comes a day when I must tell you to go, you will know that I do not truly mean it, and you will not go. This will be our secret, just between you and me: that never, under any circumstance, shall we part. Do you agree?

(THE CHILD nods as he cries.)

SKIPPER: *(To SAILORS.)* Anchors aweigh!

THE CHILD: *(Still crying.)* But I'm frightened! I'm not a beggar, I still have a lot to lose! I want to board the ship with everyone!

314

SKIPPER: *(To SAILORS.)* Put out the lights, we must slip through the ships of the coastal patrol!

THE CHILD: *(Running to the end of the pier, starts singing at the ship.)*
The sweet days of summer are here,
Awash in joy we await...

SKIPPER: No, boy. Save yourself that humiliation. The world doesn't work that way, with songs. Besides, there's something off-key about your singing, you're trying too hard to win my heart over, you're too eager to live – there's no innocence, no naiveté. It's obvious you've put on this performance before. *(To SAILORS.)* Raise the gangplank – now!

(The SAILORS begin raising the gangplank. MAN JEALOUS OF THE LIVING bursts onto the pier, exuberant.)

MAN JEALOUS OF THE LIVING: So what, the child, too? Like this?! Not just me, him too: like this?! *(Prodding THE CHILD's face.)* Look: right here there'll be a bare skull laughing to the skies! *(To THE MOTHER.)* Did you love his smile? Well you'll have two rows of smiling teeth!

(THE MOTHER gets up suddenly and paces the pier restlessly.)

SKIPPER: Anchors aweigh! Set sail!

MAN JEALOUS OF THE LIVING: *(Going wild with joy.)* And I'll lie: like this. And he will too: like this. And together: like this. And all of us: like this. Like this. Like this.

E

THE MOTHER: *(To THE CHILD.)* And why do you keep clinging to me? Go sit down! You should know that I loved your father more than I loved you. He was a choice of love, but who chose you?

315

You caused me pain at your birth, and you continue to cause me pain and to make demands of me that I cannot live up to!

So what if you're a child?! So what if you came from my belly?! Who cares, if you really think about it, whether you die? Who cares?! *(Calling to the SKIPPER.)* Skipper, I'm ready!

SKIPPER: The gangplank has been raised. Why didn't you speak up a moment ago? What makes you so sure I'll always want you? Right now I can't be bothered.

THE MOTHER: What do you mean, you can't be bothered? I'm yours! Like you said: we'll take the dress off!

SKIPPER: You forget that I'm old, that I'm easy to fire up, but also easy to extinguish.

THE MOTHER: *(Tearing her dress open at the breast.)* Here are my breasts! Look at them!

SKIPPER: Breasts are not everything.

THE MOTHER: When you touched them, you thought differently.

SKIPPER: When I touched them. Now I'm not touching. *(Shining the flashlight on her.)* What's happening to me, that nothing can rattle me anymore? I'm worried. Is it old age? The beginning of death?

(THE MOTHER kneels, sobbing, on the pier. His flashlight roams over her body.)

You understand your breasts are not trivial, don't you?

THE MOTHER: Yes.

SKIPPER: We lust for a brief moment. When it's over, we don't understand what or why we were lusting after. Until the next moment of lusting.

THE MOTHER: Yes.

SKIPPER: And the gap between the moments is longer than the sum of all the moments.

THE MOTHER: Yes.

SKIPPER: And if we give you, women, something in return for the moments of lusting, that is an act of kindness.

THE MOTHER: Yes.

SKIPPER: A coin for a beggar.

THE MOTHER: Yes.

SKIPPER: Alms for your breasts, like I would toss at a humpback for his deformity.

THE MOTHER: Yes.

SKIPPER: Know your place. It's important. Sway those humps of yours, so they arouse my pity.

THE MOTHER: Yes. *(Sways her breasts.)*

SKIPPER: *(To SAILORS.)* Lower the gangplank! A day of kindness.

(THE MOTHER abruptly turns to MAN JEALOUS OF THE LIVING, who, with a twisted face, starts whistling 'nonchalantly' and exits.)

F

The SAILORS lower the gangplank, allow THE MOTHER and THE CHILD to board, then raise it back up. The SKIPPER addresses one of the SAILORS.

SKIPPER: Begin sailing down-river with the lights off. We have at least an hour of quiet before we get to the border. I'll be in my cabin, showing it to the lady. *(He puts his hand on THE MOTHER's shoulder.)* Come.

THE CHILD: Mother?

(THE MOTHER stops, a twisted smile on her lips. THE CHILD's whole body begins to tremble. THE MOTHER exits, with the SKIPPER's arm around her. COMFORTING PASSENGER wraps a blanket around the trembling CHILD as he leans on the railing, and strokes his head.)

COMFORTING PASSENGER: Hush, child. Your mother is immersed in the exhausting labor of saving your life. The day will come when you'll understand.

THE CHILD: I already do. Everything has appeared in my dreams. My mother's breasts are taken from me. The first woman in my life turns her back on me. A warm and benevolent smile turns into a mocking wink. It was all in my dreams. Over her shoulder she gives me a smile of betrayal and mockery so painfully beautiful, then disappears. Never to return.

G (REQUIEM)

THE MOTHER with the SKIPPER in his cabin, only her voice can be heard. The COMFORTING PASSENGER tries to put THE CHILD to sleep, by singing to him.

COMFORTING PASSENGER: *The sweet days of summer are here... Awash in joy we await...*

THE MOTHER: Gently... Gently... Gently...

(THE CHILD tilts his head towards THE MOTHER's voice, but COMFORTING PASSENGER tries to divert his attention.)

COMFORTING PASSENGER: There are moments when the heart asks questions, but the mouth – better it should sing.

Child, try to think about the fact that your life and your mother's life have been saved. Think about the horizon that awaits you, think about the sea, did you know we're about to sail on the ocean?

(Little by little, THE CHILD stops trembling and he falls asleep in her arms.)

That's it, he's fallen asleep. Taken a break from his little tragedy, a breath of air before the next blow.

The magic of sleep: a person sleeping is a child, and a child sleeping is the essence of childhood. All the world's beauty, all its emotions, all its flavor and aroma, are distilled into a sleeping child.

Oh, children, you were born to break our hearts. You little people, funny gnomes in peculiar costumes, starry-eyed, innocent, askers of mad questions, plate-breakers, pants-wetters, monkeys that jump and run, get up and fall, candy-stealers with no limits or boundaries – you were born to strum our most secret strings, you were born to be irresistible to us, you were born simply to break our hearts.

Part Three: The Child

The ship, the island. Dawn.

A

The ship is approaching the shores of an island. After an arduous journey, it now looks like a ghost ship. The PASSENGERS on deck, huddled in their coats, look shattered and freezing cold. There is a driving rain and winds. Suddenly, one of the PASSENGERS calls out excitedly.

IMPASSIONED PASSENGER: I see land!

> *(The PASSENGERS crowd by the railing to see.)*

DISAPPOINTED PASSENGER: Barren, gray rock – that's all that's visible through the fog.

IMPASSIONED PASSENGER: All my life I never knew how much I love barren rocks! Rock! To set foot on a solid piece of rock – I'll never ask for anything more in my life!

WISE SAILOR: When you stand firm on the rock, you'll start wanting a ray of sunlight, too. We all know what human beings are like.

SKIPPER: Toss the rope to the pier!

B

On what appears to be the deserted pier, the PORT GUARDS come into sight, huddled in their coats, holding rifles. The SKIPPER calls to them.

SKIPPER: Where are the immigration and customs officials? I have exhausted, frozen people here, they have to get to shore at once!

GUARD: You'll have to wait. The port official arrives at eight and starts seeing people at quarter past eight.

IMPASSIONED PASSENGER: Oh, quarter past eight! Oh, the grand and splendid expectations, the fateful expectations of our lives: the expectation that a clerk will come, the expectation that a clerk will not fall ill, the expectation that a clerk's digestive system was in order this morning, the expectation of the expression that surfaces on a clerk's face when he sits at his desk, the expectation that a stamp in a clerk's hand will be brandished, that a stamp in a clerk's hand will not tarry in mid-air, the expectation that a stamp in a clerk's hand will emboss the paper, that the paper will not be lost, that the paper will not fly off in a breeze, that there will be no breeze, the expectation that the paper will be delivered from the sure hand of the clerk to your own trembling hand. Were I asked this morning what human hope looks like, I would say: a clerk at quarter past eight!

C

Through the fog enshrouding the island, appears a boy of about seventeen, dressed in tatters, walking with a limp, a broken umbrella in his hand to shelter himself from the rain, unsuccessfully.

IMPASSIONED PASSENGER: Hey, boy, how's life on the island?

LAME BOY: You think if you make an effort to ask in a natural tone, 'How's life on the island?' it'll bring your getting off the ship any closer to reality?

I come to the shore every morning to watch refugee ships arrive. It's always the same story: they get sent back where they came from.

IMPASSIONED PASSENGER: Us, they'll let in. We have permits.

LAME BOY: Everyone says that.

IMPASSIONED PASSENGER: And why do *you* come here?! To hasten our despair?!

LAME BOY: I'm a poet. I write about you people who emerge from the fog and disappear back into it. I lament your fate and I sketch it. As your faces draw near, they tell the story of your disillusionment; but all of human failure is imprinted upon the backs of your necks as they recede into the distance.

I will be the poet of the back of the human neck; that narrow slope, where the hair dwindles into a wisp, until it ends, and the creased skin begins, sweating under a filthy collar – there is the truth about man.

IMPASSIONED PASSENGER: *(Fingering the back of his neck in bewilderment. Suddenly.)*
The truth of the lame!

LAME BOY: I've seen many people, and I have many poems.

D

GUARD: The immigration official has arrived!

(IMMIGRATION OFFICIAL enters, and boards the ship at a leisurely pace. The PASSENGERS thrust their passports at him.)

IMMIGRATION OFFICIAL: Refugees again. Your permits are invalid. You cannot come ashore.

IMPASSIONED PASSENGER: The travel agent we—

IMMIGRATION OFFICIAL: The travel agent cheated you. They cheat you all, that's your lot today. You're the stuff cheating is made of.

(Sounds of protest and wailing are heard from the PASSENGERS.)

Quiet! What are you shouting for?! What are you all wailing about?! Always wailing, always hands outstretched! God, let there be a single day with no outstretched hands! One ordinary day with people keeping their hands at their sides, in a natural position! I see a hand stretched out at me with papers, I immediately feel tired and think about my pajamas!

And everyone comes *here*! To me! Everyone wants to get into the one place they can't! Forty years, not even a bird came to shit here, and now, when they're killing them – they turn up. You slit someone's throat – suddenly he prefers leprosy. Well of course!

Oh God, twenty past eight in the morning, and already I want my bed!

IMPASSIONED PASSENGER: *(Grabs hold of the IMMIGRATION OFFICIAL's hand, quietly.)* We'll pay to get off this boat.

IMMIGRATION OFFICIAL: *(Quietly.)* There are people paying more so you won't. *(Loudly.)* Leave the port! You were here – now you're gone! Out with you! God have mercy! *(Disembarks.)*

E

THE MOTHER: *(To SKIPPER.)* You're not taking us back! You know that in the place we came from, they'll kill us all!

SKIPPER: *(Gazing at length at THE MOTHER and the PASSENGERS, and they at him.)* It's not good for a person to have a face, it's not good to meet someone's eyes for

323

more than an instant. Suddenly you know him, dammit, suddenly a person is standing in front of you.

No, no I won't take you back, I've seen your faces. A pity. Human beings. *(To IMMIGRATION OFFICIAL.)* Tell the Governor of the island: I will not set sail until the passengers have disembarked.

F

PASSENGERS: *(Pointing at themselves and shouting hopefully at the shore.)* Look at us: faces! Faces! Human beings! Help us reach the shore!

(Little by little, the ISLAND RESIDENTS gather on the shore – men, women and children, all downtrodden, worn down, deformed, poor and idle. The ship's PASSENGERS behold a nightmarish scene no better than their own. Among those gathered is TOOTHLESS RIDICULER with his famished children.)

TOOTHLESS RIDICULER: Times are good: the paupers rattle their tin cups at the beggars. The empty pockets ask the empty bellies to dance. Why did you come here?

TRUSTING PASSENGER: Where else would we go?

(All at once TOOTHLESS RIDICULER's children rush forward, reaching out from the edge of the pier to the ship's PASSENGERS hoping they will toss something to them. The TOOTHLESS RIDICULER scoffs.)

TOOTHLESS RIDICULER: This is our life.

TRUSTING PASSENGER: It's better than death.

TOOTHLESS RIDICULER: It's a prolonged dying.

TRUSTING PASSENGER: At least you're breathing.

TOOTHLESS RIDICULER: In order to moan with hunger.

TRUSTING PASSENGER: *(Pointing to the throat of THE CHILD, on deck.)* This throat will be slit.

TOOTHLESS RIDICULER: Only yesterday it was swallowing cakes.

TRUSTING PASSENGER: And a week from now it will crumble to dust.

TOOTHLESS RIDICULER: It's either sooner or later.

(One of the children on the island throws a stone at the ship. It hits the TRUSTING PASSENGER in the face. He covers his face with his hands, teeters for a moment, wipes the blood off. The TOOTHLESS RIDICULER opens his mouth, either in mockery or in a silent scream, then turns to leave with his children. The TRUSTING PASSENGER kneels and calls out to him.)

TRUSTING PASSENGER: Forgive us. *(The TOOTHLESS RIDICULER stops.)* For the cakes. Forgive us. If we'd only recalled then, that one day we would die…!

TOOTHLESS RIDICULER: *(With a mocking expression that never leaves his face. Kneeling.)You* forgive *us.* We will keep on breathing when you die. Forgive us. *(He exits with his children.)*

G

LAME BOY sees ISLAND GOVERNOR approaching from a distance.

LAME BOY: *(To PASSENGERS.)* Look, the island governor is coming to the port with his wife and an entourage of foreign reporters and photographers, to christen a new warship. Call out to him! It's an opportunity! The island governor is not a man to snub the foreign press!

(Enter ISLAND GOVERNOR, GOVERNOR'S WIFE, GOVERNOR'S ENTOURAGE, JOURNALISTS and PHOTOGRAPHERS, all of whom pass by the pier on their way.)

IMPASSIONED PASSENGER: Governor, Sir, we are refugees seeking solid ground to set foot on!

(The Governor stops briefly, tries to continue on his way, but in the presence of the JOURNALISTS and PHOTOGRAPHERS, who show interest in the ship and its PASSENGERS, he stops again.)

Not to live, Governor, just not to die – not to die!

Off to the side, on the edge of the island, in a small camp, crowded, crammed in, we won't take up any space, a crust of bread, not even anything to spread on it! Nothing to spread, Governor, sir!

GOVERNOR: *(To JOURNALISTS.)* I would like to be a poor shepherd. Then I would say 'Yes' to the whole world – what would it cost me to be humane? I would be in favor of giving out everything to everyone – nothing would be at my expense. But I say 'No.' I am not a shepherd – I am the island governor. Would someone like to swap places with me?

FEARFUL PASSENGER: How can I get across to you, Governor, sir, my fear of dying?! How to get across, with which thread, from one person to another, the fear of dying?!

ISLAND GOVERNOR: Yes, the fear of dying. The fear. Who doesn't know the fear of dying? We will pray for you.

IMPASSIONED PASSENGER: With nothing to spread, Governor, sir!

ISLAND GOVERNOR: We will pray for you. We will pray for all those who dwell on this earth, who, as they tumble down into the pit, are already willing to give up something to spread. *(Suddenly bursting into tears.)* How humiliating to be human! *(To PHOTOGRAPHERS.)* Take your pictures, take them, show from up close my helpless, babyish sobbing. In fact, let the entire enlightened world see our sole natural resource: the tear! *(He turns to leave, followed by the Entourage.)*

TRUSTING PASSENGER: *(Suddenly hoisting THE CHILD up in his arms, calling out.)* Governor's wife, ma'am! A child!

(Everyone stops again. The GOVERNOR'S WIFE looks at her husband, who reconsiders briefly, glances at the JOURNALISTS and PHOTOGRAPHERS, wiping away his tear.)

ISLAND GOVERNOR: Yes, a child. And although we have seen children before, still, each child, they say, reinvents childhood. Bring the child down! We will take him!

(GOVERNOR'S WIFE extends her hands.)

H

THE MOTHER: Alone? I'm his mother.

ISLAND GOVERNOR: There are a lot of orphans here.

TRUSTING PASSENGER: Let her disembark with her child. One woman with one child.

(The GOVERNOR'S WIFE lowers her hands, angry.)

ISLAND GOVERNOR: No. The boy wasn't included to begin with. But we did you a favor, and you already want more. That creates a precedent. And what will we say on Judgment Day, to those who we turned away empty handed and died? After all, there must be consistency, especially where conscience is concerned, otherwise you get into trouble.

The child alone – or no one.

THE MOTHER: *(In a silent plea to the SKIPPER and the PASSENGERS. They all stand silent, no one can help. She embraces THE CHILD.)*

My son, my beloved child, you've had a lucky break and the Island Governor is a big enough murderer that his reputation needs to be repaired in the international press by being photographed with a rescued child in his arms.

A crack has emerged in the wall, and only you will escape through it.

(The SAILORS lower the gangplank to the pier. THE CHILD whispers to THE MOTHER.)

THE CHILD: Mother, I know you don't really mean it. I remember what you said before we sailed: 'I will never part from you. Never.'

THE MOTHER: My son, forget now what I told you...

THE CHILD: Mother, you said that then, too – that even if you were forced to, I would know you didn't really mean it, and that we would never part...

THE MOTHER: My child, listen to me, parting is difficult for you, as it is for me, but we cannot be together any longer.

THE CHILD: 'And this will be our secret,' that is what you said...

THE MOTHER: But I will return one day, you'll see...

THE CHILD: That 'never, under any circumstance, shall we separate.'

THE MOTHER: *(Shaking him.)* Something has changed! Listen to me! There's no time! I'm your mother, I gave you life, but our world is built such that life is there now, with that man. And with me—only death!

THE CHILD: I understand, Mother, I understand. We will really part. *(Whispering.)* But really, really, we won't.

THE MOTHER: *(Striking him.)* Forget! Forget it all! Forget what I said! Really, really, really, we must part! Now forget everything and go, and do not come back!

(She tries to push him toward the gangplank. He struggles with her.)

THE CHILD: Forget? What? Everything? Or only that? And how will I know what to forget and what not to? And when are you really my mother—then or now? Who is who? Who gives life? Who kills? Who laughs with me? Who *at* me? All the faces melt and drip away like in a dream – where is the face of daylight?

Teach me about the face! I am a child! You taught me to read and write, now give me the alphabet of the face!

|

THE MOTHER: *(Shouting hysterically.)* Take him from me! For God's sake, tear my child away from me!

(The SAILORS grab THE CHILD, hand him down, into the arms of the GOVERNOR'S WIFE. The Photographers take pictures. THE CHILD does not allow for an idyllic photograph – he squirms, kicks and bites.)

THE CHILD: Mother! I want my mother!

(The GOVERNOR'S WIFE tries to calm him, but after a while, when this proves impossible, she lets go of him, displeased. THE CHILD tries to run back to the gangplank. The Governor's guards hold him back, but he keeps squirming and screaming.)

Mother! I want my mother!

GOVERNOR: Let him board. It's a sad story. Tragedies, in our times, ladies and gentlemen, occur not in books, and not in faraway lands; day by day, on the threshold of our homes, beside the morning paper and the milk bottle, the corpses, too, are placed. We shall pray for them.

IMPASSIONED PASSENGER: *(Quietly, to the PASSENGERS.)* Milk for his coffee, he's clearly not lacking.

(THE CHILD runs up onto the ship, clings to THE MOTHER. The Governor and his Entourage exit. THE MOTHER shouts in desperation to the SKIPPER.)

THE MOTHER: Do something! You promised! 'I saw your faces,' you said!

SKIPPER: I'm done with faces.

(The SAILORS raise the gangplank. THE MOTHER takes THE CHILD by his hand, in appeasement and resignation.)

THE MOTHER: My child, with your own two hands you have sealed your fate. You will die. You simply got confused, child that you are. You were born into a world designed to drive you mad. You were mistaken. All your reasoning was mistaken.

(To the PASSENGERS.) But look how beautiful my son's mistake was. It will lead to his death, the mistake, and yet: how right it is, what beauty it holds! What mother's heart would not swell with pride: this is my child. And he is going to die with me.

J (REQUIEM)

LAME BOY rips his notebook of poems and throws the scraps of paper into the sea.

LOAFER: You wrote your poems to impress people, and now you're trying to impress by ripping them up. It's too dramatic, unnecessary, superfluous – you're assigning them more importance than they have. You could have just as easily published them in a book, even gained a bit of a reputation: the world would have looked the same. You'll learn one day to despair more quietly, more modestly, in silence. As one should.

Part Four: The Messiah

Field of graves. Twilight.

A

DEAD CHILDREN, shrouded in tatters, lie in a heap waiting, listening for the voice of redemption to come from above.

DEAD CHILDREN: We are the quietest children in the world, the dead children.

In the midst of playing in the yard, at the height of the greatest joy and elation, we were taken and thrown into a pit.

They say it's summer now, they say the waves on the beach are still spraying foam, the candy stores are open, all the nectar of the beloved world is awaiting only us – and we are not there!

When will we rise? When will we step into the light? How much longer will we listen to other children rejoicing outside without us?

PROPHESYING DEAD CHILD: I saw an angel, he was sailing in sunshine, he slowly dived as in a sea of honey, and came down and whispered to me: 'Rest a while longer, until we fill the quota of your friends and siblings who are destined to die as you did.'

DEAD CHILDREN: For so many years we have been hearing this promise: dead children join us every day, blood and screaming fill the land – tell us once and for all: what is the quota?

PROPHESYING DEAD CHILD: That is what I asked him: 'What is the quota?' And he understood me and smiled and whispered: 'Oh, little lambs, quiet screechers. Oh, my tender, impatient dead ones: Do you not see? The cup nearly runneth over, and the hour is drawing nigh: one more child, and the quota shall be filled.'

(Great excitement ripples through the pile of children. They begin to twitch and fidget like impatient children under their covers.)

DEAD CHILDREN: One more dead child! One more! Soon we will awaken, the light of resurrection shall shine upon us, we shall rise, brush our teeth, wash our faces – and to the sun! The sea! To splash water and to laugh about all the time we spent waiting in darkness!

SENSITIVE DEAD CHILD: In the end of days the worst newspaper headline will be: 'Boy Loses Kite and Cries.'

ARGUMENTATIVE DEAD CHILD: No, that's too terrible. At most: 'Boy Loses Kite and Finds it Immediately.'

B

IMPATIENT DEAD CHILD: But when will another child die already? As the moment gets closer – our patience runs out.

How urgent the death of the last child suddenly becomes!

OBSERVANT DEAD CHILD: He's coming! He's coming! I see him! Here comes the last dead child!

(The pile of children is gripped with renewed tension. From outside comes a tearful wail. DEAD CHILDREN tremble with joy.)

DEAD CHILDREN: Oh, how happy is he who has died a moment before the resurrection of the dead! He missed nothing! He didn't have time to lie in a grave and decompose, maybe he missed an afternoon snack, maybe a sweet, and up he is again, as if from a short nap with all of life stretching out ahead of him!

C

THE MOTHER enters, carrying the dead child in her arms. She approaches the pile.

THE MOTHER: Hello, dead children. I have brought my son. He is dead. He will lie with you.

DEAD CHILDREN: You have brought him to the right place. Put him down with us.

THE MOTHER: That's easy to say. But from the moment I put him down, I will never pick him up again, I will not smell him, I will not feel him, I will no longer have my child.

DEAD CHILDREN: We are familiar with this moment.

THE MOTHER: I am trying to postpone it.

DEAD CHILDREN: Until when?

THE MOTHER: That's the thing: I'm so used to carrying him in my arms. He is my son, you understand? He is my child.

DEAD CHILDREN: And now he is dead.

THE MOTHER: That's the trouble.

DEAD CHILDREN: And his flesh will rot in short order.

THE MOTHER: Exactly. We are not designed to contain the dead among us.

IMPATIENT DEAD CHILD: Say goodbye to him and lay him down with us.

THE MOTHER: *(Drawing back from the pile.)* No, one more moment. Another second. Here he is in my hands. He is mine. As if nothing has happened and nothing will – just me and him. Him and me. Together. And another second. And another. And another hug. And another look. And another. *(Walking away and stumbling.)* Ah, time did not stop then and it will not stop now! *(Drawing near the pile.)* Enough, my son. We shall part. One postpones and postpones–but the moment does arrive. So brief was our encounter in the world. And the moment has arrived.

THE CHILD: No, Mother. Wait. Do not put me down. Wait.

THE MOTHER: Why? Your life is over.

THE CHILD: But wait, Mother. Not with such ease. Not yet.

THE MOTHER: You're hurting me.

THE CHILD: Not yet, Mother.

THE MOTHER: As if you still pin hopes on me.

THE CHILD: Yes, Mother. I will tell you a secret: in your arms, I am full of hope.

THE MOTHER: *(Turning to the children, laughing through her weeping.)* Did you hear the gullible little one? He still pins hopes on me! He thinks death is a bad case of the flu – a week or two and you're back on your feet! My child, understand, this is really the end. You will not get up again. Lie down, give up.

THE CHILD: I will not give up. You are my mother. By giving birth to me you gave me the great promise of life. And I trust you.

THE MOTHER: *(Laughing in despair.)* He still trusts me! He trusts! He's gone utterly mad, my dead child. All the dead are crazy, lying in the earth and trusting *us*!

THE CHILD: Yes, Mother, we trust.

THE MOTHER: How cruel you are. I'm weighed down, and you are adding to my burden.

THE CHILD: What's left for me? To be a burden! I'll pull you down with me!

(A bitter groan escapes THE MOTHER's lips. THE CHILD cries out.)

I will not let go of you, Mother! Like a choker around your neck, my rotting body will hang on you, an adornment for the rest of your days. I have found my place! I have learned my lesson in life!

THE MOTHER: I will listen to you no longer. I will place you on the ground and leave.

THE CHILD: I do not believe you.

THE MOTHER: *(Bending down to place him on the pile.)* There.

THE CHILD: You wouldn't dare.

(THE MOTHER straightens up with THE CHILD in her arms and kisses him with a newfound intensity.)

I told you. She is my mother. She's making idle threats: she won't leave me, she's my mother, she won't let go until I awaken and rise. She is my mother. My mother…

(All at once THE MOTHER bends down and places him on the pile of DEAD CHILDREN.)

THE MOTHER: I've let go.

(Pause.)

THE CHILD: Mother?

THE MOTHER: *(Moving away from him and closing her eyes.)* There was a time when I didn't know this child, my son. When I was engaged – did I know who he was?

THE CHILD: *(His voice weakening.)* Mother?

THE MOTHER: *(Taking another step away.)* He didn't exist. Wonderful days. The world could have been awash in murder for all I cared – I had no child to cry over; and the face that would one day die on me–had not yet been formed.

THE CHILD: *(His voice weakening further.)* Mother?

THE MOTHER: *(Drawing even further away.)* I will call to that time: Come back, come back! Come back, great happiness, empty womb, unborn child!

THE CHILD: *(Almost inaudibly.)* Mother?

THE MOTHER: Most precious treasure, nothingness – come fill me up!

(Silence. Suddenly, with a burst of joy.) He's given up, at last. My son gave up on life. From now on he will rest, crumble, he is not the first dead child in the world, and I am not the only bereaved mother, there are many, so many partners to warm the heart. What's all the fuss about, the flailing, the shrieks, the big commotion… It will all die down, settle. My son has given up. And I, too, will rest at last.

(She walks away from the pile of children, stops suddenly, from her throat erupts what might be her voice or might be THE CHILD's, the smile of sweet memories on her face:.)

'Yes, Mother, I will tell you a secret: in your arms, I am full of hope…'

(A sob erupts from her throat when she realizes that she will never be at rest. Then she smiles again, and says, in what might be her voice or might be THE CHILD's.)

'I told you, she is my mother. She's making idle threats: she won't leave me…'

(With complete resignation:.) You won't let me rest, will you? You haven't died, you haven't given up, you will not let go, you sassy boy.

(She laughs, and carries on, as if chatting with a neighbor.)

The little ones are so stubborn, these days! They don't give an inch! Mine, when I tell him in winter to put on an extra layer – he refuses. Goes out barefoot to the yard. And in summer – the opposite: long pants and wool socks. And he's never willing to get into bed, not to mention brush his teeth. How stubborn are these little scoundrels of ours!

(She kneels to the ground, wordlessly.)

D

ARGUMENTATIVE DEAD CHILD: He's fallen asleep. His slumber will last only a moment. His grandchildren will live to hear the story of his death from his own mouth, beginning with the words: 'Once upon a time…'

DEAD CHILDREN: Once upon a time there was death. Messiah – the quota is full.

OBSERVANT DEAD CHILD: Quiet, he's on the island, I can already see him! The Messiah is coming!

(Enter the 'MESSIAH,' with a beard and overcoat, carrying two large suitcases. His appearance is reminiscent of a peddler. He looks as if he's being chased, runs in a panic towards the pile of children without noticing them, bumps into the pile, trips and falls onto the children, sees the horror, draws back in terror, incredulous. The DEAD CHILDREN tremble with anticipation, crying out prayers to him as if he were their father.)

DEAD CHILDREN: You came, Messiah! You came! Say that you've come!

(The 'MESSIAH' tries to run away. He finds himself surrounded, with no way out. He goes back to the pile and watches it for a moment.)

The miracle! The miracle! Resurrect us!

(The 'MESSIAH' tries to hide his suitcases, but they are too large, he does not know what to do with them. He starts opening one suitcase.)

OBSERVANT DEAD CHILD: Now he's going to take out his miracle salve, to heal the wounds of our flesh!

(The 'MESSIAH' opens the suitcase completely, and removes from it several watches.)

IMPATIENT DEAD CHILD: So long have we waited for you, Messiah, sir. So shattered are we by our yearning, that we cannot jest now. Please, go to work, resurrect us.

(The 'MESSIAH' hides the watches under the children's bodies.)

ARGUMENTATIVE DEAD CHILD: The second one! The second suitcase! That is where the miracle salve is!

(The 'MESSIAH' opens the second suitcase, which is also filled with watches.)

IMPATIENT DEAD CHILD: Messiah, sir, you are being so playful because you are alive, you have it good, you have not suffered in a grave for so many days, waiting for resurrection.

And you are incapable of understanding the heart of a child: we want to get up and play in the yard. The time will come when we joke around with you as, together, we bring up memories on the anniversary of the resurrection. Now rise and perform the deed! Raise us up!

(The 'MESSIAH' hides the watches from the second suitcase under the bodies.)

ARGUMENTATIVE DEAD CHILD: Still playing around.

SENSITIVE DEAD CHILD: And what do we do with Swiss watches in the grave?

(There is a silence of disappointment among the children.)

PROPHESYING DEAD CHILD: But you impatient fools, don't you get it? Messiah is burying time! Time is dead – eternity is here, like a big bear on one foot, eternity stands before us!

And Messiah is really in no hurry – why should he be? After all, eternity is dragging behind him on a chain. Messiah is playing around a little. Messiah has come to us with the biggest surprise of all, and now he wants to delight with us in the sweet anticipation of the final moments!

DEAD CHILDREN: *(Trying to take heart.)* Yes, we will delight a while longer! It is pleasant to die when the Messiah is around the corner!

E

Enter SOLDIERS, who surround the place from all sides, followed by the COMMANDER, and the WOMAN BORN FOR LOVE. At the sight of them, the 'MESSIAH' is horrified, he huddles into himself, and lies silently in the pile of children, playing dead. The Children look confused and helpless for a moment, but they soon regain hope.

DEAD CHILDREN: He's pretending! The Messiah is pretending!

ARGUMENTATIVE DEAD CHILD: He's playing dead, to surprise our murderers even more!

DEAD CHILDREN: They don't know what's in store for them!

ARGUMENTATIVE DEAD CHILD: The world goes about its business – murdering, devouring – and Messiah is already among us!

COMMANDER: *(To THE MOTHER.)* Did you put The Child down? Did you say goodbye? Come with us. Your life is only just beginning. You are needed to balance out the warring forces.

F

One of the SOLDIERS notices the 'MESSIAH' in the pile of DEAD CHILDREN.

SOLDIER: Commander, someone here is alive. He has two empty suitcases, and he is not a child.

(The SOLDIERS surround the 'MESSIAH.' He slowly rises to his knees, shaking with fear. The DEAD CHILDREN whisper among themselves.)

DEAD CHILDREN: Now he'll show them! Now he'll strike them dumb!

IMPATIENT DEAD CHILD: *(Whispering to 'MESSIAH'.)* Tell them, Messiah! Tell them who you are already!

(The 'MESSIAH' whimpers with fear on his knees before the COMMANDER, who kneels slowly beside the 'MESSIAH' facing the pile of children.)

COMMANDER: Look, they're looking to you as if expecting something from you.

(The 'MESSIAH' laughs anxiously, shaking his head vigorously. The COMMANDER, transfixed, continues gazing at the children.)

And again – the child. And again – asleep. You wake them up – they fall asleep. There's no describing the serenity.

And how much hope there is in those open mouths, and the bared teeth that hint to you: we once bit into an apple, and there are more apples.

(The 'MESSIAH' extends his hand, touches the face of one of the children, wipes the blood from his face, tidies his hair, caresses him. The DEAD CHILDREN begin to twitch with joy.)

DEAD CHILDREN: The resurrection! The resurrection! He is starting the resurrection with mercy!

(The 'MESSIAH' bursts into tears, falls on the pile of children, hugs and kisses the corpses, gathers into his arms the body of IMPATIENT DEAD CHILD.)

IMPATIENT DEAD CHILD: *(With great emotion and horror.)* Father, my father! With your merciful touch I shall awaken!

(And with the IMPATIENT DEAD CHILD in his arms, the 'MESSIAH' looks straight into the COMMANDER's eyes. The COMMANDER rises slowly to his feet, removing his pistol as he speaks.)

COMMANDER: You flatter me too much when you look straight into my eyes. As if you believe there is really something behind them. As if the fact that I have my own shape and a first name indicates something equivalent inside me.

(He points the pistol at the face of the 'MESSIAH,' who lets go, frightened to death, of the body of IMPATIENT DEAD CHILD, and crawls over the pile of children.)

DEAD CHILDREN: Now, now! The string is about to snap! The sky – to open. It will happen now! Yes, yes, this is how it happens in the movies, too – the hero falls to the floor, everything seems lost, and only at the last moment... At the very last moment...

(The 'MESSIAH' rummages under the pile of children, pulls out a watch, shows it to the COMMANDER, holds it out for him. The COMMANDER indicates that he should toss the watch to him, and the 'MESSIAH' does as he wishes. The 'MESSIAH,' like a magician drawing rabbits from a hat, pulls out more and more watches, burrowing madly in the pile of children, and hurling the loot at the COMMANDER and the SOLDIERS. Everyone catches the watches eagerly, becoming a boisterous group of boys waiting for prizes, yet at the same time fascinated and amused by the 'MESSIAH' who continues to burrow feverishly, sweating, stained by the children's blood, his eyes sparkling with terror. When he finishes, he quickly crawls off the pile, all the way to the COMMANDER's feet, expecting, like a dog, a reward. The COMMANDER, with a dismissive wave of the hand, busy with his watches, indicates that he may leave.)

COMMANDER: We have turned a blind eye. Go, evaporate, before we change our minds.

(The 'MESSIAH' quickly gets to his feet, in a hurry to leave.)

IMPATIENT DEAD CHILD: Messiah, why are you running away from the truth?

(The 'MESSIAH' freezes as if struck on his back, turns around, gazes at length at the gang of eager SOLDIERS so busy with their watches that they pay him no heed, and at the pile of DEAD CHILDREN staring back at him. He slowly walks back to the pile, kneels before it, spreading his arms wide as if to embrace all the children as one, and prostrates himself on them. The COMMANDER notices him, says, distractedly.)

COMMANDER: Oh, you again.

(He shoots him in the head. The 'MESSIAH' dies on the pile of children.)

WOMAN BORN FOR LOVE: *(To COMMANDER.)* You used to enjoy sticking the toe of your shoe into the wound.

(She raises her shoe, as if to dig its toe into the 'MESSIAH's' wound, her foot hovers in mid-air, then she lowers it. The COMMANDER laughs.)

COMMANDER: We've grown tired, ah? Even murderers and whores yawn and drink tea.

(He exits with WOMAN BORN FOR LOVE.)

DARING SOLDIER: *(To THE MOTHER.)* Come, we will help you bring up memories of your child: from the place where he came into the world, we, too, will go in and out.

THE MOTHER: *(Approaching THE CHILD's body, leaning over him as she did at the beginning of the play.)* 'See, you can live without him!' So said the Skipper, and laughed with his gold tooth, yes, he laughed like that with his gold tooth: 'See, you can, you can without him!'

(She exits with the SOLDIERS.)

H (REQUIEM)

A silence of despair prevails among the DEAD CHILDREN.

PROPHESYING DEAD CHILD: I saw an angel, he was sailing the sun, he slowly dived as in a sea of honey, and came down and whispered to me: 'Oh, little lambs, quiet screechers. Oh, my tender, impatient dead ones. There's been a small mistake in the count. Now it is final: one more child.'

(Silence of disbelief.)

This is what he told me: 'Rest a while longer, just one more child.'

DEAD CHILDREN: *(One of them trying to take heart, begins softly humming, the others join him one after the other.)*
The sweet days of summer are here,
Awash in joy we await,
The day is long, the night is far,
But already we start to fret:
Will summer be time enough? Will life be time enough?

(And while the song continues in the background, CHILD WHO CRUMBLED TO DUST, who lies some distance from the pile, like a protrusion in the earth, turns to them as if disturbed in his sleep.)

CHILD WHO CRUMBLED TO DUST: And you there, you new recruits to death, calm down.

THE CHILD: I will never stop wanting to live…

CHILD WHO CRUMBLED TO DUST: You will, calm down.

THE CHILD: At my birth, my mother gave me the great promise of life… I will never stop missing it…

CHILD WHO CRUMBLED TO DUST: Yes, the longings still rise like warm vapors from the flesh; but for how much longer will you have flesh?

Look at me: a flattened mound in the sand still hints that I was there. That too shall pass. How has it all crumbled into a big one-and-the-same?

THE CHILD: *(Crying.)* No, I will not give up!

CHILD WHO CRUMBLED TO DUST: But that is what you used to say when they put you to bed, remember? You sobbed bitterly. Your heart pounded with lust for life and games: you so loathed to leave the pleasures of life behind you till morning.

You said, 'No, no, I will not fall asleep!' But by the second 'no,' your eyes were closing. A massive force, heavy as lead, pulled you down, until you were diving down, the world falling away, vanishing into darkness, and you with it. Calm down.

(The Children's singing slowly dies out. THE CHILD's speech grows heavy.)

THE CHILD: No… No…

CHILD WHO CRUMBLED TO DUST: Calm down.

END

www.ingramcontent.com/pod-product-compliance
Ingram Content Group UK Ltd.
Pitfield, Milton Keynes, MK11 3LW, UK
UKHW020719280225
455688UK00012B/418